"YOU'RE GOING TO KILL THIS ONE!"

"Greg kept ripping up the towel into strips. 'And this is how you're going to do it,' he said and proceeded to tie Lynel Murray up. He put one around her mouth, one around her eyes, and tied her feet together. She was lying on her stomach.

" 'Come here,' he said.

"I looped a strip of towel around her neck like he told me to and started to pull. Greg was standing there watching me. Well, I just couldn't do it by myself.

"Finally, he took one side and started pulling while I was on the other side. I pulled a little, then had to let go. I tried again, but had to let it go. My fingernails were digging into my palm and cutting my hand. Greg got mad because I wasn't doing it. He pushed me out of the way. 'I'll do it myself!' "

REAL HORROR STORIES!
PINNACLE TRUE CRIME

SAVAGE VENGEANCE   (0-7860-0251-4, $5.99)
By Gary C. King and Don Lasseter
On a sunny day in December, 1974, Charles Campbell attacked
Renae Ahlers Wicklund, brutally raping her in her own home in
front of her 16-month-old daughter. After Campbell was released
from prison after only 8 years, he sought revenge. When Campbell
was through, he left behind the most gruesome crime scene local
investigators had ever encountered.

NO REMORSE   (0-7860-0231-X, $5.99)
By Bob Stewart
Kenneth Allen McDuff was a career criminal by the time he was
a teenager. Then, in Fort Worth, Texas in 1966, he upped the ante.
Arrested for three brutal murders, McDuff was sentenced to death.
In 1972, his sentence was commuted to life imprisonment. He
was paroled after only 23 years behind bars. In 1991 McDuff
struck again, carving a bloody rampage of torture and murder
across Texas.

BROKEN SILENCE   (0-7860-0343-X, $5.99)
The Truth About Lee Harvey Oswald, LBJ,
and the Assassination of JFK
By Ray "Tex" Brown with Don Lasseter
In 1963, two men approached Texas bounty hunter Ray "Tex"
Brown. They needed someone to teach them how to shoot at a
moving target—and they needed it fast. One of the men was Jack
Ruby. The other was Lee Harvey Oswald. . . . Weeks later, after
the assassination of JFK, Ray Brown was offered $5,000 to leave
Ft. Worth and keep silent the rest of his life. The deal was ar-
ranged by none other than America's new president: Lyndon
Baines Johnson.

*Available wherever paperbacks are sold, or order direct from the
Publisher. Send cover price plus 50¢ per copy for mailing and
handling to Penguin USA, P.O. Box 999, c/o Dept. 17109,
Bergenfield, NJ 07621. Residents of New York and Tennessee
must include sales tax. DO NOT SEND CASH.*

PROPERTY OF THE FOLSOM WOLF

Don Lasseter

PINNACLE BOOKS
WINDSOR PUBLISHING CORP.

PINNACLE BOOKS are published by

Windsor Publishing Corp.
850 Third Avenue
New York, NY 10022

The P logo Reg. U.S. Pat. & TM Off. Pinnacle is a trademark of Windsor Publishing Corp.

First Printing: January, 1995

Printed in the United States of America

10 9 8 7 6 5 4 3 2

FOR THE VICTIMS

From the beginning, through three years of research, more than a hundred interviews, long hours in courtrooms, formidable mountains of documents to read, and two cross-country treks, my purpose in writing this book was twofold. More than anything else, I wanted to commemorate Corinna Novis and Lynel Murray, the wholesome, innocent young victims of brutal, incomprehensible murders, and to give admiring recognition to the most courageous people I have ever known, their parents. Donna Novis, Bill Novis, Nancy Murray, and Don Murray, along with their families, survived abysmal, heartbreaking pain that most of us can not even imagine.

The second goal was to examine the lives of the couple accused of the killings with the hope of understanding what drove them into a vortex of destruction and death. If there was any hint of rationalization for the heinous acts, I wanted to discover and understand it.

Acknowledgments

A few of the people I interviewed asked me not to use their real names in the text. I have honored that to protect their privacy.

Other than the rare pseudonyms, the story is true. There are no fictional or composite characters. Dialogue is re-created from court documents, police records, interviews, and testimony.

Finally, please permit me to acknowledge:

—My agent, Susan Crawford, Crawford Literary Agency, who always had the right word at the right time,

—My editor, Paul Dinas, of Pinnacle Books, who knows the right words when he sees them, and is a master at sorting out writers' scrambled words, and

—The most important person of all, without whom all of these words would be wasted; You, the reader. I thank you.

—Don Lasseter

Foreword

A buzz of excitement rippled through the gallery when Cynthia Lynn Coffman stepped through a side door and entered the cavernous, baroque courtroom. With a combination of sensual elegance and prim vulnerability, Coffman strode gracefully to one of the chairs reserved for defendants, eased into it, crossed her shapely legs, and stole a quick glance toward the other end of the table where James Gregory Marlow sat.

Seasoned trial watchers and members of the news media packed the court in San Bernardino, California, on Halloween day, 1988. Curiosity about the two defendants was widespread throughout the county and much of the state. The couple faced charges of kidnapping, raping, sodomizing, robbing, and murdering beautiful, innocent Corinna Novis, age twenty. Almost two years had passed since the brutal crime.

When the savaged body of another victim, Lynel Murray, age nineteen, was discovered in a motel room on November 13, 1986, in a different county, news watchers were shocked and sickened. Detectives found Corinna Novis, buried in a deserted vineyard just ten miles from San Bernardino. She had been missing for a week and when she was discovered, the public was outraged at the descriptions of her cruel, violent death. Morbid fascination blended with anger when Cynthia "Cyndi" Coffman, twenty-four, and James Gregory "Greg" Marlow, thirty, were apprehended and accused of both sadistic murders.

Newspapers had headlined both homicides, guessing that the killings were for "sexual gratification." The news media had also announced that investigators might link the couple with other unsolved murders of young women in the region.

Before the bailiff's announcement that court was in session, reporters and spectators whispered among themselves asking the questions on everyone's minds. Why would a young *couple* rape and kill? Did Cynthia Coffman actually participate in the rape? Included in the prosecution's list of charges was the crime of sodomy. Could the state prove that a woman had sodomized a female victim? Was that physically possible? What on earth could have motivated them, if they had, indeed, committed such repulsive acts?

Two compelling questions, it was speculated, might not be answered in this courtroom. In addition to these charges, would Marlow and Coffman face a second trial for raping and killing Lynel Murray, in neighboring Orange County? And had they murdered a man in Kentucky? It was rumored that Kentucky authorities were waiting for the outcome of both trials before deciding on a course of action.

Could this quiet, pretty, demure woman, who seemed so vulnerable, really be guilty of such heinous behavior? Was she the rarest of all predators . . . a female serial killer? Or was she, too, a victim? Had she been the puppet of a brutal, dominating partner?

Some of the men in the audience were astonished at how attractive Cyndi Coffman appeared. News photos of her, emaciated and dirty, with stubbly hair, had not done her justice, they decided. She seemed delicate and feminine with a luxurious growth of dark brown hair billowing in shiny waves over her shoulders, fashion-model cheekbones, exotically tilted green eyes, and her willowy figure that was kittenish, yet catlike. A soft white sweater and a blue pleated skirt gave her the appearance of just having left a college campus. But there was something about those eyes. Did they have a hint of cold malice or cruelty in them? Female spectators, more than men, thought so.

Shock would ripple through the audience when they learned that Coffman's shapely derriere was tattooed with the blue scroll, *Property of Folsom Wolf.*

Newspapers and television had informed readers that Cyndi was from a middle-class, Catholic family in St. Louis, Missouri, and was the mother of a young son who now lived with relatives of her ex-husband. She was intelligent and had worked steadily for several years after graduating from high school.

How on God's earth, observers asked, could this woman have landed in a courtroom so far away from her home and family, facing these charges? Perhaps it was really the fault of her co-defendant, James Gregory Marlow.

Marlow sat in the other defendant's chair, staring at a blank piece of paper on the table in front of him. Frown lines in his forehead burrowed deeply under his thinning widow's peak, and his wide-set eyes were troubled. His face was thicker, fleshier than it had looked in news photos. The gray suit he wore stretched across his muscular back and his biceps threatened to burst the seams. He did not return Cyndi's glance when she entered the courtroom.

The dramatic story of James Gregory Marlow, Cynthia Lynn Coffman, and three murder victims, was about to unfold before the jury. Over 175 witnesses would testify and it would take a staggering ten months to complete. Sensation seekers would be immersed in violence, aberrant sex, parental abuse, compulsive love, incest, and murder. They would vicariously descend into shadowy depths populated by drug dealers, hillbilly-bikers, and killers. A young man's violent death would be recalled in detail. The idyllic, wholesome lives of two young women would pass in review, and end abruptly in horror.

Spanning seven states and several lifetimes, the journey would reveal the hellish relationship of a couple who had met each other just six months before the murders they were accused of committing.

Prologue

Predawn, November 15, 1986

Three flashlight beams probed the chilly darkness, skipping and bouncing through tangled grapevines and across weed-choked clods of earth. Tumbleweeds drifted into the paths of the three searchers, casting spiderweb shadows from the circles of dim light. The men walked slowly, silently, through gloomy rows in a desolate vineyard, sequestered from a sleeping world.

Detective Dick Hooper arced his flashlight back and forth, carefully scrutinizing each foot of ground between the vines. Shivering, he tugged the collar of his sport coat tighter around his neck and ears.

Following the lead of a small spotlight that beamed from forty yards away, Hooper and two other investigators made slow progress, examining each shadow, kicking aside dead branches and foliage. At last, they divided the vineyard into sectors to make the search more efficient.

Now separated from the other searchers, Hooper felt the eerie seclusion call up echoes from his past.

His memory pieced together unlikely images from his U.S. Navy career, twenty years earlier, spent in the desert at White Sands, New Mexico. He recalled the distant flash and roar of test missiles fired into the clear, star-studded sky. Back then, the desert had seemed infinite, and the loneliness a way of life.

Hooper glanced into the night sky above the vineyard. Just like White Sands, it was cold and crystal clear, with glittering stars trying to compete with the nearly full moon. Clouds that had threatened rain all day had retreated, leaving frigid temperatures that pierced his light clothing.

"Over here!" The shout from one of the other men cracked the silence and startled Hooper. He hadn't realized that he was so tense.

"Over here. I think I've found. . . ." Hooper broke into a run, nearly stumbling over brush and clods. A rush of adrenaline tugged at him. If the shouting voice was right, then what his team dreaded was going to become a horrible reality.

"Look," came the voice as Hooper arrived. "There's been some digging here. They tried to camouflage it. Look at that tumbleweed and brush over the dirt. I almost overlooked it."

Hooper dropped to his knees and began to claw at the recently turned earth. He knew he was being impulsive, but he couldn't . . . didn't want to resist. He had to know. *Don't let it be her. Let her still be alive.*

Scooping away the brush and dirt, Hooper still clung faintly to the hope that he wouldn't find what he knew was there. His fingers stabbed again into the sandy soil, and he touched cold, rigid human flesh.

Hooper leaned forward again to gently scrape away the dirt. As the soil was removed, Hooper could gradually see the form of a delicate hand with manicured red fingernails. Then, in a slow-motion sequence that would replay in Hooper's mind for the rest of his life, the hand seemed to bend ever so slightly at the wrist, and the forefinger curved into a beckoning position. His throat constricted. Controlling his emotions, he rose and walked a few yards away to let the other men continue the unearthing task.

Later, in the cold morning light, when the body was completely uncovered, Hooper looked into the shallow grave. The young woman lay facedown, her left arm wrenched behind her back. Her left hand, which Hooper had discovered, was still in the beckoning posture. Her green-and-black striped blouse was slightly rumpled and the black pants were barely soiled by the sandy earth. She wore no shoes.

This was the second brutally violated body of a beautiful young woman he had seen in just thirty-six hours.

One

"Let's steal your ex-boyfriend's car, and use that to go to Kentucky," Greg Marlow half-suggested, half-demanded of Cynthia Coffman.

"No, I'm not taking Sam's car," she replied. "It's in terrible shape. Probably wouldn't even make it that far. And besides, the license tag is expired."

"Well, we've got to have something to drive back there to get my inheritance."

Cyndi wasn't sure she entirely believed the story Greg had told her about an inheritance. It wouldn't be his first lie about money. He had really hooked her with his grandiose descriptions of the Appaloosa ranch that he and his ex-wife had "owned" over in Victorville, that had "made all kinds of money." And she had never seen a penny of all the big bucks he had made for "killing someone in prison."

"What about that new little red pickup truck your friend over in the trailer park has? You've got a key to it, don't you?" Greg asked, with a little smirk.

"Yes, I've got a key, but he trusted me with that. He told me I could use it in an emergency."

"Well, this is an emergency," insisted Greg. "We've gotta get to Kentucky. C'mon, let's see that key."

As Cyndi withdrew the key from her wallet, her reluctance diminished and the idea of taking the pickup became more agreeable. Maybe there was some truth to Greg's story of his father dying in Kentucky and leaving him a big bankroll or a farm. Even more appealing was the thought that en route to Kentucky, they could go through St. Louis and see her son, who was living with the parents of Cyndi's ex-husband. She hadn't even talked to the little boy on the telephone for weeks, and she missed him. Maybe she could even figure out a way to grab him from her ex-mother-in-law's custody and take him to Kentucky.

Cyndi was still bemused by the crazy events of the last two months. She had moved to Barstow to be with her boyfriend, Sam Keam, but that relationship had withered, and was dying even before the idiotic events that sent them both to jail. She and Sam had been arrested shortly after a brawl in front of a convenience store when he had been attacked by four men. She was released after a few nights in jail, but Sam had been held longer. His cellmate, Greg Marlow, had been freed before Sam, and had paid a call to the apartment where Cyndi awaited her boyfriend.

There was something about the masculine, tattooed visitor that released the juices of excitement in Cyndi. Wearing a tight T-shirt when he stood at her doorstep, his chest was granite solid and his biceps glistened in the desert heat. She couldn't believe how quickly she had agreed to spend time with Greg, then give her body to him. Maybe if the sex hadn't been so mind-boggling, she wouldn't have been entangled in a new relationship so soon. She even liked the nickname he had acquired in prison, "Folsom Wolf," which stemmed from the dramatic picture tattooed on his side of a crouched wolf, snarling, ready to attack. The tattoos of a flaming swastika on his chest, bearded vikings on both shoulders accompanied by a skull on the left shoulder, full-color portraits on his right forearm, and assorted other decorations, didn't bother her. They were truly works of art. Only one set of letters on his skin vexed Cyndi and caused her jealousy to flare—the name of his ex-wife inscribed on his penis.

Now, here he was, pressing her to steal a pickup truck from her friend. She wasn't exactly sure why, but she found Marlow extremely persuasive.

A little after midnight, still astonished that she had agreed to steal a car, Cyndi stealthily inserted the key into the ignition of the red Nissan pickup, started the engine, and eased silently out of the Lenwood trailer park, seven miles from Barstow. Outside the front gate, she followed Greg's borrowed car for thirty-five miles, through Barstow, across barren desert back to Newberry Springs.

The following morning, just after sunrise the couple emerged from a tiny trailer house. Greg opened the truck door, and found a set of tools behind the cab. He gave them to Paul Donner as payment for the food Greg and Cyndi had consumed in Donner's house.

In a storage room, Greg found some black paint. He asked Paul for permission to use it so that he and an ex-con pal could paint the truck. License plates stolen from an off-road vehicle on the other side of Newberry Springs, were screwed on the rear of the truck, and the original plates buried in desert sand. That evening, Cyndi and Greg loaded the Nissan with clothing, boots, and skis she owned, along with the ones they had stolen from Sam Keam.

Preparing to leave Newberry Springs and drive to Kentucky, Cyndi was concerned about the finances. She and Greg had a little less than sixty dollars in cash, and enough "speed" to last a few days. She figured they would make it somehow.

Dust roiled behind them as they bumped across the hot pavement toward I-15, rolled to a stop, and merged into the eastbound freeway traffic.

At a gas stop in Las Vegas, Greg noticed that red paint was visible next to the white trim around the big NISSAN letters on the tailgate. Instead of reentering I-15, he drove twenty-five miles to Lake Mead, where they rested awhile before he recruited Cyndi to use her lipstick liner brush, with a small can of black paint, to touch up the telltale red showing on the tailgate. Two years later, Cyndi would recite the details of that incident in a dramatically different context.

Returning to I-15, they sped across the bottom of Nevada, angled through the northwest tip of Arizona, and drove a little less than a hundred miles into Utah. They celebrated crossing each state line by parking and making love in the cramped pickup cab.

In a cheap motel that night, they counted the remaining money and agreed that it wasn't going to take them very far. Cyndi had skied the slopes of Brian Head previously and knew a few of the locals. She found an acquaintance, to whom she sold her skis and boots, along with Sam Keam's. That sale provided enough gas, food, and beer money to continue the trip.

Woodland Park, Colorado, was the next stop. Greg looked up Elmer Lutz, a contractor who built microwave telephone relay towers on mountaintops across the nation. Lutz and Greg had met at a tower site where Marlow had worked as a temporary laborer, and Greg was wondering if the contractor needed any help in Colorado. "Not right now," Lutz told him. "But I've got a job coming up in Georgia in a few weeks. Might be able to use you down there." After providing the couple overnight accommodations, Lutz scribbled an Atlanta telephone number and suggested that Greg give him a call.

Disappointed that Marlow wouldn't be able to make a few bucks with Lutz, the couple drove on to Colorado Springs where an old buddy of Greg's gave them shelter for a couple of nights. Cyndi would always remember the stop: "You know how

Colorado is during the summer, all the wildflowers growing everywhere. Greg was walking around picking flowers for me. It was fun, just a lot of fun. Very sweet and nice."

Money was still a big problem, though, so Cyndi produced some jewelry and pawned it. They didn't get enough cash to pay for any more motels or food, so Cyndi and Greg drove the seven hundred miles to St. Louis, straight through. They arrived at the home of Cyndi's grandmother on July 2, at ten o'clock that night. The elderly woman was startled to see her granddaughter, since Cyndi's last visit had been Christmas, 1984, a year and a half earlier. But "Gram" welcomed her granddaughter along with her brawny friend, and served them some of her birthday cake left over from the previous day.

Cyndi was anxious to talk to her parents. As soon as she had wolfed down the cake, she started trying to telephone them, but several attempts were unsuccessful. Finally, a few minutes past midnight, Cyndi's mother, sounding dead tired, answered. The conversation lasted only a few minutes, during which Cyndi suggested a visit that same night. Her mother did not sound encouraging, and turned Cyndi over to her stepfather, Carl Anderson, who said, "It's really late, and your mother and I are exhausted. How about . . . why don't you come over in the morning?"

When Cyndi replaced the phone in its cradle, she was crying angrily. Within a few minutes, she and Greg went to bed and he asked her about the phone conversation. He would later describe her reaction: "She was mad, kind of crying. She said that her mom didn't want her to come over there. Then she said that she didn't even want to go, and didn't want to talk about it any more."

In the morning, Cyndi's gloom was obvious. She had talked about visiting her son and possibly taking the boy with her to Kentucky. But they did not drive the short distance to the Coffman home where the child was living. Their explanations for that decision were widely divergent when they later talked about it. Cyndi blamed Marlow, saying that he refused to go pick up the child because they didn't have enough time. They had to get on to Kentucky.

Marlow explained, "Her and I talked about it in the bedroom. She said she didn't want to go over there. We decided to come back at another time when we didn't have a stolen car and . . . get him another time. That was Cyndi's idea. So she borrowed ten dollars from her grandmother because we were out of money again and we took off to Kentucky."

Once a coal-mining town, squeezed between railroad tracks and Federal Highway 27, Pine Knot, Kentucky consisted of scabrous wooden buildings along a main drag resembling a boarded-up Old-West town. A couple of miles north, new homes with green lawns and half-acre ponds were sprouting, but the center of Pine Knot survived with only

a few stores, a tiny brick post office, and a dispro-
portionate number of greasy auto repair shops.

Street signs are as scarce as paved roads around
Pine Knot, and numbers on the houses don't exist.
It is easy to get lost in the country lanes that me-
ander between brooding pines, dogwood, and
shimmering poplars, especially at three in the
morning. Greg had spent several years of his youth
in this region and felt a certain familiarity with
the topography, but was having difficulty finding
his friend's house. He told Cyndi to keep driving
around, until he finally gave up, and they stopped
at a dilapidated gas station where there was a pay
telephone.

Greg called a cousin who agreed to meet him at
the gas station. The relative arrived within minutes
and guided the lost pair to the mobile home of
Greg's friend. Greg knocked on the bedroom window of the cracker-box structure. The sleepy occu-
pants looked out the dirty glass, recognized Greg,
and bellowed an invitation for him, Cyndi, and the
cousin, to come on in.

When it was light enough to see, Cyndi found
that she wasn't particularly impressed with her surroundings. "It's a hick town," she would recall.
"Pine Knot is right next to Revelo and Stearns.
They're little bitty towns. Old tires scattered everywhere. Most of the people I saw had real long
hair, and all of them had motorcycles. They looked
like bikers."

Like many of the citizens living in small shacks
or mobile homes dotting the wooded hills and val-

leys, Donald Lyons preferred to be called by his nickname, "Lardo." The bearded man, who stretched
his dirty hair into a pigtail, limped from an old
injury, which didn't make it any easier to carry his
260 pounds on his six-foot frame. Over morning
coffee and marijuana, Greg and Lardo reminisced
about old times and caught each other up on recent events. Later, they drove around and visited
other friends and relatives, from whom Greg
learned some bad news.

He really had expected a modest inheritance.
His grandmother, Lena Walls, with whom he and
his half sister, Coral, had spent a great deal of
time as children in California, had died. (His father was still alive.) But what little property she
owned had already been swallowed up by relatives
and neighbors. If any of it had been intended for
Greg, it was not coming his way.

As with most events in the life of James Gregory
Marlow, the inheritance was just another disappointment. "The hell with it," he shrugged.
"There are other ways to get money." For now, he
and Cyndi would just enjoy being with his wild
friends.

Lardo and his woman held a Fourth of July
party that Cyndi would not forget. Fifteen people
gathered in the residence where beer, booze, pot,
and methamphetamines were in ample supply.
Marlow smoked prodigious amounts of weed and
guzzled booze until he was fall-down drunk, but
Cyndi denied that she was loaded. "No, I didn't
get drunk. Greg did though, and got his ear

pierced. A friend of Greg's (was there), that he had grown up with, named 'Duce.' That's the only name I know him by. He took a sharp little poker that Greg had on his key chain and stuck it through Greg's ear. And then he takes a diamond that he had in his own ear, and puts it in Greg's ear. Later that night we went to bed and Greg passed out. The door was locked, but Duce kicked it in and said he wanted his earring back. I was in the bed with no clothes on. And he came in and yanked the earring right out of Greg's ear."

When the hangovers had healed the following morning, Marlow straddled the back of Lardo's big motorcycle, and the two men roared off to a place called Roundtop Road. It was, according to Greg, "down in the bottom of a holler," a gathering place for good ole boys to sit around, get high on homegrown weed, and figure out how to score some more. A friend of Lardo was there, a guy they called "Killer."

After some general "bull-slinging," Shannon "Killer" Compton began talking about someone called "Wildman," whose real name was Greg Hill. Hill, Marlow later recounted, was going to testify in court against an acquaintance, and some of the local boys didn't want that to happen. Killer made it clear that Wildman Hill should be silenced and admitted that he had agreed to take care of the problem but had been procrastinating. He enlisted Greg Marlow's assistance. Several thousand dollars would be given to Lardo for the job, and Lardo would pay Marlow five thousand bucks.

Marlow indicated to Killer that he would have to think about it, and returned with Lardo to the mobile home.

That night, he told Cyndi, "I've got a snitch to kill," and asked her what she thought about it. Cyndi wasn't surprised because Greg had told her that he had been a hit man. She would one day be asked about her reaction, and she could only remember thinking, "What a fine mess I had gotten myself into."

Greg, when asked how Cyndi responded, said, "She thought it was a good idea to get some money so we could get a place and get jobs." He claimed that he tried to convince her that it would be better to wait for the job in Atlanta promised by Elmer Lutz. But Cyndi, he said, insisted that they should take the fast money, now.

They argued for a little while and Marlow said, "Heck with it then. Let's go out there and . . . take a look at it."

Crowded into a van with Lardo and Killer the next morning, Marlow traveled twenty miles east, twisting and winding on I-92, through Hollyhill and Jellico Creek, across I-75 at Wayne County seat, Williamsburg. Through the historic town, the group crossed the Cumberland River, passed fourteen more miles of farms and decrepit mobile homes, and stopped near a whitewashed cabin surrounded by pasture in "Dead Man's Holler." Killer pointed to the cabin and announced that it was the home of Wildman Hill.

Back at Lardo's that evening, Killer handed Greg a little .22 caliber pistol.

At five A.M., Greg woke Cyndi, and they sleepily dressed before getting into the black Nissan. Fighting drowsiness, they duplicated the trip of the previous day, drove around in the early light near Wildman's house, slowed near a white wood-frame church two hundred yards from the house, and aimed the truck up a steep gravel road. It was all the little vehicle could do to ascend the thickly forested hill which formed a ridge between Dead Man's Holler and the next little valley.

At the top, they proceeded another hundred yards before parking near a scattering of tombstones, called Upper Mulberry Cemetery. Greg pulled a sleeping bag and some blankets from the truck, and placed them at a strategic point in the woods where they could sit and observe the house, down in the "holler."

Cyndi and Greg spent most of the day there, sleeping and watching. Greg recalled that they whiled away some of the hours by having sex several times. Cyndi remembered that Greg was getting impatient and angry and began to turn into "Wolf." That meant, she said, "His voice starts going monotone, his eyes change, his facial expressions change, and it's just like he becomes a different person."

The next morning, according to Coffman, Greg forced her to take off her blouse and bra, remove a bandanna that had been looped around her waist as a belt, and wrap it around her breasts like a bikini top. She was going to act as bait to lure Wildman up the hill.

Greg waited in the woods near the parked pickup while Cyndi scrambled down the steep gravel road, turned at the church, and walked to Hill's house.

She knocked on the door and waited. When it opened, a stocky twenty-eight-year-old man, barefoot and rumpled, wearing blue jeans and a black T-shirt emblazoned with the words *Harley-Davidson*, stood there pushing his long tangled dark hair back from his forehead, and rubbing the sleep from his eyes. Gregory "Wildman" Hill squinted at her and grunted, "Yeah?"

"Could you help me?" she asked him. "My truck is stalled and I need someone to help me get it started."

"Yeah, sure," he muttered, scratching a three-day growth of beard and scanning her slim body. "Just a minute, I got to put my boots on." In addition to pulling on battered brown cowboy boots, he tucked a handgun between his spine and the waistband of his dirty jeans.

Wildman Hill drove Cyndi in his battered red Toyota sedan two hundred yards to the church, turned right, and tried to ascend the hill, but his car wouldn't make it. Instead, he parked, and they climbed the gravel road afoot, to the pickup. The hood was propped open, giving the appearance that something was wrong with the engine. Hill asked her to try to start it while he poked his head into the engine compartment.

When he leaned out to give her instructions, he was startled to see a man charging toward him. Greg Marlow yelled, "What are you doing up here with my sister?"

Hill started to reply, "She just asked me to help her with . . . ," but before he could finish, Marlow lunged toward him. Wildman twisted, and simultaneously reached for the pistol in his waistband. The two men struggled for a moment, and a gunshot cracked the morning silence, echoing across the misty hills.

Greg Marlow described it. "He turned around and I kept walking toward him, and he pulled the gun out. I grabbed his arm . . . grabbed the gun, and I shot him."

Cyndi said, "I was standing by the door of the truck. The hood was up and Marlow was talking to him. And I heard a shot go off. I saw Marlow. He wiped off the guy's gun, laid it back down. We got in the truck and left." They bounced down the hill, leaving the victim lying in the dirt, mortally wounded.

Speeding away from the parked Toyota, past the old church, they drove to "a little store right down on the highway and got a couple of sodas and went back to Pine Knot."

A couple of days later, Cyndi was in the bedroom of Lardo's house, when "Greg came in and threw a wad of money at me and told me to count it." She spread the bills across the bed, then stacked them by denomination. She counted five thousand and fifteen dollars, in hundreds, fifties, twenties, and fives.

TWO

July 1986, Pine Knot, Kentucky

It had always been a dream of Greg Marlow's to own a Harley-Davidson motorcycle, and he finally had enough money to buy one. He gave the stolen pickup truck to a relative in the backwoods of McCreary County, and started shopping.

Two days after he and Cyndi had left Wildman Hill dying in a pool of blood, Marlow found just what he wanted, a big brawny "hog," a Harley-Davidson. He paid three thousand dollars in cash for it, promptly painted it, and named it "Big Red." Greg and Cyndi rode the bike to their "wedding" on July 11.

"It was what you call a biker wedding," Cyndi explained. "It is not a legal wedding, it's just a group of friends who get together and somebody says something, you know, now I pronounce you man and wife." Her bridal gown was a sleeveless blue summer dress, given to her by Lardo's wife.

Cyndi's face was not the typical bride's, though. It was, as she later described, scratched and bruised. On the day before the "wedding," she said, "We went outside, and we were under some trees and all of a sudden he started hitting me. Then he started dragging me around the yard by my hair and my arm. All the way around the yard to the front yard. And he kept hitting me and saying things, for a good hour or two. Finally, he put a choke hold on me and I passed out. When I woke up, I was still in the yard."

When Cynthia was asked why Marlow had treated her in this manner, she stated that she had no idea. She did recall that someone, one of the guys Marlow knew, had asked, "Why did you drag her around, why are you beating up on her?"

According to Cyndi, Marlow's answer was short. "He knocked the guy over the deck and dislocated the guy's arm." After that, no one else interfered if Greg wanted to beat her up.

Trooper-Detective Colan Harrell, at age thirty-nine, had been with the Kentucky State Police for seventeen years, and had traded in the crisp uniform for plain clothes in 1974. A trim man, two inches short of six feet, Colan was a native Kentuckian, born in Corbin, just fifteen miles up I-75 from Williamsburg where he lived and worked. In the same town, he had earned a B.A. degree from Cumberland College, a beautiful campus of red brick buildings, trimmed in white, surrounded by expansive lawns.

Anyone meeting Colan Harrell probably wouldn't guess his profession. His lilting drawl, easy laugh, and friendly manner seemed more suited to a public relations job or a corporate business executive. The image was offset only by the wad of Taylor's Pride tobacco bulging in his right cheek, and the use of a Styrofoam cup as a spittoon. Light complected, with blue eyes, and a wave of sandy hair looping down over his forehead, Harrell loved his job, and was respected by citizens and colleagues alike. Williamsburg had a city police force, County Sheriff's officers, and Colan Harrell from the State Police. Harrell worked with the other groups to investigate everything from murder, to robbery, to marijuana deals.

Colan Harrell faced a far more serious crime in July 1986. Accompanied by Chief Sheriff's deputy Jim Brim, a trim six-footer who could play the role of young Lyndon B. Johnson, Harrell stood at the top of the ridge above Dead Man's Holler, and looked at the body in the brush. It had been there three days, lying facedown, in ninety-degree heat, and maggots were already doing their repugnant work. The victim had been shot through the head, from right to left.

A relative of Greg "Wildman" Hill had discovered the body, and summoned police. When Harrell and Brim arrived, they found no murder weapon, but recovered it on the following day. The relative had picked it up near the body, and figured he might as well keep it, but reconsidered and turned it over to the police. Colan Harrell knew Greg Hill from several run-ins he'd had with the law, mostly minor infractions, and regarded him as a "rounder." Just one week earlier, the officers had responded to a complaint of a loud, boisterous, drunken party at Hill's cabin, and had "discouraged" a rough crowd from irresponsibly firing their weapons in all directions. Hill's daddy, Jerome, was the retired principal of Liberty Elementary School, and had tried his best to keep his son, along with two brothers and two sisters, on the straight and narrow. But Greg, the officers later told a writer, "got mixed up with the wrong crowd, and done business with the wrong people."

Greg Hill had visited his parents all day on the Sunday prior to his death, and whipped up a big batch of chili, his cooking specialty.

His family made no mention of Greg's activities in the marijuana business.

Despite intensive and meticulous investigation at the crime scene, Colan Harrell, Jim Brim, and a team of officers were unable to turn up any clues that might lead to the identity of a suspect in the murder of Greg "Wildman" Hill.

While staying in Pine Knot, Cynthia Coffman later said, she and Greg occupied themselves by going with friends on "pot hunts." ("It means you go through the woods and all kind of land looking for marijuana plants.") They went on maybe fifty pot hunts during the two months they spent in Kentucky.

One day, Cyndi recalled, they were on a pot hunt, climbing a hill on Big Red, the motorcycle.

"There was a hill you had to climb, and the clutch plates were slipping. Greg was having a hard time getting up this hill because the ground was wet. So I leaned up and told him, 'I'm getting off.' He just went and left.

"I walked through this . . . what we call a holler . . . 'cause it's back in the woods and very far and few between houses. A friend of Lardo's was on the way to Lardo's house and he gave me a ride the rest of the way back."

When she arrived at the house simultaneously with Greg, Cyndi said, "He pulled up on the bike and started hitting me, because I was stupid, I was out with these guys, and he was looking for me and thought I fell off the bike. And he ended up taking me . . . dragging me down the street to a creek and starts yelling and hitting me. He's got his gun, his .45 in his hand."

Cyndi's voice became tense. "And then finally at one point he shot the gun off right next to my head and the bullet just went right by my ear."

The malfunctioning clutch plates on Big Red did need attention, so Marlow took the bike apart to make the repairs. Cyndi remembered, "We were down in Duce's basement and Greg had Big Red in there up on blocks. He had me sitting on the floor, yelling at me. And he came over and hit me and told me how stupid I am and I don't know anything."

Gesturing toward her face with one hand, Cyndi pointed to a spot where she said she had been struck. "He had one of the clutch plates in his hand and he hit me in the face with it and cut open my face. There is a scar right above this bump I have on my face." Immediately following the blow, Cyndi later reported, she felt the urge to urinate, but he wouldn't allow her to go to the bathroom. "So I had to urinate in a cup."

"Did it occur to you to leave this man because of the beatings you were sustaining?" Cyndi was asked.

"At this point, I was more afraid of him than ever, because after he had killed that man, he told me he had sent the names and address of my son and family to his friend. And they knew that if . . . they knew to get me or my family if I ever did anything against him."

There was one more incident of beating before they left Kentucky, Cyndi said. "He was kicking me with his steel-toed boots and I thought he had broken my leg. And the next day I was taken to a doctor to have it X-rayed."

Before she could go to the doctor, though, Cyndi recalled, "Greg told me to sit in the yard and he went riding off on the bike. He was going too fast and he wrecked it. When he came back after the crash, he had scratches on his back and shoulder and said, 'Well, now you can go to the doctor, 'cause I need to go, too. It will be just like you fell off the bike, too.' "

They received treatment under the names of Mr. and Mrs. Glen Campbell.

There were more gatherings with Lardo, Automatic, Duce, their buddies and their women. Marlow kept glancing at Killer's girlfriend. It wasn't because he found her irresistibly attractive or sexy. He just liked the tattoo on her right arm. It spelled out the words *Property of Killer.*

After more than two months in Kentucky, Greg and Cyndi left to go to Atlanta to find work with Elmer Lutz, the microwave tower contractor. They stopped in Knoxville, Tennessee, for a short visit with another of Greg's relatives, and to trade Big Red for a Cadillac, an early 1970s model. Marlow later complained that he had agreed to the trade for Cyndi's sake because he thought she was pregnant, but she wasn't.

In Atlanta, they found Lutz, and for the first time in the four months that Cyndi had known Greg, he went to work, doing general labor at a microwave tower installation. His job duration turned out to be short, though. He worked only four days.

On the evening of the fourth day, Cyndi recalled, "It was Thursday night. Greg had come home from work to the hotel and he said that Elmer and these other guys wanted to go to the bar and we were going with him. So we went to the bar and there was a pool room in the back. We were drinking tequila and beer. And the other guys that Greg worked with were playing pool."

Greg got into an argument with another bar patron, and while he was doing that, Cyndi said, "The cue ball where his friends were playing pool got stuck. I knew how to get it out. You just roll another ball down and it knocks the cue ball out, so I did that for them."

Later, according to Cyndi, she and Greg left with Elmer Lutz to meet some of the other men and get something to eat at a restaurant. "And all the way driving there, Greg kept—he made me drive—and he kept elbowing me as hard as he could in the ribs. It got to a point where Elmer told him, 'Man, just let her drive, you know. What are you hitting on her for? Just let her drive.'

"We got to the restaurant and while we were waiting to be seated, Greg looked at me and I knew he had changed to Wolf. He said, 'We are not eating.' I thought, oh no, not another beating. So I grabbed the cigarette machine and he pulled me off and drug (sic) me outside."

When some men ran out and told him to leave her alone, Greg rasped, "You'd better tell them to get out of here or I'll kill them and you."

She shouted to the men, "It's okay. Don't worry about it. Everything is fine." Cyndi's voice was a whisper in describing the incident.

Greg cooled down, and because they were afraid the police had been called, they moved to another restaurant. The other men went in to eat, but, Cyndi said, she and Greg stayed in the car. "While they were in eating, he was beating me in the car. He had me down on the floorboard clubbing me and punching me. And there was blood on the leather seats of the car and on the windshield from where my nose and my mouth were bleeding." Finally, they returned to the hotel.

"I thought the beating was over. Instead, we got in there and he starts really beating on me. He's kicking me in my ribs and punching me. All of a sudden he said, 'Where is your scissors?' I had a little pair of mustache scissors, but I wouldn't tell him where they were. He tore up the whole room and found them."

Seeming near tears, Cyndi continued, "He comes over and sits on me, and he asked me, 'What do you want to lose, your hair or your eye?' I told him I didn't want to lose either one. He told me that I had to make a choice. So I said don't take my eye, 'cause I knew that the hair would grow back.

"He sat on me and cut all my hair off as close as he could with the scissors, then he took me in the bathroom and tried to shave it with a razor, but the razor wouldn't shave it. So he told me to sit on the toilet seat and he said, 'Now I'm taking your eye. It won't hurt. I know exactly what I'm doing. I'll just poke it out and you won't even feel it. It will bleed just a little bit.' "

That went on for half an hour, Cyndi recalled. "Then he made me strip naked. I was too slow so he ripped the rest of my clothes off. And he opens the door to the motel room. We are at the far end. And he tells me to get out. I asked if I could put some clothes on. He said, 'No, you're going just like you are. It's okay, you'll be back with your own kind anyway, the niggers out there.' "

After she had been on the second-floor landing outside, naked, for several minutes, Cyndi said,

Greg opened the door and told her to get back in the room. "He pulled me back in there and he tells me to lay on the bed." With her voice breaking, she said that Greg forced her to lubricate him with petroleum jelly. "And he sodomized me. It was really painful."

On the following morning, when Marlow woke up, he squinted at Cyndi, groaned, "Oh, no," and rolled over to go back to sleep. Several hours later, when he woke again, he and Cyndi found that Elmer Lutz had pushed a check under the door as final payment for Greg's four days of work. It was obvious that he had been fired.

With Cyndi wearing a baseball cap to hide her baldness, they left Atlanta and returned to Kentucky to stay another month.

After several pot hunts and an aborted try at burglary, Greg stole a maroon Dodge station wagon, stuffed it with their meager belongings, and hit the road again. They lingered for a while in Knoxville, at the home of his relative, who grew tired of the freeloading and gave Greg $150 and an invitation to leave. The couple headed west to Page, Arizona, where Cyndi had lived for eighteen months after she left St. Louis. Out of cash again, they visited two of her old friends' places to try to borrow some money. An ex-boyfriend, shocked at her thin, bald appearance, told them that he couldn't help. Ten miles out of Page, in Greenhaven, a woman named Judy, with whom Cyndi had lived, was also stunned:

"I went to the door . . . and I don't have an

outside porch light, so I opened it all the way. Cyndi (was there) wearing a green military jacket with a hood over her head, and a bandanna tied around her head. When she walked into my trailer, and pulled the hood down, I saw that her hair was no longer than my fingernails."

Conversation followed, and Judy asked why Cyndi's hair was so short. Marlow explained that they had been in Kentucky where he was a lineman for a power company, and that he and Cyndi had been camping out. Then, according to Judy, Cyndi filled in the details: "She started to tell about chiggers getting in her hair and laying eggs and you couldn't kill the eggs. The only way to get rid of the eggs was to shave the hair. I'm from North Carolina, and I know different."

Judy was also curious about the tattoos she saw on Marlow's arms, and asked if it hurt when he got them. "It didn't hurt half as bad as the one on the end of my dick," he sneered. The rude comment insulted Judy, and angered her because it was said in the presence of her child. She told Marlow that his "cussing" was inappropriate, and that she was not able to give them any financial assistance.

Driving away, in a serious pinch for money, Greg and Cyndi brainstormed possible sources for money. Cyndi knew that her ex-boyfriend's parents kept a safe in their Page home. It took only a few minutes to locate the house, where a few passes verified that no one was home. After casually sauntering into the backyard, Greg lifted Cyndi through an open window so she could unlock the back door. They found the small safe, concealed it in a cardboard box, and managed to carry it to the car without being seen. Outside town, on an isolated country road, the couple was elated to discover that the safe wasn't even locked, and then disappointed to find that it contained only personal papers and twelve silver dollars. Greg pocketed the coins and used a small folding shovel to bury the safe, with the papers still in it, in the soft desert sand.

They spent the night with another of Cyndi's ex-roommates in Big Water, Utah, ten miles north of Page. All of the folks they visited in the vicinity would remember the bizarre pair.

Fleeing Page, en route to Barstow again, Greg started talking about a "hit" he could do that would earn them ten thousand dollars, according to Cyndi's later recollection. He didn't tell her where he had learned of it, but divulged that the victim would be a pregnant woman in Phoenix, Arizona, something about a fouled-up dope deal. He talked of the Arizona hit for several days, she said.

Back in Newberry Springs, California, Greg sold the stolen car. "The title was in the glove box," Cyndi claimed, "so he put my name on the title papers and sold the car to a woman."

The tiny, secluded desert community was ideal for hiding, so Greg and Cyndi sought out his old friends, Paul Donner and his wife. Once again, the

Donners allowed them to sleep in a little backyard trailer house and to share meals.

Sitting around the Donners' living room one evening, sharing drugs and conversation, Cyndi ran into trouble. After doing a line of speed, Cyndi recalled, she developed stomach pains, and audibly groaned. "I made a noise and Greg got mad and took me out to the trailer and told me that I was in the house moaning for Paul. We came out of the trailer and as usual he took my clothes off of me and taped my hands behind my back, and taped my legs, and started beating up on me. He told me he was going to put me out in the desert and maybe if I was lucky Paul would find me before the coyotes did."

Marlow didn't throw her to the coyotes, but he did keep her awkwardly bound for nearly two hours, Cyndi complained.

Newberry Springs offered very little opportunity for making money legal or otherwise, so Greg decided that he and Cyndi should head for Fontana, near San Bernardino, where his half sister, Coral Willoughby, lived.

Their welcome had been worn thin with the Donners since neither Greg nor Cyndi were contributing to the cost of food. The night before they left, Greg told Cyndi that he would keep Paul busy long enough for Cyndi to sneak into a loft and steal a pair of rings. One was later pawned and the other traded for methamphetamines.

Early in October, Greg and Cyndi boarded a Greyhound bus to Fontana. They found their way to a cousin's home, where Greg asked for a place to stay while his "truck was being fixed." There was really no truck, but his relative accepted the story and agreed to provide temporary shelter.

During the brief stay, Greg Marlow acted on one of his fantasies. Tattoos seemed to turn him on, and in Tennessee a new one had been inscribed on his left forearm. It depicted a crawling spider equipped with oversized human male genitalia, in full color. The subject of tattoos was on Marlow's mind.

At Killer's house in Kentucky, there had been a poster of a tattoo artist decorating the buttocks of a woman. Greg had been fascinated by it and had pointed it out to Cyndi several times. He had also admired the tattoo on the arm of Killer's girl-friend, the one that made her the "property of" her man.

"He brought it up several times," Cyndi recalled. "And then when we weren't doing anything, he brought out a tattoo gun that Killer had given him, and told me he was going to tattoo me. I really didn't want it, but he said I was getting it anyway. So I told him that if I had to have it, at least I wanted to be the one to write the letters."

"First," she said, "he tattooed W-O-L-F on my ring finger and told me that it was like a wedding ring. He put two little squiggles, like lightning bolts, next to the letters. They stand for white supremacy. Then I wrote the letters *Property of Folsom Wolf* on a piece of paper."

When she completed designing the scroll, Cyndi

removed her jeans and panties, and lay on the bed, facedown. Marlow used the pattern that she had drawn and began probing the skin of her left buttock with the tattoo needle.

"He kept going over and over the part that says *Folsom Wolf* and made it real dark. He just went over *Property of* once, so it's real light. It got to the point where I couldn't take the pain any more, so he said he'd just leave it like that and go over it again later. But he never did.

Three

By the third week of October, Greg and Cyndi had exhausted the generosity and patience of his cousin in Fontana. The list of potential benefactors who might provide free room and board had dwindled to one: Greg's half sister, Coral. Carrying boxes and a duffel bag, they hitchhiked to Colton, and walked to the home of Coral's friend, Eve Matin. She remembered Greg from his childhood years in the region, and welcomed the couple. After a short visit, Greg used her telephone to call Coral. Within an hour she arrived to drive them to the home she shared in San Bernardino with her husband and his brother.

Greg introduced his companion to Coral as "Cynful." After exchanging greetings, Cyndi explained her close cropped hair by telling Coral that her head had been infested with chiggers in Kentucky. "I had to cut all my hair off to get rid of them." Greg affirmed the story.

During the next five weeks in the Willoughbys' house, Marlow and Coffman slept in the living room, either on the couch or sleeping bags. Coral and her husband occupied the original bedroom, while his brother used a cobbled add-on room. There was an air of dissension from the beginning, and tempers flared over the cost of food and expenses. There were also some problems regarding the division of methamphetamine.

One evening, Cindy remembered, "Greg, Coral, and me went over to the Matins' house and Greg started dividing up some speed on a mirror. He divided three lines first, then he took half of mine and put it on his line."

According to Cindy, Coral told Greg that he wasn't being fair and Cindy agreed with her. Greg started yelling, "Fine, you can have the whole fucking thing," and pushed it at her.

"I knew I had done it and was going to get it again. So I pushed the mirror back and said, 'No, that's okay, I don't want any more. Go ahead, you and Coral can have it.' " Greg seemed under control and Cindy thought maybe she had escaped a beating. A little while later, though, during a trip to a drug dealer's house to buy more speed, he punched her ribs so hard she thought they were broken.

The connection's house was near the intersection of Sierra Avenue and Jurupa Street, where there was an abandoned grape vineyard. Greg and Cindy would visit the area again, in just a few days.

Outside the dealer's house, Greg's attack continued, according to Coffman. "He'd smack me. He usually didn't punch me in the face, he hit me in the ribs. It's like he didn't want to leave big bruises on my face or something, so he would punch me, like, in the legs or the arms or my ribs, but (on) my face, he mostly slapped me."

Ceasing the pummeling, Greg got in the car and announced, "I'm leaving you here."

"Can I have my purse?" Cyndi pleaded, moisture welling in her eyes. "What about my stuff? Can I have my stuff?"

"You ain't gettin' nothin', bitch."

Coral hit the accelerator, spinning the tires in gravel, but the car moved only a few feet before stopping again. Greg yelled, "Get your fucking ass back in this car." Cyndi meekly climbed in, trying to hold back the tears.

Back at the Willoughbys' house, Greg ordered her into the bedroom. "I knew he was Wolf again," Coffman whispered, recalling the details. "I went into the bedroom and he started kicking me, hitting on me. He kicked me in my shin and cut my leg open. He kicked me in my personal area, and I still have problems with that. And he kept hitting and punching."

After a short respite, Marlow left the room, and returned with something in his hand.

Coffman was in pain and asked him for aspirin or something to relieve her discomfort. "I was laying on the bed and he comes back in and handed me four pills and told me to take them to make the pain go away. I took all four of the little white tablets. After I took them he just started laughing and he said, 'Boy, are you a dumb bitch. That's cyanide. You're going to die now.' I was crying and he just stood there laughing at me. He goes,

'When you die, I'm going to take all your clothes off and I'm going to leave you on the corner for the niggers. They can have you.'

"After that," Cindy continued, "he told me, 'Bitch, get in the bathroom.' He made me sit on the toilet seat, and he pushed a lit cigarette in my face. He says, 'I'm going to ask you some questions, and I want the right answers. Did you fuck Paul?' I told him no, I've never been with Paul. And he goes, 'Liar.' And he took a knife and shoved it in my leg." That was the last thing Cyndi remembered. She passed out for the next twenty-four hours.

According to Coffman's recollection; she spent Halloween, 1986, lying on a couch in agony, "With a Kotex stuck to my leg to stem the bleeding. I had him get me some tape, and I butterfly stitched it myself."

There is often a pattern with men who brutalize their mates. Immediately following a traumatic beating, they frequently smother the victim with apologies and kindness. Coffman claimed that Marlow was like that. "Oh, he'd be real nice to me. He would take me to the bathroom, he'd cook for me, he'd tell me he loved me. (He was) sorry and it shouldn't ever happen again." It was her fault, though, Marlow told her, because she made him turn into the Wolf.

The apologies and kind treatment assuaged Coffman until a few nights later. They were lying on their sleeping bag, when Marlow rolled Coffman over on her stomach, mounted her from behind, held a knife to her throat, and softly whispered that he wanted to kill her while they were having sex. Fortunately for her, he completed the sex act, but not the killing.

Sex sometimes took place in the Willoughbys' shower stall, too. Cyndi and Greg always showered together, using it frequently to make up for the missed baths during their cross-country travels.

As usual, there was a critical shortage of money. Marlow talked about the possibility of robbing a "connection," because dope dealers would never go to the police, but nothing came of it.

The Willoughby brothers were not very enamored with their guests. Sick of the freeloading pair, they finally suggested that Greg and Cindy should seek other accommodations. Coral took exception to the threatened expulsion of her half brother, and angrily snapped, "If they go, so do I."

On Thursday evening, November 6, the volcanic tensions spilled over. Coral's husband repeated that her brother and Cynful were no longer welcome. Furious, Coral began packing, and grabbed a .22 caliber Marlin semiautomatic rifle from the closet. Her husband snatched it away from her, holding it by the barrel.

"That's mine," Coral screamed.

"Wrong," he barked, swinging the weapon in a wide arc. It slammed against a wall, breaking off the wooden stock. As he turned back, he saw Greg Marlow, wearing combat fatigues, boots, and a T-shirt, standing in the doorway, glowering. His right hand held a pistol aimed at Willoughby's head.

Coral recognized it as the .22 caliber revolver that her grandmother had given her.

"Calm down," Marlow snapped, and grabbed Willoughby's right arm. Coffman appeared, curious about the fracas. Marlow told her to go to Willoughby's van and get a pair of handcuffs he had seen there. Marlow had frequently admired the manacles that hung from the rearview mirror.

Assuming that he was going to be shackled, Coral's husband watched as Cynful returned with the handcuffs. Instead, Marlow pocketed them along with the keys he scooped off Willoughby's dresser. While Cyndi and Coral loaded clothing and boxes into her Buick Skylark, Marlow continued to hold the gun on Willoughby. At last, he backed away while maintaining eye contact and slid into the car with Cyndi and Coral. The trio sped away, leaving Willoughby breathing a sigh of relief.

With no specific plans in mind, the trio stopped at the Matin house. No, they were told, it wouldn't be a good idea for them to stay there. At least, Greg asked, could they store their clothes there for a few days? The Matins relented that far.

During the previous week, Greg had visited an old pal from his teen years, named Richard Drinkhouse. Marlow had once dated his sister, and Coral had gone out a few times with Richard. Alternatives for sleeping quarters were down to zero, so Coral drove the Buick to a decrepit, single-story apartment on Foothill Boulevard that may have been a motel in more prosperous years when the thoroughfare was part of Route 66.

No one was home at the Drinkhouses' residence, so they went to the convenience store where Richard's wife worked, and got her permission to stay one or two nights. She told them her door was unlocked, so they drove back and took sleeping bags and a few clothes into the shabby dwelling. Richard Drinkhouse returned to find his apartment occupied by the threesome. He and Greg sat up most of the night, talking over old times and recent problems.

On Friday morning, at Greg's suggestion, Cyndi put on the blue dress she had worn at their "wedding" in Kentucky. Then, with Coral, they paid another visit to the Matins. Explaining that he needed some nice clothes so they could apply for jobs, Marlow borrowed a brown suit and tie along with a white shirt. His muscular body stretched the seams as he squeezed into it.

While Coral drove them to the Redlands Mall, where she worked in a sandwich shop, Cyndi and Greg talked again of the possible hit in Phoenix and how they could acquire enough money to make the trip. At the mall, Greg accepted the car keys from his sister as she stepped into the sandwich shop, and headed outside with Cyndi. They had to find a way to get some money.

After fruitlessly drifting around all day, the couple arrived again at Coral's workplace late Friday afternoon. They wolfed down sandwiches, Coral's treat, then returned to the car to wait for the end of her shift.

"That's the one we are going to get," Marlow said, nodding toward a new white Honda CRX that had just pulled into the parking stall, nose to nose with the Buick Skylark in which Cyndi sat. "She's the one."

Cynthia Coffman glanced through the windshield in the direction Marlow had indicated. She shivered. The flimsy blue dress she was wearing, her Kentucky biker-wedding bridal dress, provided scant protection against the November chill she had tried to escape by getting into the car. Greg still stood outside, leaning on the open passenger's door. He tugged at the ill-fitting borrowed suit and jutted his chin upward as if trying to pull free of the tight shirt collar and brown necktie. Cyndi watched as the girl Marlow had pointed out left her Honda and walked toward the glass doors of the Redlands Mall entrance. She was an attractive girl, with long brown hair rolled on the back of her neck, and a nice figure enhanced by snug black pants and green-and-black striped blouse she wore.

"She's just a kid. She's not going to have money or anything," Cyndi argued.

"Oh yes, she will. She'll have money. Look at her car."

When the girl entered the mall, Cyndi emerged from the Buick and walked toward the Honda with Greg. She agreed that it was a nice little car that would easily get them to Phoenix where they could do the job that promised several thousand dollars. It would probably be great on gas mileage, too, like the Nissan pickup had been. At least she wouldn't be stealing this car from a friend.

They leaned over to peer into the Honda, hoping that the girl had left the keys in the ignition. But she hadn't.

"Okay. When she comes out, you stop her and ask her for a ride," Greg instructed. Then he hurried into the mall to give Coral the keys to her Buick they had borrowed. Confident that he wouldn't need his sister's car anymore that evening, he walked back outside to wait with Cyndi.

The young woman who had left her shiny new Honda in the parking lot was named Corinna Novis.

Four

Corinna Del Novis was born in Gooding, Idaho on January 3, 1966. Her parents, Bill and Donna Novis, had made the thirty-seven mile trip from Fairfield, where they lived in an old hotel, so that Donna could be close to Bill's family during a difficult pregnancy.

Bill Novis, too, had been born in Gooding twenty-six years earlier. His childhood was spent on his parents' homesteaded farm, five miles from the center of the rural town. Glenn Novis, Bill's father, had labored for years to clear the rolling fields of lava rock, had drilled a well to irrigate the barley and alfalfa, and as the boy grew, taught him to milk the cows, mow the hay, and perform the multitude of tasks necessary to work a dairy farm. Clear air and homegrown food nourished the youngster into a strapping six-foot-two, leather-muscled youth with large strong hands that could easily draw the milk from thirty-five cows, toss bales of hay onto a truck bed, and wrestle the farm machinery through the plowing, tilling, or harvesting chores, all in one day.

Bill loved the farm and the town, and felt a sense

of gratitude to his father for picking a place to raise his five children where the water was clean, where doors were left unlocked, and where the twenty-eight-hundred townspeople knew and trusted each other. Gooding had changed very little since its inauguration as a town on November 14, 1907, and the local folks were perfectly satisfied to keep it that way.

Before he graduated from high school in May 1958, Bill Novis had entered the U.S. Army Reserve. At the end of his active duty in March 1959, he returned to Gooding to continue working on his dad's farm.

Bill's sister and two of her friends, like many of the high-school girls in Gooding, enjoyed parading up and down Main Street during the lunch break, and Bill liked to drive in from the farm and watch the parade. One of his sister's friends, a sixteen-year-old sophomore named Donna Govia, had been in Gooding only one year. Donna's mother was a native of the little town, but had moved to California where Donna and six siblings were born. In 1961, however, the mother had decided that the environment in Gooding was more wholesome, and returned to rear her children there.

Bill thought the skinny little sophomore with the waist-length hair was really cute, but she didn't like him. "I always thought I was a pretty good kid," he would later say, with an easygoing drawl. "But she thought I was part of the Wild Bunch."

The three girls needed a ride one afternoon, and Bill was happy to accommodate them. In the car, "We got to talking and Donna finally agreed to go out with me."

There were several dates, and then several more. "I don't know," Bill remembered. "I guess I kinda grew on her. Being that Donna was my sister's friend, we double-dated. Went together about a year, then got engaged, and got married in August 1962. Went to Yellowstone National Park on our honeymoon." It was the beginning of a love that would develop, grow, and endure.

Within the first year of marriage, Bill and Donna had a daughter. They agreed that it would be Bill's job to name any daughters they had, and Donna would name sons. Bill was a fan of a popular singer named Brenda Lee, so their first daughter became Brenda Lee Novis.

During that first year, Bill continued to milk cows on his father's farm, but came to the realization that he wanted to move out and start a new life for his wife and daughter. They found a small house in Gooding and he, deciding to use the knowledge he had gained in the Army, bought a truck. He started hauling hay for the local farmers. His brother, who lived in Eugene, Oregon, and worked in a plywood mill, came to visit and was impressed with Bill's entrepreneurial efforts. "Why don't I buy a truck and we'll go in together and start a hay-hauling company," he offered.

The two brothers expanded to hauling grain during the long Idaho winter, when snow flurries periodically covered Gooding County roads. Bad weather sometimes reduced the hauling-business income to subsistence level, so the fledgling truckers were struggling to survive. A hay-and-grain broker in Fairfield liked the honesty and reliability of the Novis brothers, and offered them a contract for year-round hauling if they would relocate to Fairfield. They moved their families there to an old hotel in September 1965.

Three months later, Bill drove Donna to Gooding where she could be near his family when their second daughter was born.

Once more, it was Bill's turn to come up with a name. A rock star named Ray Peterson had a national hit, singing "Corinna, Corinna, where've you been so long?" Bill liked that.

Corinna Del Novis was never mistaken for a boy. "I could dress her up all in blue when she was tiny," Donna laughed, "and people would say, 'Oh, what a cute little girl.' " She was a completely feminine baby, who was bubbly, happy, and rarely cried.

On March 23, 1967, when Corinna was fourteen months old, Bill and Donna rounded out their family with a son. Donna, at last, had the privilege of dreaming up a name for her child. After considerable pondering and worrying, she came up with a marvelously original name: William Novis, Jr.

The children loved each other, and they adored animals. Corinna was especially fond of cats. And she fell head over heels for the horse that her parents gave her soon after she entered Frahm Junior High School. Both girls were given horses, and Corinna named hers Linda.

"Corinna was the luckiest one person you ever

laid eyes on," beamed Donna. "She didn't know the first thing about horses. But she tried to learn, and then entered a horse show. The very first time, the judges awarded Corinna the blue ribbon." She would eventually earn a trunkful of ribbons and a shelfful of trophies with her beloved Linda.

When Corinna was in the eighth grade, from out of the blue, she found a new interest. She announced to her mother that she was going to become a cheerleader. With her usual enthusiasm, she worked at it feverishly, and went to her first five-day cheerleader camp that summer. By the time she entered Gooding High School, everyone agreed that Corinna was going to be one of the top cheerleaders until she graduated. With her attractive figure, pretty face, big dark green eyes, shoulder-length brown hair, sunshine smile, and athletic skill, she was a natural.

In addition to her cheerleader skills, Corinna found a place on the varsity track team. She excelled in the three-hundred-meter hurdles, and was on the mile-relay team. She competed in the state championships in Moscow, Idaho, four years in a row.

With her driving work ethic and mercurial energy, Corinna found a variety of ways to earn extra money. She was a frequent baby-sitter; one couple simply would not allow anyone else to look after their son. In addition to a washing airplanes stint, she worked as a housecleaner for a teacher and the school principal. And she would later serve tables at the Lincoln Inn where farmers and folks gathered in the center of town to eat or have a friendly drink.

Corinna's income from these various part-time jobs allowed her to pay her own entertainment expenses without burdening her parents. Donna would recall that Corinna never wanted to be a burden in any way.

"I knew that I could totally trust my kids. When they were out late, I always knew exactly where they were. Sometimes, other mothers would call me to find out where their children were because they knew that my kids confided in me. I never had to stay up all night wondering."

Corinna graduated from Gooding High School in May 1984, with seventy-one other members of her senior class. She had accrued a respectable 3.1 grade point average, despite her many extracurricular activities. She immediately started making plans to attend the College of Southern Idaho in Twin Falls, twenty miles to the south.

At C.S.I., Corinna enrolled in a medical office procedures program, designed to be completed in one and one-half years. She would complete the requirements in one year. Recruited to join the track team at the college, she declined in favor of joining the cheerleader squad. What little spare time remained, she used as a volunteer for the American Red Cross and as a swimming teacher and lifeguard at the college swimming pool. She pulled one youngster from the pool who was nearly drowned, and was credited with saving his life.

A good-looking football player from Hagerman frequently joined the social scene in Gooding. Corinna had seen Mike McFadden many times during high school, at dances, at the Dairy Queen, or at Fall Holes, a popular gathering spot on the Snake where teenagers liked to gather, pop open a few beers, and join hands to leap over the white cliffs and plunge fifteen or twenty feet before splashing into the deep green water. They had often attended the same social gatherings, and they naturally became friends. That was before he went away to California to Redlands University, following his graduation from Hagerman High in 1982.

During the Thanksgiving break in 1984, when Mike came home for the holiday, he and Corinna ran into each other again, and agreed to get together after a C.S.I. football game. Something clicked. When he returned to California, they found excuses to frequently telephone each other. The Christmas holiday reunited them briefly, and the relationship grew during the next few months with letters and phone calls saying how much they missed each other.

On that Valentine's Day, Corinna and Mike decided that their relationship was mutually exclusive; they would go steady. Mike felt a deep happiness on his marathon return trip on Sunday.

After graduation from C.S.I. in May 1985, Corinna eagerly waited for the summer break at Redlands University, which would start in June, so that Mike could come home.

"We never missed one day of being together that summer," Mike McFadden recalled. "She'd ride her bicycle the ten miles over to my house to meet me for lunch. I was working with my dad's horses, as a trainer and veterinarian assistant. In the evenings, I'd work out in the weight room or I'd run, training for the next football season at Redlands. She would stay and help me work out, by timing my wind sprints or jogging with me."

"Mike lived in a really nice place," Donna said. "And Corinna knew she was always welcome there. But you know, the kids felt just as comfortable in our little house, and spent a lot of time here, together."

September came, the leaves changed colors, and it was time for Mike McFadden to journey back to Redlands University to resume his studies and play strong safety on the football team.

Corinna was never one to mope around. Outwardly, her smile was just as bright, and her schedule of work and play just as hectic. But she missed Mike, and she wanted to get started with her future. She wondered if she should move to California where she could be with the man she loved and take advantage of greater job opportunities. She talked a lot with her very best friend, her mom, who naturally preferred that her daughter stay near home.

At last, they reached a compromise. On the first day of April, Corinna boarded a Greyhound bus bound for Redlands. She would go there for a few weeks to see Mike and to find out if she wanted to make it permanent.

Corinna stayed in Redlands with Mike for almost five weeks. Her urge to be self-supportive was as strong as ever, so she took jobs at a doughnut shop and an aerobics studio. Her jobs and his school left little time for social activities, but they treasured their time together. At the end of the trial period, Mike drove her back to her parents in Gooding. She kissed him goodbye when he climbed into his car to return to Redlands and promised to be with him as soon as she could.

The next few weeks were a time of decision. After many discussions that lasted late into the nights, and some considerable resistance by Donna, Corinna at last concluded that it was time to make a change. She had been working as a waitress at the Lincoln Inn in Gooding, and had saved enough to support herself for a few months. She bought an airline ticket, and rode with her family to Twin Falls. She kissed them goodbye, told them she loved them, and boarded the plane for California.

When she arrived in Southern California to stay, in June 1986, Corinna Novis could not have been happier. There was a world of fun, opportunity, and love waiting for her, and she planned to share it with the man of her choice, Mike McFadden. Nothing could possibly interfere with their golden future.

While Corinna searched for her own place to

live, she shared Mike's apartment, just a few blocks from the campus of Redlands University. Mike would resume his studies there in September and continue playing strong safety on the football team. They had the whole summer to play, but Corinna's work ethic would not allow full-time leisure. She launched a job search the first week. Mike worked part-time at the college racquetball court.

Corinna landed a part-time job in Redlands with a State Farm insurance agency operated by Jean Cramer, whose son was Mike's fraternity brother. Until the job expanded, Corinna also dished up ice cream at a local store. She enjoyed working, and became fiercely loyal to her employers. Later, when the insurance job grew to a full-time position, she would still drop in at the ice cream parlor, and if they were busy, would help out free of charge.

As the summer dwindled away, and Mike McFadden faced the rigors of full-time classes and football, he began having doubts about a permanent relationship. He wondered if they both were perhaps too young for such a commitment. He and Corinna discussed it, and even though it was a "tough decision," they decided to taper off the relationship and just remain good friends.

Transportation became a problem after the breakup, so Corinna purchased a baby-blue moped equipped with a white basket on the front to carry books or insurance papers. Wearing her white helmet, Corinna was easily recognizable zipping around Redlands and the university campus. By now, she lived by herself in a comfortable one-bedroom duplex apartment two miles from the center of town.

An increasing amount of her time was spent on campus, dedicated to her continued deep interest in cheerleading. Utilizing the skills she had learned back at Gooding High School and C.S.I., she volunteered to coach the university cheerleaders, and became a regular part of the program.

A visit from Brenda, Corinna's sister, helped offset the hurt of her broken romance. Corinna agreed to return the visit soon, and she kept her promise in October. The reunion with Donna and Bill Novis was celebrated by the purchase of a new Honda CRX to replace Corinna's moped.

Once more Corinna waved goodbye to her beloved family and drove the car back to Redlands.

On Friday, November 7, Corinna had accepted an invitation to a fraternity party, but planned to meet some friends first. She made an appointment for another friend to manicure her long red fingernails at 5:30 P.M. in downtown Redlands. She was anxious to share the news that a cousin was coming to visit on Monday. As soon as she finished work, she hopped into the white Honda CRX and rushed over to Cho's liquor store to buy some non-tobacco cigarettes she had promised to bring to a buddy. The proprietor, Frank Cho, noted how pretty Corinna looked in black pants and a green-and-black vertical-striped blouse, with her hair pinned in a roll.

Corinna left Cho's and headed to the Redlands Mall to do some last-minute shopping and to buy a new pair of earrings.

Five

No more than ten or fifteen minutes passed before Corinna Novis exited the glass doors, and hurried toward her sparkling little Honda. Just as she
opened the driver's door, Cyndi Coffman approached her, and said, "Excuse me. You look like
a student. Are you going over to the college? Our
car is broken down and we sure could use a ride
over there."

Greg and Cyndi would later say that Corinna
Novis agreed to give them a ride and allowed them
to get into the Honda with her. The Novis family
would passionately dispute the idea that Corinna
willingly let two such disreputable-looking people
into her car. Even though Coffman was wearing a
dress, they pointed out, she looked strange with
her butch haircut, and Marlow's tough biker image
was not successfully disguised by a suit. "Their
whole story about Corinna picking them up was
the biggest crock," Corinna's sister, Brenda, protested. "There was no way she would do that. She
was very cautious when I visited her, and she
would never pick up a hitchhiker or a stranger
asking for a ride." Corinna's father said that he

firmly believed that she was forced into the car, and Corinna's mother emphasized that even though her daughter was from a small rural town where people trusted each other, she was not naive, and definitely would not have agreed to give two tough-looking people a ride.

So Corinna, either willingly or by force, drove her Honda out of the mall parking lot, past the gaunt eucalyptus trees at the driveway exit, and onto Redlands Boulevard. Marlow sat in the passenger's seat, with Cyndi on his lap. The sun had dropped down over the horizon, dragging the temperature down with it.

When Corinna turned onto a dark street, toward Redlands University, Marlow jerked suddenly, revealed the gun he had concealed under the suit coat, and jammed it into Corinna's ribs. "Okay, pull over to the curb," he ordered. The startled girl complied.

"I don't have anything . . . ," Corinna appealed to her captors, but they paid no attention. Cyndi slid off Marlow's lap and out the passenger's door, skirted the car, and squeezed in next to Corinna. Marlow pulled Corinna toward him, forcing her onto his lap so that Cyndi could drive the car.

After circling a few blocks, Cyndi found the on-ramp to I-10, known locally as the San Bernardino freeway, accelerated into the Friday night commuter traffic and headed west in the direction of Los Angeles. Corinna began to plead with Cyndi Coffman. But she wasn't begging for her own safety. "Please," she asked, "please don't hurt my car. It's new, and I'm really trying to take care of it. Please don't wreck it or anything."

Coffman ignored her. She listened instead to Marlow, who told her, "Head toward Rick's house." She knew that he meant the shabby apartment of Richard Drinkhouse where they had spent the previous night.

They drove west on the freeway for twenty minutes, past San Bernardino, between a twin row of towering eucalyptus trees, past the site of the old Fontana steel mill, before Greg finally told Cyndi where to exit. She pointed the car in the direction of the silhouetted mountains to the north and after a couple of miles, recognized Foothill Boulevard. Soon, Cyndi saw the run-down cluster of single-story apartments on her right. She pulled into the rutted driveway, eased between the two rows of battered dwellings, and parked in front of unit number 106.

Marlow dragged Corinna with him as he got out of the car, and the trio walked under the tar-papered overhang that served as a porch. Cyndi followed Corinna, carrying the girl's purse. Greg tapped at the door, which was opened by a twenty-eight-year-old, corpulent, short, seedy-looking man, barefooted. Richard Drinkhouse, in the fashion of his peers, wore a stringy black beard outlining his round, swarthy face, and dressed in jeans and a stained T-shirt. He limped back from the door, favoring his left leg which he had broken several months earlier in a motorcycle accident, and allowed Greg, Cyndi, and their captive, to enter. Ignoring the frightened stranger, Drinkhouse grunted "Hi" to his boyhood pal. The only answer came from Corinna, who weakly returned his "Hi."

Without any conversation Greg and Cyndi pulled Corinna through the cluttered living room past scarred and dusty maple furniture, a grimy green-flowered French provincial couch, and a blaring television set with exposed wires leading to holes in the cheaply paneled wall. Empty beer cans and full ashtrays littered the place. Leaving their host standing in silence, the trio turned through a doorway into an equally messy bedroom. Greg ordered Corinna to sit on the unmade bed, where piles of soiled clothing spilled onto the dirty brown carpet.

When Corinna obeyed, Greg quickly snapped one loop of a pair of handcuffs on her right wrist, and connected the other end to a decorative arch in the wooden headboard. Cyndi sat down in a chair near the entry to a roughly tiled bathroom and shower, which reeked of mildew. Greg returned to the living room.

Richard Drinkhouse had plopped back on the couch to watch television. Greg studied him for a moment, then volunteered, "We brought her here, Rick, because we need to talk to her. We want to get her bankcard number, you know, that secret number you gotta have so we can use her card to make money come out of a machine at the bank. Cyndi used to have a card she could do that with."

Drinkhouse nodded, and Greg returned to the

bedroom. Muffled conversation from his friends and their captive was unintelligible to Drinkhouse. His curiosity got the best of him so he got up and shuffled toward the bedroom door, pretending to be after his shoes, but in reality trying to see what was going on in there. He could see Cyndi sitting in a chair at the end of the bed, but his view of the captive girl was obstructed. Only her legs, from the knees down, were visible.

Cyndi noticed their seedy friend hovering near the door. She glanced his way, then toward Greg, and nodded her head toward Drinkhouse.

Drinkhouse sensed that he shouldn't be prying, and went back to the living room. Greg stalked through the door and gave him an order. "Just stay on the couch and watch TV."

Shortly, Coral had finished her shift in the sandwich shop at Redlands Mall and stopped by Richard's apartment. Greg came out of the bedroom again, at the same time Coral entered the living room. "Hi, Coral," he greeted her. "I need to get some of my stuff out of your car." They stepped outside together.

Greg leaned close to Coral's face and whispered, "Coral, I've got someone here." Coral looked puzzled. Greg continued, "Now don't freak out on me." Coral still wasn't entirely sure what he meant, but shrugged it off.

When they reentered, Greg cleared up his cryptic comment. He told Coral about the girl in the bedroom and how he planned to take money from her bank account. Cyndi again disappeared into the bedroom, followed shortly by Greg, leaving Coral to watch TV with Richard. Within a few minutes, Drinkhouse could hear running water in his shower.

When Cyndi Coffman later described the events in the apartment that night, she told the following story:

"I was sitting in the bedroom with the girl when Greg came back in and told me to make him a cup of coffee. When I brought it to him, he was still sitting there trying to get the PIN (personal identification number) out of her. That's when I told her to do what he said. Give him the number. And she gave it to him.

"After about a half hour, he taped her mouth, and said, 'We are going to take a shower.' Then he took her clothes off and put her in the shower. I was standing in the bedroom and didn't say anything. He took his clothes off and climbed in, with the shower on, and I knew what was going to happen, so I just turned around and walked away. I knew he was going to rape her.

"I went into the living room where I had left a pair of jeans and a shirt, and I took them back into the bedroom and changed into them.

"When he climbed out of the shower, he said, 'Why don't you help her get dressed?'

"I said, 'Take the handcuffs off her, and she can dress herself.' He did it, and she got dressed."

***

Marlow told the story a little differently:

"I can't remember exactly the times, but . . . um . . . Cyndi got into the shower with that lady. And she asked me to get in the shower, too, so I did. Cyndi took her clothes off first, then helped the girl take her clothes off. They got in the shower together, and I got my clothes off and got in with them.

"Cyndi wanted to see me be with a girl. And she pushed us together, and I couldn't . . . a lot of times I couldn't get it up for Cyndi. That's why she flirted around a lot and would give me oral sex.

"So, in the shower, I couldn't do anything . . . it wasn't doing anything for me, so Cyndi gave me oral sex there, too. After she was done, she started to kiss around on the lady. Then we all got out and got dressed."

He also stated that Corinna gave her PIN to Cyndi while they were in the shower.

But neither of them would completely reveal what happened within the tiled walls of that dark, moist, mildewed cell. Neither of their stories accounted for subsequent evidence that the helpless captive had been sodomized.

The main thing Drinkhouse could remember about the episode was hearing the shower running for five to ten minutes, and that when Greg came out of there, wearing only his trousers and a towel over his shoulder, he had wet hair. He couldn't tell if Cyndi's hair was also wet because "it was so short."

When Cyndi entered the living room, according to a later account, she carried Corinna's purse and dumped the contents onto a coffee table. She or Greg had previously taken the bankcard from it, so she sifted through the remaining contents but found little worth keeping other than a few dollars in cash. She reportedly said, "This bitch has got four IDs."

Seeing the money, Greg asked Cyndi and Coral to go to a nearby 7-Eleven convenience store to get some cigarettes and Pepsi. Drinkhouse asked for some beer. Cyndi went to Coral's car with her, struggled to remove a bulging duffel bag from the backseat of the Buick, and lugged it into the apartment. Then, the two women left in the Honda to make the purchases. Cyndi also used Corinna's money to partially fill the gas tank of the little car.

While they were gone, Greg was back and forth between the bedroom and the living room. Drinkhouse stayed on the couch, but while Greg was in the bedroom with the captive girl, overheard her ask, "Are you going to take me home now?"

"As soon as they get back," he heard Greg reply.

Shortly after Cyndi and Coral returned, Coral told the group that she was going to leave. Greg and Cyndi stepped to the door, waved, and watched Coral's taillights disappear from the driveway.

Minutes later they brought Corinna into the living room. Drinkhouse saw that the girl, whose hair was damp, had gray duct tape over her mouth, her wrists handcuffed behind her back, and a jacket, "like a green flight jacket," draped over her shoulders.

According to Greg Marlow, Drinkhouse then spoke up, saying that he deserved something for the use of his place. "I want a thousand dollars for you bringing that girl over here." Marlow also claimed that Drinkhouse said, "You can't just let her go 'cause she is . . . she'll bring the cops right back here to me."

"What do you expect me to do? Put her under some rocks or something?" Drinkhouse never acknowledged such a conversation.

Marlow was still wearing the suit pants and white shirt he had borrowed, but tossed the coat and the brown necktie into the Honda. Before he and Coffman got in, they realized that they couldn't risk allowing Corinna to sit up where she could be noticed, so they pushed her into a reclining position behind the seats, still bound and gagged with tape. They covered her with blankets and a sleeping bag. Cyndi climbed into the driver's seat.

Out of the driveway, she turned right on Foothill Boulevard. The commuter traffic had given way to Friday night social traffic; a constant stream of bright headlights and the rosy glow of hundreds of taillights. Marlow and Coffman wanted something a little more private and secluded.

She drove six blocks and turned left onto Sierra Avenue, toward I-10. As they approached the freeway, she and Greg argued about going to the house of a drug dealer, but couldn't because they only had fifteen dollars.

Crossing over the busy freeway, they continued south on Sierra, which leads into the rural countryside. All that Coffman and Marlow could see to their right was vacant land, and to their left, a large abandoned grape vineyard. The heavy traffic was left behind; only the headlights of an occasional car probed the gloomy night.

The little car started bumping along a narrow, dusty, dirt road into a dead vineyard. Cyndi drove about one hundred yards before braking to a halt. Marlow stepped out, removed the blankets and sleeping bag from atop Corinna, and pulled her out of the car. He freed her hands and peeled the duct tape from her mouth.

Marlow ordered Coffman to buy some drugs at the dealer they'd argued about minutes before. Thinking that Greg wanted to rape the young girl again, Cyndi took off for about twenty minutes, then came back.

A short time later, Marlow and Coffman were on the road again back to the city.

In the cold dark vineyard, surrounded by tangled grapevines and weed-choked clods of earth, Corinna Novis lay facedown in a shallow grave. She had been brutally strangled with a ligature, perhaps a necktie, and her face had been pushed into the sandy soil with such force that her mouth was packed with dirt. It would be theorized that it took two people to perpetrate the murder. The young woman, who worked so hard and always had a smile for everyone, was no more. She had endured a prolonged night of pitiless, abusive lust, and finally cruel, deadly violence that tore away her life. The horror and pain for her was over, but the agony for others was just beginning.

Six

"Are you okay now?" Cynthia asked Greg, as she drove the Honda away from the somber vineyard.

"I'll never be okay now," he groaned. "Not ever again I don't think." The drooping corners of his mustache exaggerated his frown. "Let's head over to Matin's place so I can get out of this monkey suit, and give it back to the guy who loaned it to me," Greg said, pointing toward Colton. Cyndi headed the Honda east along Foothill Boulevard. Less than five miles behind them, silence once again enveloped the dead vineyard where the still warm body of their victim lay, covered by a few inches of sandy soil and some hastily improvised camouflage of weeds and brush.

Greg and Cyndi had killed, ostensibly to steal enough money to enable them to travel to Phoenix to kill again. They had the car they needed, but hadn't yet stuffed their pockets with the anticipated cash from Corinna's bankcard.

In Colton, at the Matin house, they were surprised to see Coral's car parked at the curb. Cyndi braked to a stop behind the Buick Skylark and Greg went into the house. He greeted Coral, who was there alone, peeled out of the suit, and donned his familiar camouflage pants, boots, T-shirt, and army fatigue jacket, clothing he had left there earlier. Following a quick, whispered conversation with his sister, about the location of a bank, he and Cyndi sped away.

A little past nine P.M., Cyndi and Greg stopped at a 7-Eleven convenience store, had a cold drink, then drove across the street to a First Interstate bank. Cyndi parked a few feet away from the automatic teller machine, and while Greg waited in the car, she anxiously inserted the card in the machine's slot. Following instructions on the video screen, Cyndi tapped out the six digit PIN number Corinna had given them, anxiously glanced toward Greg, and waited. Nothing happened. She frowned, and read the message on the ATM screen, which told her that she had entered an incorrect identification number.

Once more, Cyndi carefully punched each button to enter the code Corinna had given them. It was still incorrect.

"Damn! She lied to us," Cyndi hissed.

Back in the car, Greg ranted furiously, incoherently. Cyndi could understand only: ". . . that damn bitch! We gotta find that number." On the outside chance that Corinna had written her secret code on any of the assorted documents stored in the glove compartment, Greg began pulling its contents out and, with Cyndi's help, examining the various papers, holding them up to the amber glow of overhead lights. They didn't find the number, but they did discover a street map which, when unfolded, revealed a small, inked circle indicating a location in Redlands. "Bet that's where she lives," Cyndi exclaimed.

"Okay, let's go over there and see if we can find the right number to that bank machine."

After getting lost a couple of times, Cyndi stopped a few yards past a long gravel driveway which disappeared into the darkness along a row of green cinder block, single-story apartments. When no one was in sight, they strolled into the driveway, straining to see the apartment numbers, and cautiously circumvented the dim cubicles of light filtering from windows. Crunching slowly along the gravel surface about thirty yards, they passed under the shadowed canopy of an enormous walnut tree, walked another seventy yards, and stopped in front of the last apartment. Greg fumbled around the doorknob, inserted a key and the door to the dark apartment swung open.

Stopping briefly in the small, immaculate living room, they let their eyes grow accustomed to the darkness, then went into the single bedroom where they risked switching on a light. Cyndi attacked a file cabinet, while Greg rifled through the pockets of Corinna's clothing in the closet. He found a few dollars in bills and change, then began to survey the room for anything else of value.

Cyndi snatched a folder from the file cabinet, peeled out a handful of papers which she threw on the bed, and in a loud, hoarse whisper, said, "Look, here it is. Here's her bankbook and her code number. Damn, looks like she just took some of her money out a little while ago."

Excited, Greg intensified his search, hoping to find some of the money Corinna had taken from her account, but was unsuccessful. He found a box that had contained a new telephone answering machine, but the unit had already been installed and the container was empty. He tossed it on the bed. "Hell with it then," he complained, "we'll just take some of this stuff to sell, then go to the bank and get the money."

Greg kneeled, deftly unclipped a telephone cord from the wall connection, and wrapped it around the answering machine. He handed it to Cyndi, and picked up a brown portable typewriter from a table. They had been in the apartment for over a half hour, and it was time to leave.

It was nearly eleven P.M. when they arrived back at the Colton house they had visited earlier in the evening. Cyndi sat in the Honda and waited while Greg went to the door where he was met by Coral. "Coral, we got a telephone answering machine I wanna sell to pick up a few bucks. Know anyone might buy it?"

Coral turned toward her ex-boyfriend, Curtis Matin, who was wondering where his suit was (he finally found it three days later, wadded and soiled, in a spare room), and asked, "Curt, you want to buy a recorder?"

"Nah," he replied, as he stepped to the door and glanced outside where he saw the white Honda parked at the curb.

Greg faced Coral's friend and asked, "How about a pistol? You wanna buy a pistol?" Matin declined.

Coral thought she might know someone who would be interested in the answering set, so she, Greg, and Cyndi piled into Coral's Buick to visit some underworld cronies. It was a waste of time.

A few hours before dawn, Coral dropped them off again at the Honda. "Let's go back to the bank and see if that code number will work to get the money," Greg said, directing Cyndi to resume her chauffeur role. At 4:49 A.M., still in darkness, Cyndi approached an automatic teller, this time next to the Redlands Mall where they had abducted Corinna. She inserted the card and carefully punched the PIN number.

The machine responded with a message on the screen asking what transaction to conduct. Cyndi eagerly keyed an inquiry to determine the amount of money in Corinna's checking account. She saw the readout on the screen and cursed. There was a meager $15.05 balance. She punched another button, only to find that a savings account had been closed out. Because Corinna had less than twenty dollars in the bank, the minimum required for transactions, and no arrangement to withdraw advances, Cyndi walked away, empty-handed again.

Exhausted from a night of greed, violence, and death, the couple returned to the apartment of Richard Drinkhouse to sleep for a few hours.

On the following morning, Saturday, November 8, Greg Marlow and Cyndi Coffman were still in need of cash. They left the Drinkhouse apartment in the Buick with Coral, and visited a couple of Greg's acquaintances to try to sell the typewriter, but found no takers. At last, the trio drove to a pawn shop in central Fontana, and Cyndi, by herself, carried the machine into the cluttered store. After a few moments of haggling, Cyndi agreed to leave the typewriter in exchange for thirty dollars. She identified herself as Corinna Novis, produced a driver's license to prove it, and signed Corinna's name on the pawn ticket.

With money in their pockets, they drove directly to the connection's house and bought a quarter-gram of speed for twenty-five dollars. Coral returned Greg and Cyndi to the Honda and the couple drove to a secluded, rustic wooded area, Lytle Creek, to loaf away the day and enjoy their booty. They did attend to one bit of "business." Cyndi took some of the things out of Corinna's purse that she didn't want, buried them, and refilled the purse with her own personal items.

The sky above Lytle Creek glowed coral and scarlet as the sun dropped through the haze of Los Angeles County, west of the picturesque canyon. It had been just twenty-four hours since Greg and Cyndi had abducted a beautiful young woman from Redlands Mall to rob her of enough money to pay for their planned journey to Phoenix, but they sat in Lytle Creek—homeless, hungry, and broke.

That night, teaming once more with Coral at the Drinkhouse apartment, the trio decided to try to sell Corinna's answering machine. They hurried to the home of one of Coral's friends who had no use for the device but volunteered to steer them to someone else who might. She squeezed into the car and gave directions to another house, just five blocks away.

The woman carried the answering machine to the door, and disappeared into the house. In a few minutes she returned, and handed a small bag to Greg, who glanced inside it and saw about a half-gram of methamphetamine in a plastic bag. He grunted his assent to the trade.

After dropping her friend off, Coral drove them to Mike Willoughby's house in San Bernardino to get "an outfit or rig," a hypodermic needle to inject the methamphetamine. Greg and Cyndi went inside while Coral waited in the car. She was eventually coaxed in and the group remained there, injecting the drug, talking, and sharing cold pizza, until almost three in the morning. When the speed was all used up, Coral returned Greg and Cyndi to the parked Honda.

Standing at the curb between the Honda and the Buick, in the early morning darkness, Greg did an unusual thing, as if he had a foreboding premonition that there might not be many more opportunities. He hugged his half sister, Coral. Such a show of affection between the siblings was rare, but he did it, and she would remember it years later.

Then, almost embarrassed, he asked her for directions to the beach and she, puzzled, gave them to him. Greg and Cyndi said bye to Coral, hopped into the Honda, and were off into the night. They wound their way through the vast network of freeways from San Bernardino County to Orange County, traveling over sixty miles before veering from the freeway at an off-ramp about twelve miles north of San Clemente, where Richard Milhous Nixon's home once served as the Western White House.

The beach area, where "all the rich people lived," should provide easy pickings; a ready victim to be robbed, easy money, and, perhaps, another beautiful young female victim who could be brutally used to satisfy carnal lust.

Bright rays of pink dawn had not yet reached Dana Point when Cyndi and Greg arrived on Sunday morning.

Like predators watching for a kill, Cyndi and Greg waited in the marina parking lot until the cliff shadows receded and warm morning sunshine drove away the chill ocean mist. But it was too early. Their potential prey was still asleep. The couple decided to extend the hunt northwest, along the coast.

Cruising along California State Highway 1, known locally as Pacific Coast Highway, Greg and Cyndi entered Laguna Beach, another popular resort community and mecca for artists, tourists, skin divers, and sunbathers. They passed a Taco Bell and Kentucky Fried Chicken restaurant. Neither of the fast-food restaurants was yet open. It didn't matter, they didn't have any money anyway.

Past Laguna Beach, through wealthy Newport Beach, Cyndi and Greg finally pulled to a stop at surfers' paradise, Huntington Beach. Exhausted, they flopped down on the sand and let the roar of the surf and the squawking seagulls lull them to sleep.

When they woke, the sun was high in the sky and the Sunday beach crowd, sparse in November, sprawled on colorful towels or waded in the chill ocean water.

"We've gotta find another one," Greg muttered. "Didn't get any money from that girl. We'll just have to look for another one."

Seven

On Monday morning, November 10, Jean Cramer, the owner of a State Farm Insurance agency in Redlands, was surprised and worried. Corinna Novis had always telephoned if she was going to be late, but Cramer had heard nothing by midmorning. Something must be wrong, because the reliable young woman wasn't answering her home phone either. A growing sense of distress tugged at the worried agent until she could no longer rationalize it, so she drove over to Corinna's apartment. The Honda wasn't there, but Cramer tried the door anyway. Peering through the closed outer screen door, she saw that the entry door was ajar. After tentatively pushing it all the way open, Cramer stepped inside and gasped at a "sauna-like" blast of hot air. She called out, "Corinna, are you here?"

Only silence answered her. Cramer glanced around, noted the refrigerator door was open, then stepped into the bedroom. It was in disarray, with dresser drawers open and papers scattered on the bed. In the bathroom, none of Corinna's grooming items were missing. She obviously hadn't packed for a trip. Cramer grabbed the telephone and called the police. While waiting for their arrival, she called Mike McFadden.

Since their breakup, Mike had still kept tabs on Corinna, and had verified, less than a week ago, that she planned to attend the Friday night gathering. He hadn't seen her there, but in a crowd of over two hundred people, he might have missed her. He had really started worrying when he didn't see her at the Saturday football game, either. Mike knew that "for all the world" she just wouldn't miss watching the cheerleaders she coached or watching him play. It was peculiar, too, that when he tried to telephone over the weekend, neither she nor her new answering machine picked up his calls. He'd thought about driving over there, but didn't want to interfere if it was anything personal, perhaps related to someone new in her life.

The relative Corinna was supposed to meet at the airport was puzzled, too, by her cousin's failure to show up. And the manicurist friend was no less troubled.

By the time Mike joined Cramer and the police at Corinna's apartment, he was convinced that something terrible had happened. But all he could do was wait by a phone, like Cramer, and hope that she would call soon. Other friends began printing posters to distribute around Redlands asking for help in finding Corinna Novis.

***

On that same Monday morning, James Gregory
Marlow and Cynthia Coffman started cruising the
beach communities again. Hunger gnawed at their
stomachs, demanding satisfaction, and the need
for food transcended the hunt for human prey. Finally, they realized that they had a way to steal a
few more bucks when Cyndi remembered the meager fifteen dollars and five cents that was in
Corinna Novis's checking account at First Interstate Bank. It didn't take them long to find a
branch just a couple of miles off Pacific Coast
Highway in Laguna Niguel. Cyndi withdrew
Corinna's checkbook, driver's license, and a pen
from the purse they had taken from her.

After a few minutes of practice forging Corinna's signature as it appeared on the stolen
driver's license, Cyndi wrote a check for fifteen
dollars, then strode confidently into the bank to
cash it. The bank clerk dutifully checked a computer screen to assure adequate funding in the
account and asked for identification. Cyndi presented Corinna's driver's license, and the clerk
compared the signatures, entered the license
number on the back of the check, and counted
out fifteen dollars.

After filling the tank of the Honda with gas and
their stomachs with some cheap fast food, the couple resumed their search for a new victim. Cyndi
was driving, still in Laguna Beach, when Greg's
head snapped sharply to the right. A shapely
blonde woman, walking along the sidewalk, was approaching a parked red Corvette.

"That's the one," he barked at Cyndi, in an eerie repetition of the words he had used when he pointed out Corinna Novis. "Turn the car around. Go!"

Cyndi remembered her reaction. "I just looked at him. And I turned the car around and went, and by the time we got back to where we had seen her before, she had disappeared. But just about at that point, we see the car coming this way. We're going this way (the opposite direction) and . . . he told me to follow her. We followed her for about ten minutes. Then we lost her. It was about five o'clock in the afternoon, when the sun goes down."

Attempting to locate the red Corvette, Cyndi and Greg repeatedly circled the area, but without success. They parked and waited, but neither the blonde in the red car nor any other prospective victims appeared.

At about 9:30 P.M., high-school senior Heather Voss and her friend Penny May Orth were in trouble. It was Heather's seventeenth birthday, and the couple was driving to a friend's house in Huntington Beach to celebrate. They had just passed the Huntington Inn on Pacific Coast Highway, and turned right, when the transmission malfunctioned on Voss's old Dodge Colt. They coasted into the rear parking lot of the inn, and were sitting in the dark, wondering what to do, when they saw a White Honda CRX pull into the lot. The muscular driver, the girls observed, must have been inexperienced behind the wheel because he jerked the car each time it moved. The back of the car appeared to be filled with blankets and clothing.

The man stepped out, walked over to the stranded couple, and asked if they needed help. After Voss explained the problem, the man said, "Well, hang on a second," and conferred with his passenger, a slim woman with short hair. Voss would later report that she heard the man ask, "Should I?" and the woman replied, "Yes." When he returned, he looked under the car and told the women that he would need a jack.

Penny said that she knew someone in the adjacent mobile home park who would give her a ride to her car, she and Heather could drive to a location where they could obtain a jack, and then they would return. She asked if the Honda driver would wait. He gave no firm commitment.

Within minutes after her departure, Penny arrived in her car to pick up Heather. The couple in the Honda had parked in a corner of the lot, and the two girls pulled next to them to ask again if they would wait. The man said, "Okay, I might be here." But thirty minutes later, when Penny and Heather returned with a jack, the Honda was gone.

In Laguna Beach three hours later, hungry again, Greg and Cyndi pulled into the parking lot between the Taco Bell and Kentucky Fried Chicken restaurants they had passed on the previous day. Cyndi later described it. "We went in the Taco Bell, ordered food, went outside in the car, and ate it. It (the restaurant) was getting ready—after we had gotten our food they were probably only open about five or ten more minutes."

An assistant manager, working the night shift at the Taco Bell, would later tell a far different account of Cyndi Coffman's visit to the restaurant.

Cyndi's recollection continued. "After we had finished eating, Greg told me to give him my ID, that he had to throw my ID away. I asked him why. He said, 'Because you can't have it on you. What if we get pulled over? You can't have your ID.'"

Cyndi gave Greg some of her identification cards, along with Corinna Novis's driver's license, checkbook, and several other items. "He took it, and his own ID, and he wrapped them all up, mine and his together, and he wrapped hers (Novis's) individually in a different bag. He got out of the car and said he was going to throw them away. And he was gone a few minutes, and he came back to the car."

Leaving Cyndi in the car, and carrying the Taco Bell bag containing the ID cards, Marlow walked across the lot toward the Kentucky Fried Chicken restaurant, turned, and went to the trash Dumpster at the rear of the building. He glanced around in the darkness, tossed the bag toward the Dumpster, and returned to the car.

It was late, and they were tired and drove up an inclining street to a residential neighborhood in the hills of Laguna Beach, to sleep again in the car. They parked on a quiet street, and curled up in the little Honda.

The distant roar of commuter traffic stirred a cramped, unbathed, rumpled pair out of uncomfortable, groggy sleep in a little Honda on Tuesday morning. Cyndi felt grimy and grumpy as she looked at her hands. The long fingernails she so carefully cultivated were dirty and unpainted. That depressed her even more.

At the Kentucky Fried Chicken restaurant in Laguna Beach, Armando Hernandez could hear the pleasant rhythm of the crashing surf and crying seagulls only a block away from his workplace. He had completed picking up Monday night's trash, even some that had blown over from the Taco Bell across the parking lot. It was only 9:30 A.M., and he had nearly finished his clean-up work. As he tossed the last bag of trash into the Dumpster, something on the ground, near a trash compactor, caught his eye. Some cards had partially spilled out of a Taco Bell bag that had apparently fallen from the Dumpster.

Hernandez leaned down to examine the find, nudging the bag with his foot. *Well*, he thought, *that's Taco Bell stuff. I'd better call the manager over there.*

The Taco Bell manager, David Cook, summoned by Hernandez, kneeled to examine the discovery. He thanked the finder, picked up the bag, stuffed the spilled items back into it, and carried it back over to his restaurant. There, he examined the material more closely. He found several different identifications and some checks along with a red wallet. Something looked peculiar to him. On one of the checks, there were repeated signatures of the name on one of the ID cards.

Looked like they were trying to do some forging, he thought.

If they were ever going to get to Phoenix, to score the lucrative kill, Greg and Cyndi had to resume their search for someone to rob.

"We drove around again looking for people," Cyndi said. "We never did find anybody. We went back to the same spot where the Corvette had been parked, but it never came back that day."

After spending more than an hour waiting for the Corvette, Cyndi and Greg hit the road again, driving northwest on Pacific Coast Highway.

"We drove around to different places," Cyndi recalled. "We were still looking for someone, and wound up in Huntington Beach at the Prime Cleaners. We were driving through there, and we parked by the (athletic) club that's right next to it. Greg saw a woman walking out of the dry cleaners and he told me that she was by herself, and that would be a good place to rob the woman by herself."

***

In Redlands, Det. Joseph Bodnar was growing more concerned about the disappearance of Corinna Novis. The sincerity of her boyfriend, Mike McFadden, and one of her other friends Bodnar had visited the previous day at the missing girl's apartment, had impressed him. No one had seen the girl since last Friday, and he knew that the likelihood of finding her would diminish with each passing day. He knew of the missing person posters that had been spread throughout the city and the Redlands University campus. Maybe they would help turn up a lead soon.

Now, on Tuesday the eleventh, Bodnar was encouraged when the call came from Laguna Beach informing him that Corinna's ID, along with two other people's, had been discovered. An inventory of the items found by the Taco Bell manager included an Idaho driver's license, an ATM card, and some blank checks from Redlands, all in the name of Corinna D. Novis; an Arizona driver's license, with a Page address, for Cynthia Lynn Coffman; and a medical emergency card for James Gregory Marlow.

Surely, these documents would have an immediate effect. Bodnar allowed a glimmer of optimism to take hold, and prayed that they would find the missing girl alive with this Coffman and Marlow. He hurried across the hall to tell Scotty Smith.

Detective Sergeant L. Scott "Scotty" Smith had just been assigned to the Novis case. Built like a fireplug, and blessed with clean-cut good looks, a disarming smile, and soft-spoken manner, he was a prototype of the ideal cop who could talk to a classroom of kids or a cell full of violent felons with equal ease. At twenty-six, he was one of the youngest detectives in the history of Redlands. He didn't know it yet, but he was starting to work on his first homicide case.

The two detectives immediately requested printouts of any criminal history related to the names Cynthia Coffman and James G. Marlow. There were minor infractions on Coffman and an outstanding warrant related to her failure to appear in a Barstow court; with Marlow, they thought that they had pulled four sevens on a Las Vegas slot machine. Marlow's extensive record revealed robberies and prison time, which certainly suggested that he could be involved in the disappearance of Novis. The officers felt a slim sense of relief that no homicide charges were listed. Cynthia Coffman was either another victim or an accomplice. Coffman's address in Page, Arizona, at least suggested a place to start looking, and, they hoped, might provide the first link in a chain leading to the missing girl. Before calling the Page police, Smith and Bodnar arranged to put out an all points bulletin in San Bernardino County, as had been done in Orange County, to be on the lookout (b.o.l.o.) for Marlow, Coffman, and, of course, Corinna Novis.

In San Bernardino, Marlow's name was not unfamiliar to some of the local law enforcement officers. One was dispatched to see if Marlow's half sister, Coral Willoughby, might have some knowledge of his whereabouts.

* * *

After Tuesday's sunset, Greg and Cyndi parked in a lot behind the Huntington Beach Inn on Pacific Coast Highway. A decision had been made to rob the dry cleaning store, but first they needed to change the license plates on the Honda. He spotted an unattended car in a dark corner of the lot and figured that he could steal the plates from that car and put them on the Honda.

Cyndi described the events. "Greg got out of the car and tried to change plates. And he came back and he was mad because his fingers were too big—he couldn't get (them) behind it to hold the bolt to turn. He told me to go and switch the plates." She added that, in his anger, he kept punching the sensitive stab wound on her leg, and bit her arm, telling her how stupid she was.

She removed the plates from the car, but when she returned to Greg, they discovered that the stolen license plate was useless. The expiration date was long past.

After one more failure, they at last replaced the Honda plates with some stolen ones.

Broke again, they needed some money for food. Marlow went to the soft-drink-dispensing machine in a passageway of the inn, waited until no one was around, and managed to break into the coin box. When he and Cyndi counted the stolen coins, they found that he had taken nearly twenty dollars, more than enough for a fast-food dinner. After they had satisfied their hunger, they found a secluded spot, and spent a third night in the car.

On the morning of the fourth day of their hunt in the beach towns, Wednesday, November 12, Greg was absolutely determined to find a new victim. But that day, for the first nine hours, was a duplicate of the previous three. Cyndi described that morning. "We drove around again, doing the same thing, looking, got some food to eat, and the day just went on. Around four or five o'clock he said, 'Let's just go back and rob that (dry) cleaners.' "

Eight

On May 31, 1967, Lynel Murray was born in the Edwards Air Force Base military hospital. Nancy Murray had heard that giving birth was traumatic, but she was amazed at how easy Lynel's delivery was. She thought, *I could do this again.* She would.

"That was the year the Indianapolis 500 was rained out on May thirtieth," Don Murray would recall. "I had to work the next morning. When I got off at noon, I drove across base to the hospital listening to the race on the radio. When I arrived at the hospital, I got to hold my little daughter."

Don thought that the doctor who delivered her looked exactly like Dr. Ben Casey, the infallible television medic portrayed by actor Vince Edwards.

One of Nancy's best friends, when she was in high school, was named Lynel. It was a beautiful name, Nancy thought, and one she'd never heard before. She decided while she was still a student that if she ever had a baby, she was going to name it after her high-school chum.

Lynel Murray was a perfect baby with sunny

blond hair, her parents' blue eyes, and the complexion of a Viking. She learned to talk early, and "never stopped talking." She was an "incredible chatterer" her mother would recall, just like her paternal great-grandmother, Dorothy Ann Harlan. "Mrs. Harlan, bless her heart, was just like Lynel. You'd walk into a room, and she would start talking. You could walk out, return an hour later, and she would still be talking, and she would never know you'd been gone. She was one of the neatest ladies in the world. Lynel inherited it directly from her."

As a baby, Lynel was rarely grumpy. But when she was, it was quite easy to change her mood. "All you had to do was feed her," her family would reminisce. "Then she would become one of the jolliest people in the world. It was a lifelong pattern with her. You feed her, and then she could not stop laughing. When she was older, she would sit at the dinner table and cry because she was laughing so hard."

A highly controversial military event in January 1968 changed many lives, and filtered down to Don and Nancy Murray. Commander Lloyd Bucher, in charge of a U.S. Navy intelligence-gathering ship, the *Pueblo*, surrendered his vessel and crew to North Koreans who seized it. The sailors would be in captivity for the remainder of the year. Threats of hostilities between the United States and Korea erupted, causing the United States to reinforce military installations in Japan. Itizuki Air Force Base, 123 miles from Korea, across the Sea

Of Japan, was reopened. A few months later, Airman Don Murray was stationed at Itizuki.

Nancy and baby Lynel followed in September. Enlisted men were not entitled to free transportation for families, so Don sold everything he could to scrape enough money together for their plane fare. They found housing in an old bachelor officers' quarters building.

Lynel was a big hit among the military families and the Japanese citizens. Everyone wanted to touch her for good luck, in awe of the sky-blue eyes, blond tresses, which sharply contrasted with the round-faced Japanese babies and their coal-black hair. "We couldn't take her anywhere without someone picking her up and carrying her around," Nancy boasted.

Just before New Year's Eve, 1969, Nancy felt sick, and realized that she was pregnant again. The new family member arrived on August 22. Lynel and her little sister would always be amused at the time separation between them; two years, two months, and twenty-two days. In the 1960s, more girls' names from the Soviet Union became known to Americans, and Nancy thought they had nice, exotic sounds. She chose a modified version of Anastasia for her new baby: Stacey Murray.

Tensions eased between Korea and the United States, allowing a phaseout of Itizuki Air Force Base. Don Murray, now a staff sergeant (E-5), remained as a spokesperson for the office of information until February 1970, when his four-year military tour was completed. He, Nancy, and the two children returned to civilian life in Southern California and settled in Glendale.

Two years in smog-choked northern Los Angeles County was plenty for the Murrays. Nancy made some lifelong friends there, but she and Don wanted to move. They bought a house in Fountain Valley, one of the bedroom communities of Orange County. He hoped the upper-middle-class region would provide a haven for his family, free from snarled traffic, pollution, and crime.

Not all marriages are destined to last forever. Don and Nancy Murray both loved their two blonde, beautiful, little girls, but other stresses and strains gradually pulled the couple apart. Marriage counseling helped temporarily, but the gulf between them grew during 1975 until they separated, and on the day after Christmas, they agreed to divorce.

It seemed to Nancy that the best way to handle it, for the girls and herself, would be to seek a whole new environment. When she was growing up, a neighbor boy had been her best buddy, and they had maintained contact. She learned that he was going to move to Troutdale, Oregon, outside of Portland. It seemed as good a place as any to start over.

Lynel and Stacey Murray entered new schools in January 1976 in Troutdale, in the fourth and second grades. They attended different schools, and missed each other sorely during the daytime. The

change troubled both children. Instead of making
new friends, they relied upon each other for companionship. Nancy's friend, who became her fiancé, built a playhouse for Lynel and Stacey in "a
patch of woods." Endless hours of romping and
exchanging secrets in their private domain occupied the little girls' afternoons.

Southern Californians don't adapt easily to rainy
climates, and Troutdale had more of the wet stuff
than Nancy or the kids liked. It was gloomy. The
romance between Nancy and her fiancé became as
gray as the storm clouds and faded away, too. "You
can't marry a friend you've known that long,"
Nancy explained. "You love him dearly, but you
can't build anything from there." The urge to return to the area of her birthplace was irresistible.
Back in the sun of California's southland, Nancy
soon bought a condominium in Huntington Beach.

Absent from the condo more than she wanted
to be, Nancy still felt the necessity of working two
jobs much of the time. During the day, she acted
as a hostess-agent for a real estate developer, and
she spent evenings as a waitress at a Charley
Brown's restaurant. Lynel had inherited natural
enthusiasm for interaction with people from her
mother, a characteristic Nancy always had that
made both jobs easy for her. Regular customers
often asked for her tables at Charley Brown's. Men
were pleased when she greeted them with her
sunny smile and kidding repartee.

* * *

Conflict between teenage daughters and their mothers is the norm, and the relationship between Nancy and Lynel was no exception. The head butting started when Lynel was fourteen. Nancy's long working hours and home duties drained her by the end of each day. Exhaustion fueled misunderstanding, and led to hurt feelings.

Just before her sixteenth birthday, Lynel decided she wanted to try living with her father.

Don Murray had married again and lived twenty miles north of Huntington Beach in a comfortable ranch-style home on the edge of La Habra. In an unusual twist, Don had met Jacqueline at the marriage counseling service he had attended with Nancy in 1975. They were married two years later and had two daughters of their own.

Lynel and Stacey adored their two younger siblings, while Holly and Erin idolized the older girls. They were together nearly every weekend, with Don generally acting as chauffeur.

On St. Patrick's day, 1983, Don drove to Huntington Beach to pick up his oldest daughter, following her request to live with him. Expecting to see Lynel and Nancy at each other's throats, he was surprised when he found them in the driveway, hugging each other and sobbing hysterically. *If they love each other so much,* he wondered, *why do they want to live apart?* On the return trip, Lynel continued crying, and was morose for days. Jacque enrolled her in the new school and encouraged Lynel to interact socially, but she couldn't shake the doldrums. A local boy was fascinated with Lynel, but she gave him no encouragement.

Don and Jacque had been overjoyed to have Lynel with them, but realized the teenager was lonesome for her friends at Villa Pacific, and for her mother and sister. The feeling was mutual with Nancy, Stacey, and Lynel's pals. Three months later, the trio was reunited again in the Huntington Beach condominium. Don and Jacque were sorry to see Lynel go, but recognized that her loyalty and love for both sides of her family had been strengthened by the experiment.

When Lynel started telling her mother about a high-school classmate, Robert Whitecotton, who was having domestic problems, Nancy figured Lynel was simply transferring her care for stray pets to troubled people. She was only partially correct. Lynel's early interest in Rob may have been sympathetic, but it would eventually turn romantic.

The two youngsters met as sophomores while attending Edison High School in Huntington Beach. As a team, they had an idea to assist fellow students who had problems and needed to talk about them. Lynel and Rob conceived the idea of establishing a peer counseling center. They recruited volunteers, worked with the faculty and administration, and saw their plan implemented into a smashing success. A small trailer house was placed on campus, and distressed students were given permission to visit the center any time they needed to talk over a serious predicament, be it related to drugs, alcohol, sex, or any other contemporary plight.

From that foundation, the relationship between Rob and Lynel blossomed into dating, then love.

On November 12, 1986, Lynel and Rob had a date. He would meet her at the condo as soon as she got off work. They planned to rent a movie, get some pizza, and have another evening together at home.

Lynel's hours at Prime cleaners were 2:30 to 6:30 P.M. She reported to work a few minutes early, looking especially pretty in her black outfit, leaf-shaped earrings, and a pendant hanging on a delicate gold chain around her neck, the one she always wore. Her left ring finger was encircled by a gold band with six diamond chips.

Lynel made an entry on a wall calendar, then tackled the afternoon duties.

Nine

When Cyndi recited her version of the events that night, she just recalled that she and Greg sat outside the Prime Cleaners waiting for it to close. Asked what she was doing during the wait, she replied, "Sitting there, standing in front of the car, sitting on the hood of the car, walking around, walked around the store a couple of times. One time, he told me to walk all the way around so I could look in the store and see if she (the employee inside) was the only one working or if somebody else was working with her, because when we first drove in, there was another guy in the store with her."

Walking around and sitting were not the only activities of Cyndi or Greg during the wait. Linda Schafer, a local resident, dropped off some clothes after six P.M. at the Prime Cleaners. Before going in, she saw a woman loitering in the parking lot. "She was extremely thin. Very, very thin. I thought tall, but maybe because she was so thin. And she had almost no hair. Her head was almost—no hair. She had very tight jeans on, very tight jeans."

Linda Schafer took her bundle of clothes into the dry cleaning establishment. When she left the building, she saw Cyndi and Greg together, and was astonished to see how they were behaving.

"They were standing maybe about the second building over perhaps. And in this incredible embrace, (a) passionate kiss. In fact, she had one leg wrapped around his lower leg." Schafer described how Marlow and Coffman then noticed her, and separated. "I could see their lips move. I believe they spoke to each other."

The encounter gave Linda Schafer "an uneasy feeling." As soon as she was in her car, she carefully locked the doors, and left the parking lot.

About two or three minutes before closing time, 6:30 P.M., Cyndi said, she and Greg entered the Prime Cleaners.

Lynel Murray greeted the couple, and prepared to serve them. The nineteen-year-old girl, with the long honey-brown hair and radiant smile, had no reason to believe that she was in danger.

According to Cyndi, "She pulled out one of those slips of paper that they fill out for your dry cleaning, and he (Greg) said he wanted his coat cleaned. He had his coat in his hand, so that's when she pulled out a piece of paper. And then he pulls the gun out and told her to get in the back."

Lynel complied with the demand, hurrying to the back of the shop. Marlow told Cyndi to get the keys and lock the door. She found the store keys on the counter, locked the entry door, and flipped a sign around to indicate the store was closed. Cognizant that the building had plate-glass windows in front, and there were no curtains or blinds to obscure the vision of potential witnesses, Greg found the light switch and turned it off.

"Empty the cash register," he directed Cyndi. She hastily snatched approximately two hundred dollars from the till and handed it to Greg. Marlow pulled the handcuffs from his pocket, the same ones he had used to bind Corinna Novis, and snapped them onto Lynel Murray's wrists. He had conveniently brought duct tape, too, and ripped a piece from the roll to tape her mouth closed.

"We need a change of clothes," Marlow said. "Get some clothes for us." Cyndi rummaged through the racks of cleaned clothing, and picked a zebra-striped black-and-white knit dress and a white sweater for herself. Greg joined her, and lifted a gray suit, a brown corduroy coat, and two white shirts from the movable racks. Cyndi stripped off her dirty jeans and shirt, and slipped into the dress.

"Go get the car," Marlow instructed, "and pull it up to the back door." Cyndi hurried outside to follow his orders.

As soon as she stopped at the back door, Marlow

emerged, pushing Lynel in front of him. Just as they had with Corinna, Marlow held the captive girl on his lap, while Cyndi drove.

"Go to that hotel where we were last night," Greg told Cyndi, who drove the two miles to the Huntington Inn. When she pulled into the rear parking area again, and stopped the car, Greg handed her fifty dollars of the stolen money, and instructed her to go to the office and get a room for them. "Put it in her name," he said, and handed Cyndi a credit card and driver's license he had extracted from Lynel Murray's purse.

At the desk, Cyndi began to make entries on the registration form. When she came to the blank space for an address, she hesitated, then made one up: 4764 Oak Lane, Barstow. But she couldn't remember the zip code for Barstow, and was afraid the clerk would recognize a phony one. She quickly fished a card from her purse, and copied the correct zip code. At the blank space for a car license number, she simply glanced outside, and entered the license number of a Datsun she saw parked there.

She started to hand the clerk the fifty dollars that Greg had given her.

"That will be fifty-four dollars," the woman told her. Not wanting to attract attention or make a fuss, or go back to the car for the extra four dollars, Cyndi made a decision to use Lynel Murray's credit card.

"May I have your telephone number, please?" asked the clerk. Cyndi hesitated for a moment, then fumbled around in her purse. She wasn't sure whether to make one up, or say she didn't have a phone. She finally pretended to read one from a piece of paper she pulled from her purse. The transaction was completed at 7:20 P.M., when Cyndi accepted the key to room 307, and returned to the car.

At the same time that Cyndi began checking in, Lynel Murray's boyfriend, Robert Whitecotton, waited at the Murray condominium. It was seven P.M., thirty minutes after closing time, and Whitecotton was concerned. Lynel was supposed to meet him there at 6:45 for their video-rental date. They'd both been looking forward to it.

Although Lynel was rarely late, Stacey Murray wasn't alarmed. She had worked at a dry cleaner long enough to know that there were sometimes reasons to work a few extra minutes. But Rob was edgy. "Something's wrong," he groaned. "I'm going over there to see if I can find her."

In front of the Prime Cleaners, Whitecotton cupped his hands around his face and pressed closely to the glass, but could see no movement in the dark interior. Lynel's old blue "junker," the 1976 Oldsmobile *La Bomba*, still stood in the parking lot. A tight sensation gripped the pit of the young man's stomach.

Striding quickly, and running his fingers through his dark hair, Rob circled the building to check the double glass doors in the front, the side door near the drive-up window, and the rear door. All were solidly locked. He called out repeatedly, but the only answer was silence.

Whitecotton knew that Lynel had been there at 6:20 P.M., because he had called her to verify their plans for the evening.

"I can't talk right now," she had told him. "There's a customer here." Her voice and manner had given him no reason for alarm. But he was dismayed now. Walking rapidly, Whitecotton checked the supermarket across the street to see if Lynel was doing some last-minute shopping. No luck. He ran to a nearby gas station. Maybe she had gone there because of car problems. No, the attendant hadn't seen her.

His concern became torment. He nervously jerked the handset from the cradle at a pay telephone, and called Stacey to see if Lynel had arrived home yet or telephoned.

"No," Stacey replied. "She's not here, and I haven't heard from her." Now, she, too, was worried. She rushed over to the cleaners to see for herself if the problem was as serious as it sounded. It was. Before reaching the panic stage, she returned home again to assure herself that Lynel hadn't found her way to the condo. Disappointed, Stacey telephoned Charley Brown's restaurant, where her mother had arrived about an hour earlier to work the dinner shift.

It took Nancy less than sixty seconds to explain to her boss that she was leaving to search for her missing daughter.

* * *

Desperately trying to think what to do next, Whitecotton called the owner of the cleaners, and asked if he knew anything about where Lynel might be. He didn't, he said. The frantic sound of the young man's voice alarmed the owner. He agreed to come to the store to look inside for any clues to her whereabouts.

Knowing that he sounded like an alarmist, Whitecotton called the Huntington Beach Police Department and reported what little he knew.

Greg and Cyndi glanced around to be sure no one could see them. Forcing Lynel Murray ahead of them, they hurried to the hotel room, which was on the ground floor, adjacent to a breezeway. Marlow immediately hustled the captive girl into the bathroom, left her there, exited, and closed the door. She was still bound by handcuffs and muffled by duct tape.

As Cyndi Coffman described it: "He came out of the bathroom and told me to go to the bank, and I told him that I had used the credit card to get the room, because it was fifty-five dollars instead of fifty." Her memory was one dollar different from the registration clerk's recall. "He got real pissed and started throwing me around the room, telling me, 'How could you use a credit card for five dollars, how stupid can you be?' He picked me up and threw me on the bed (and) knocked me off the bed." She complained that when she hit the floor, she broke one of her long fingernails "real far down."

Greg beat her, she claimed, for a "half hour, forty-five minutes. I kept trying to tell him, because he was yelling, because he thought that I had used the credit card for five dollars and paid for the rest of the room with fifty dollars in cash. And I kept trying to tell him, no, I used the credit card for the whole thing. He kept yelling, 'How stupid can you be? They'll catch you when you use a credit card for five dollars!' I said I didn't use it for the five, I just used it for the whole thing. He wasn't paying any attention. He was the Wolf."

Finally, she said, he stopped for a minute. "I got up and grabbed the little plastic thing the money was in and handed him the money. Then he told me, 'Oh, I'm sorry,' you know. That was it. 'Go to the bank. Get me some food.' "

Cyndi recalled that she left to find a Bank of America. "That's the bank she (Murray) had a card to. She had already given him the number while they were still—we were at the Prime Cleaners."

Driving southeast, along Pacific Coast Highway again, Cyndi traveled nine miles to Corona Del Mar to find a Bank of America where she could use Lynel Murray's credit card at the ATM, called Versateller. At 8:19 P.M., she punched in the identification number Lynel had divulged and withdrew eighty dollars from the savings account. She then keyed in an inquiry to find out how much remained in the checking account. The readout on the screen indicated a balance of $64.41. Immediately, Cyndi withdrew sixty more dollars.

Retracing her route from the hotel, Cyndi stopped at a McDonald's restaurant. She ordered "two Big Macs, two Quarter Pounders, two orders of French fries, and three sodas." One of the Big Macs and a soda, she later said, was for Lynel Murray.

She had been away from Greg and his captive "at least an hour and a half." When she arrived back at room 307, Marlow was angry.

"Where have you been? What took you so long?" Greg snarled.

"First, I went to the wrong bank," she explained, describing a stop at a nearby Bank of America administrative building. "Then I finally went to the right one, and I stopped and got some food."

Cyndi told of her explanation to Greg, then related a chilling detail. She said that she noticed that both Marlow and Lynel Murray had wet hair.

"I knew what had happened. He had done the same thing that he had done [before]."

Cyndi resumed her description of that night's events: She spread the McDonald's food on a table, and she and Greg began to devour it. Lynel was sitting on the bed, trembling, cringing in terror, no longer gagged but still handcuffed. At the couple's insistence, she moved from the bed to a chair near the table. She couldn't eat the hamburger Cyndi handed her, but tried to sip some of the cola drink.

Between bites, according to Coffman, Greg told

her that if she wanted to take a shower, she'd better hurry, because they had to get out of there. She quickly stripped out of the dress, and started her shower. Marlow grabbed a towel, and began wiping down everything in the room, Cyndi recalled, to eliminate any fingerprints.

When she had completed the shower and dressed, Cyndi said, Greg walked into the bathroom and began ripping a towel into long, narrow strips and wetting them. "You are going to kill this one," she quoted him as saying.

"No!"

"Yes, you are."

Her story continued: "He kept ripping the towel. And he goes, 'And this is how you are going to do it.' Then he walked out of the bathroom with the pieces of towel and proceeded to tie Lynel Murray up. He put one around her mouth, one around her eyes, and he tied her feet together. He told me to 'Come here.' I (looped) the towel around her neck like he told me to and I started to pull the towel. She was lying on her stomach. And I just . . . started to pull. Greg was standing there watching me. Well, I couldn't do it. And so he took one side and he started pulling while I was on the other side. I pulled a little bit and then let it go and then I pulled again a little bit and then let go. He got mad because I wasn't doing it. And he just took the other side and told me we would do it that way. I was pulling on one end and he was pulling on the other. I stopped again because my fingernails were digging in my hand

and cutting the palms and I said I couldn't do it. And he pushed me out of the way and said, 'I'll do it myself. Get out of here.' "

According to Cyndi, she went to the second bed, sat on it with her back to Marlow and the kidnapped girl, and concentrated on a John Wayne movie on television. She didn't watch Marlow or the girl, nor could she hear any sounds.

Cyndi finally heard Marlow, she said, start criticizing her because she couldn't do anything right. Then he told her to run some water in the bathtub. She complied, filling the tub about six-inches deep.

"I ran the water in the tub," Cyndi recalled. "And when I got done turning off the water, I walked back in the bedroom and he picked up Miss Murray and took her in the bathroom and put her head in the tub. He put her head in the water and her legs were over the toilet. And then he came out of the bathroom."

She continued: "We started getting ready to leave. And he went back into the bathroom. He urinated on her."

Cynthia Lynn Coffman and James Gregory Marlow silently scrambled around the room picking up their few possessions and things that had been scattered around the room including Coffman's fingernail which he pocketed, hurried to the Honda, and drove away into the gathering fog.

Lynel Murray's body lay facedown, her right leg on the toilet seat, her left leg on the floor; the upper part of her torso stretched over the rim of the bathtub and leaned limply down toward the water where her face was submerged. Her black skirt was twisted and the blouse partially ripped open. The panty hose and maroon bra she had worn were missing. Deep bruises marked her back, ribs, and face. Both of her eyes had been blackened. Her neck, scalp, and nose were battered and bruised. The necklace chain she treasured was missing, and would never be found.

Her left hand, with the long red fingernails, was twisted behind her back.

Over an hour after they had left the Huntington Inn and the savagely murdered body of another beautiful young woman forty miles behind them, Cyndi and Greg pulled off the San Bernardino Freeway at Vineyard Avenue in Ontario. They eased past several rows of towering queen palm trees in the parking lot of the six-story Compri Hotel, and walked through the long canopied entryway, into the plush lobby, a little before midnight. Using Lynel Murray's credit card again, Cyndi registered for a room for two. They rode the elevator up three floors, and went to room 333.

Inside the nicest room Marlow had ever seen, much less slept in, the couple decided to dress up and go out to eat. They had noticed an all-night restaurant on the other side of Vineyard Avenue. Marlow put on the gray suit he had stolen from the Prime Cleaners. Cyndi donned the sweater she

had taken, and the couple sauntered through the
parking lot, across Vineyard, and into a Denny's
restaurant.

The waitress noticed the couple as soon as they
entered. The woman in the black-and-white dress
stood out because of her closely cropped hair, the
man because of his thinning hair and full mustache drooping down over the corners of his
mouth. But what mostly caught the waitress's attention was their conduct. While waiting near the
cash register to be seated, they were locked in a
loving embrace. She was giving him a hug and a
passionate kiss, and when the hostess approached
to guide them to a booth, she recalled, "They were
hugging so I had to wait until they were through."

After being seated, Marlow seemed serious and
glum, and remained silent. But Cyndi, the waitress
noted, was ebullient and smiling brightly. She ordered food for them, requesting "hearty steak and
shrimp" for two. The waitress tried chatting with
them, and Cyndi was responsive but Marlow
wouldn't speak or look at her. When the waitress
walked away, Cyndi waited a few moments then
followed her into the lounge area to order a half-
carafe of Chablis wine.

At the conclusion of the meal, the couple
stopped at the cash register to pay the bill, twenty-
three dollars and thirty cents. Marlow waited at
the door, while Cyndi produced Lynel Murray's
credit card. When the transaction slip was handed
to her, Cyndi generously added a tip of ten dollars
to the bill, and signed Lynel's name. It was 1:34

A.M., Thursday, November 13, when Cyndi Coffman and Greg Marlow left the Denny's restaurant, detoured to a convenience store to buy a bottle of champagne, returned to the Compri Hotel, and went to their room to enjoy the plush accommodations afforded them by the killing of Lynel Murray.

Ten

At about the same time that Cyndi Coffman had left Greg Marlow alone with Lynel Murray to run her errand for money and hamburgers, approximately eight P.M. on Wednesday, November 12, Hoosang Movafaghi, the owner of the Prime Cleaners, arrived at his establishment. Robert Whitecotton, Nancy Murray, and Stacey Murray were waiting there for him. He greeted the worried boyfriend and family, and unlocked the front entrance.

When the owner turned the lights on, it was immediately obvious that the cleaners had been ransacked. Clothing lay scattered on the floor and the empty cash register drawer stood open. "There was not even a penny left," Movafaghi recalled. He moved rapidly to the telephone and called the police.

While waiting for the police to arrive, and surveying the damage, Movafaghi's eyes fell on a wall calendar near the front desk. He felt a catch in his throat when he noticed an entry for the following day, Thursday. Lynel had dutifully noted on the calendar that she would be an hour late on Thursday because she had a math test at Golden West College. He hoped that she would be able to return to her family and take her test. "She was very responsible, very kind," Movafaghi whispered.

The panic clutching Robert Whitecotton intensified when he found Lynel's schoolbooks lying on a rear table. He knew she wouldn't have left them unless she had been forcibly abducted.

Ordinarily, police reports of missing persons are not taken very seriously within the first twenty-four hours, unless there are unusual circumstances to indicate foul play. When the police arrived at Prime Cleaners, and matched the name of the missing employee with the report that Robert Whitecotton had called in earlier, they realized that this missing persons report was serious.

There was little they could do that night, though. Patrol units were routinely alerted to be on the lookout for anyone matching the description of Lynel Murray. A helicopter circled the area above Prime Cleaners, scanning for anything suspicious. Whitecotton, Nancy Murray, and Stacey left to begin the agonizing process of searching, hoping, and waiting.

After a uniformed officer had secured the cleaners building, police criminalist Dale Hachiya arrived to collect and preserve any physical evidence available. He and another officer took photographs, dusted surfaces for fingerprints, and collected cigarette butts that were left inside. When they completed their work, they left the scene of the burglary and probable abduction.

* * *

Cyndi and Greg checked out of the luxurious
Compri Hotel in Ontario on Thursday morning,
November 13. Still wearing the striped dress taken
from Prime Cleaners, Cyndi used Lynel Murray's
ID to cash a check in the hotel lobby before she
and Greg left to leisurely travel the twelve miles to
Fontana. Now they had enough cash to visit the
connection again, near the vineyard where the
body of Corinna Novis lay, still undiscovered. They
felt like rewarding themselves with some more
methamphetamine, so they splurged and bought
two grams for one hundred and eighty dollars.

Knowing that syringe needles were available at
the San Bernardino house where they had spent
much of the night on the previous Friday, they
drove there to use the newly acquired drugs. Greg,
wearing the stolen gray suit with combat boots,
startled the two male residents and a female visitor, when he and Cyndi barged in. Wondering
where Coral was, Greg sent Cyndi into the bedroom to telephone some female acquaintances.

"No, she's not here," said the voice on the telephone. "But she told me the police have been
around this morning asking questions." The woman gave Coffman the number of another friend
where Coral might be found. Cyndi nervously dialed it.

The second call rattled her even more. "The police picked Coral up this morning," she was told.

Cyndi leaped off the bed, ran into the kitchen

where Marlow was talking to the host, and announced that Coral was in custody. Frowning and shaking his head, Marlow moved aimlessly into the living room, sat down, and idly reached for a newspaper on the coffee table. He was stunned when he saw the photos on the front page of Corinna Novis and a car exactly like the Honda CRX. Greg and Cyndi both read the article describing the mystery of the missing girl and asking readers to be on the lookout for her car.

"We gotta ditch the car," Marlow said.

Within minutes, they had gathered a few items from the house, including their remaining gram of methamphetamine, and sped away again in the Honda.

A few miles away, an acquaintance of Greg Marlow was also studying the picture of the car in the newspaper. He recognized it as the one he had seen the couple using a few nights earlier. He stroked his stubbly chin, recalled a time that Greg had beaten the hell out of him, and reached for the telephone.

Well-wishers at the Murray condominium tried to reassure each other that Lynel would be found safe and healthy. Inside the dwelling, misery, heartache, and tension gripped the family. None of them had slept all night. Neighbors brought food and words intended to comfort. At six that morning, a devoted group of friends had made flyers picturing Lynel and asking, *"Have you seen this girl?"* They posted the notices on telephone poles, in markets and stores, or anywhere that might attract the attention of any possible witness. Lynel's school buddies filled her front yard, sitting in quiet groups, whispering or just staring in stony silence.

Stacey Murray was crazy with grief. She couldn't sit still, just waiting in despair for the phone to ring. Perhaps, she thought, she could ease her mind by concentrating on work at school. There, she found that it was impossible to stop worrying, so she returned home accompanied by a classmate. Her pain wasn't reduced when the friend asked, "Why would someone steal your sister?"

Driving aimlessly for a while, Cyndi Coffman tried not to do anything to attract the attention of the local police or the California Highway Patrol. Finally, she and Greg agreed to head north, on winding Highway 18, into the towering San Bernardino Mountains. Cyndi was not entirely unfamiliar with the area. She had skied the slopes of Big Bear the previous winter with her ex-boyfriend Sam Keam.

Resisting the temptation to hurry, they twisted along the curves of aptly named Rim of the World Drive. At a tourist stop, named Santa's Village, a few miles south of spectacular Lake Arrowhead, Greg told Cyndi to pull off the highway onto a dirt road. She negotiated the turn, bumped along a dusty, rutted trail, made another turn, and coasted to a stop under a large ponderosa pine tree.

"Take some of that Armor All, spray it on the car, and wipe all the prints off," Greg instructed Cyndi. While she tackled that, he began unloading the car, scattering some of the contents on the ground. He disappeared for a few minutes with an armload of the items from the car, then reappeared, and led Cyndi back to the highway on foot.

They crossed Highway 18, and Greg threw a full pillowcase toward a trash can. He kept the duffel bag. Still wearing the gray suit and the black-and-white knit dress they had stolen from the cleaners, they stuck out their thumbs to hitchhike to Big Bear City, the town on the south shore of the lake with the same name.

No more than fifteen minutes passed before a car pulled over and the driver offered them a lift. A couple, with three children inside the car, generously agreed to take them to the lake, eight miles away. "They were from back East," Cyndi recalled. "So we talked about that, and then just made small talk the rest of the way. There had been a motel that I had stayed at previously, in Big Bear, so we went there." The vacationers drove away, completely unaware that they had transported a pair of killers.

Arriving at the Bavarian Lodge hotel at noon, Cyndi again used Lynel Murray's credit card to register for a room. To explain the absence of a car, she told the receptionist that it had broken down up the road a ways. The woman accepted the explanation, picked up the telephone to verify the credit card, and tried to hide her amusement at the "city people," who had no idea how to dress for the mountain weather.

"The lady that was working there," Cyndi explained, "was having a problem getting it to go through to the operator or whatever they call it on credit cards, and finally just said, 'I'll do it later,' and she gave us the key."

They climbed the stairs to room 28, threw the duffel bag on the bed, and stayed only a short time to do some speed. Outside again, they walked a quarter-mile to the Alpine Sports Center, a store that specialized in skiing equipment and athletic clothing. "We went there," Cyndi said, "because there was a Jacuzzi at the Bavarian Lodge and we wanted to go in it. We didn't have any suits, so we went over there to get swimsuits."

Lynel Murray's credit card was still paying off like the mother lode, so they figured they might as well get what they wanted. As they marched into the Alpine Sports Center, a man followed directly behind them. Jim Bollingmo, the store owner, had been running some errands and returned just as Marlow and Coffman entered. He thought they looked "unusual" and noticed that Marlow was wearing "logging boots" with a three-piece suit, and Cyndi had very high heels on with her black-and-white dress. He watched them as they walked over to the gun and ammunition display case.

At that point, Sharon Chamness, a store employee, approached them to offer assistance. She chatted briefly with them, particularly with Marlow, who mentioned the need for bathing suits, and that their car had broken down at Santa's Village. He also asked where he might rent a car, or if there was public transportation available. Sharon didn't know of any auto rental agencies, but told him about Mountain Transit, a local bus system.

When Cyndi and Greg were ready to check out, they had swimsuits, designer sunglasses priced at eighty dollars each, a knit hat, and a scarf. Sharon Chamness took the credit card from Cyndi, and called the authorization center to get credit approval. There was a delay, and while they waited, Greg turned to Cyndi and with an edgy voice asked, "Y'know what's takin' so long?"

Cyndi said, "There shouldn't be a problem. I haven't charged anything."

Jim Bollingmo overheard the comments and stepped over to the counter. He chatted with Marlow who repeated the story about the car being broken down.

"What kind of a car is it?" Jim inquired.

"A white Honda," Greg responded with surprising candor.

"Where did it break down?" he was asked.

Again, with uncharacteristic honesty, he said, "On the way up a hill in Santa's Village."

Marlow again asked about rental car availability. Bollingmo couldn't think of a local rental agency, but suggested that Dial-a-Ride might provide some transportation locally.

Bollingmo remembered: "He asked Sharon, our salesperson, if there was a problem with the card because it was taking a long time to get an authorization. And he mentioned that a couple of times previously they had used the card and they had problems getting an authorization there, too."

Marlow, he later said, was nervously pacing back and forth, but Coffman seemed a little calmer.

At last, the authorization came through, and Cyndi signed *Lynel Murray* on the transaction slip. Marlow asked Bollingmo where they could get some jeans. He directed them to Leroy's clothing store.

Cyndi and Greg rode the one mile to Leroy's in a Dial-a-Ride van. The van driver remembered that when the couple left her vehicle, other passengers commented on what a good-looking girl the female was.

April Dawn Shelton-Wedge, the salesperson at Leroy's, noticed the couple throw some paper cups in a Dumpster outside the front door, then enter the store at about 4:30 P.M. She thought the man's footwear looked peculiar with the gray suit that he wore. "They were clunky, dark-colored logging-type boots." She also noticed Cyndi's short hair.

Marlow picked up some clothes and approached the counter while Cyndi continued to shop in the woman's section. He placed a pair of tube socks, a brown sweater, and a ski hat on the counter and asked, "Is there any place around here that's good to go to eat?"

April cheerily replied, "Yes, the Iron Squirrel."

"Do you know where we could get a car?"

She wasn't sure, so she turned and asked another employee, who suggested that the Big Bear Airport had auto leasing. April passed on the information to Marlow.

"Thank you," said Marlow. "Sure is cold up here, a heck of a place to be stuck when it's so cold."

From a few feet away, Cyndi asked the salesperson if they had black jeans in her size, and April went to help her. She couldn't find them in black, but did find a blue pair. Cyndi took them, along with a sweater and more sunglasses, to the counter. Marlow stepped outside while Cyndi brought out Lynel Murray's credit card.

April Shelton-Wedge tallied the total charges, $255 plus change, and entered the figure on a credit card transaction slip. She took the card from Cyndi, and slid it through the slot of an on-line computerized authorization machine. The readout message indicated "Call In." April called the toll-free number to get an okay on the card.

A query came from the service agent on the line asking if the card user was still in the store. April didn't feel that she could answer aloud. The agent asked her to stay on the line and keep the user in the store as long as possible.

"What's taking so long?" asked Cyndi, her brow furrowing.

"The machine's down and I have to wait for it to come back up so I can run it through again," the salesclerk lied.

Cyndi went outside momentarily, then returned, and asked again what was taking so long.

"Well, I'm on hold and they're playing that dumb music."

"You're still on hold, huh?" asked Cyndi. "Is there a Bank of America near here, with a Versateller?"

"Yes," April told her, and gave her directions.

"Okay, give me the card, and I'll just go get the cash and pay for it." Cyndi charged out of the store and disappeared with Marlow.

The telephone rang in Nancy Murray's condominium. Instantly, the tormented mother snatched it up. A representative of the Bank of America wanted to find out if a woman who was attempting to use Lynel Murray's credit card was authorized to do so. Nancy gasped, and asked for a description of the user.

"Oh, she's medium height, thin, and has very short dark hair." Nancy had been clinging to the hope that if Lynel was kidnapped, she was still okay. Her first reaction, at the caller's description, was to wonder why the abductors had cut her daughter's hair off. Then, she gathered her wits, and told the caller to notify the police. As soon as the conversation was completed, she asked a companion to telephone an officer she knew, Det. Dale Mason at the Huntington Beach Police Department.

Another telephone call was made from a Big Bear merchant, who preferred to remain anonymous, to the San Bernardino County Sheriff's Office. Two people, the caller reported, were behaving suspiciously and using Lynel Murray's credit card. They might even be the ones in the newspaper story.

Francisco Martinez, sweeping the breezeway at the Huntington Inn, heard the hotel maid's frightened scream. The houseman dropped his broom and trash bag and ran toward room 307. Stumbling toward him, the maid was crying hysterically and speaking in Spanish. She pointed toward the room she had just left. After hearing her brief, horrifying description of what she'd seen, Francisco bolted into the room to see for himself. He stopped short at the bathroom entry, automatically reaching to flip on the light switch, and froze when he saw the body of Lynel Murray, with her face submerged in the shallow water of the bathtub. He ran out to call the police.

A patrol supervisor from the Huntington Beach Police Department arrived at the hotel at 3:43 P.M.

on Thursday, November 13. He secured the room, then radioed headquarters for the Homicide Unit.

It took the busy officers at police headquarters only a few minutes to link the description of the body found at the hotel to the girl missing from the Prime Cleaners. But policy required some additional investigation before relatives were notified.

Detective Richard Hooper arrived at the hotel almost simultaneously with Det. Odie Lockhart. Hooper had planned to visit the hotel anyway. By sheer coincidence, a good friend of his was staying there. Tom Dorsey, a member of the San Bernardino Sheriff's Office, had business in Huntington Beach, and had previously notified Hooper to arrange for a friendly get-together. But Hooper would have to postpone that for a while. He had a murder to investigate.

"Hoop" Hooper was just a few days away from his forty-fourth birthday. His youthful, unlined face, crowned by thick, dark hair that was styled in a classic flattop, belied his seventeen years of law enforcement experience. Close to six-feet and solidly built, Hoop could look intimidating as hell when he put on his "bad cop" face, or assume a handsome look of benign innocence. Under most circumstances, his countenance was placid and friendly, with eyes sparkling through silver-rimmed glasses. His voice was tinged with a gravelly effect, and he had a speaking delivery that was direct and articulate, like a seasoned drill sergeant.

"This one's yours, Hoop," his supervisor told

him. Homicide cases are assigned to detectives in rotation, and it was simply Hooper's turn to take the next one. That meant that he would be fully responsible for organizing the investigative effort and directing the activities of assisting detectives and other support personnel.

Detective Odie Lockhart joined Hooper to carefully search room 307 for anything that might lead to a suspect. Criminalist Dale Hachiya, who had worked the crime scene at the cleaners the previous day, arrived with colleague Jeff Thompson to join the detectives in scrutinizing every inch of the murder scene. Bright strobe flashes reflected from the bathroom mirrors as the two specialists photographed the body and the room from every possible angle.

The investigators noted that one of the beds was still made up, even though a pillowcase was missing, while the other bed had blankets pulled to the floor revealing rumpled, bloodstained sheets. There were also dark stains on the toilet seat, and cloudy pools of blood in the bathtub water. They collected wet strips of towels, a bathmat with a shoe print on it, a bloodstained pillow from under the bathroom sink, and a piece of duct tape from the bathroom floor.

When a medical examiner carefully lifted Lynel Murray's head from the water, Hooper observed that she wore three earrings on one ear only, while the other ear, even though pierced, had none. Two of the earrings were gold loops, but the third one, which caught Hooper's eye, was a distinctive elongated leaf shape.

Before the body was removed to be transported to an autopsy lab, more photos were taken of the towel strips that bound her. One four-inch-wide strip was pulled tightly into her mouth, around her head, and tied. Another band of the torn towel covered the first one. A third strip circled her throat, but it was not tied at the back. More strips around her waist lashed her right arm to her side. Her left arm had been bent and wrenched behind her back. There was a sticky adhesive material around both ankles.

Lynel Murray was still wearing black panties, a black blouse, partly open with a button missing, and a black skirt. She wore no bra, panty hose, or shoes. A pair of shoes was discovered pushed far under the bed.

Jeff Thompson continued to search, and found two more items in the room. A black button, with unraveled, broken threads, was nearly concealed in the carpet. It matched the buttons on the dead girl's blouse.

When Thompson examined the bed that was still made, he saw that one corner of the bedspread, the part that covered the pillows, had been pulled back when the missing pillowcase had been removed. Thompson folded the spread back to its normal position, and uncovered a small metallic object. When he picked it up, he saw that it was an "earring back." He compared it to the one still attached to the leaf shaped earring Lynel was wearing. It matched perfectly.

Richard Hooper and Odie Lockhart knew it was going to be a long evening. They still had to interview employees of the hotel and other guests, in an effort to locate any witnesses who might help solve the murder of the beautiful young woman.

South of Lake Arrowhead, a sheriff's helicopter battered the air over the green pine treetops, zigzagging and circling, trying to cover the area before nightfall. Sitting beside the pilot, a deputy squinted into the afternoon sunlight. A bright glint reflected from something below, and when the lawman shaded his eyes, he spotted a little white car partially obscured by trees, not far from Santa's Village.

Outside Leroy's clothing store in Big Bear, Cyndi and Greg waited a few minutes, until 4:45 P.M., then saw the Dial-a-Ride van approaching. They jumped aboard and, being the only passengers, sat on the front seat. The driver asked where they wanted to go.

"I'm hungry," Marlow told him. "Are there any fast-food places around here?"

"Yeah, there are a few. There's a McDonald's down the road a piece, right next to a Seven-Eleven."

"Okay, take us there."

"Right. That'll be two dollars and fifty cents," the driver said, and started the van rolling toward the east end of town.

Before he had driven more than a couple of minutes, he heard the couple start arguing.

"You pay the fare," Cyndi said to Greg.

"No, you pay it," Greg snapped back.

The driver glanced into his rearview mirror, and watched the pair. He later described what he saw. "The gentleman seemed a little nervous. He just kept fidgeting with his hands and he was looking around—he just seemed uneasy."

The argument continued for a few moments, until Cyndi finally took some money from her purse, then "got some money from the gentleman," and paid the driver.

Without warning, the couple suddenly asked to be let out, well short of McDonald's. The driver obliged them, and drove away after they had stepped down from the van.

Cyndi's subsequent explanation for their hasty departure indicated that they both must have been nervous. "We were in the front seat of the Dial-a-Ride and we heard something over the radio that said something about 'Stop by here, we want—better drop your money off.' So we knew something was wrong. And we asked the driver to stop, and we got out.

"We got out and started on the run," Cyndi remembered. "Running, walking, taking back roads, trying to get out of town. We ran for a long time. At least an hour or two."

Winding down the day at the Huntington Beach Inn, Dick Hooper had just completed interviewing a hotel guest when the buzzing tone of his pager sounded. He hoped it wasn't going to be something that would extend his already long day; he was starting to feel the effects of a nagging bronchial infection and needed some rest. He found a telephone and called the communications center.

"Hoop," the sergeant told him, "it looks like we have a suspect in your case. Someone has been using your victim's credit card up at Big Bear. Dale Mason got a call from a friend of the family, and we're talking to the San Bernardino County Sheriff's Department."

When Hooper hung up the phone, he forgot the sore throat, immediately dialed the front desk of the hotel, and asked to be connected to the room of Tom Dorsey, his visiting friend.

"Tom," Hooper said, "I'm here at the hotel. I've got a homicide in room 307. Why don't you come on over here?"

"Yeah, sure," Dorsey replied. "C'mon, Hoop, stop kidding around. Where are you really?"

"No, man, I'm serious. Get yourself on over here." Hooper filled in some of the details.

Dorsey was astonished. Before hurrying through the corridors to meet Hooper, he telephoned his wife to describe the incredible turn of events. She listened, then commented that their friend, Scotty Smith, was working on a missing girl case in Redlands and wondered aloud if there was a connection. She was the first person to suspect a link between the two crimes.

When Dorsey found Hooper, he shared his wife's remarks.

Keeping the possibility of a link in mind, Hooper told his friend, "I just found out we have a suspect or a pair of them, running around up in the mountains around Big Bear. That's a big area. Lots of space to get away. You've worked that area. Any suggestions?"

Dorsey had one. There were only three roads leading into or out of Big Bear. Seal them off and no one was going to get out of there unseen. He grabbed the telephone, and made some calls to put his thoughts into action.

Shortly after Dorsey's telephone call, a deputy sheriff stepped into the lobby of the Bavarian Lodge. He had been delegated the task of checking motels to see if anyone had registered using the name Lynel Murray. "Do you have someone checked in by this name?" he asked the desk clerk. When she raised her eyebrows and replied that she did, the deputy could barely restrain the urge to shout when he called headquarters to report his success.

* * *

The temperature at Big Bear was in the low-forties during the day, biting cold by Southern California standards. When the sun slid down over the western hills, a teeth-chattering chill pierced the thin mountain air. Clouds had been threatening rain all day, periodically parting enough to let the nearly full moon bathe the lake and forest in pale light.

Shivering and tired, the two fugitives decided not to go back to the hotel. They didn't know if they could be traced through the use of Lynel Murray's credit card, but they figured it would be better not to take chances, so they chose not to check into another hotel.

At the east end of Big Bear Lake, Cyndi and Greg turned from the main thoroughfare, Highway 38, onto Starvation Flat Road, which led into a forest of stately ponderosa pines. They walked in the darkness toward a two-story chalet-style mountain home, still under construction, on the left side of the dirt road. In front of the house stood a portable outdoor toilet they knew would be useful. On the right side of the road, a boulder-strewn hill rose about fifty feet above them.

Making their way between the trees and rocks, the duo struggled up the rise opposite the house, and stopped at the top to look into a crevice between several large granite boulders. It formed a shallow cave.

Greg crawled into the crevice, found that it would shelter them, and beckoned Cyndi to follow him. They hadn't eaten anything since the steak and shrimp at Denny's the night before. They squatted in the cold cave, shivering and hungry, like two wild animals.

They did have their speed, and gladly used the last of it during their cramped, miserable night in the cave. It was too cold to sleep, anyway.

Nancy Murray opened the front door of her condominium at 9:30 P.M., and her heart began to pound. Detectives Dick Hooper and Odie Lockhart stood outside, their faces solemn. Still reaching for any glimmer of hope, she looked over their shoulders. Maybe Lynel would be behind them, coming safely home.

"I'm really sorry, Mrs. Murray," Hooper whispered. He gently held his open hand toward her. In his palm was the ring Lynel had worn that morning.

For Nancy, the world spun out of control. She heard herself scream as she drowned in overwhelming pain. Don Murray, standing behind her, caught her when she collapsed.

On Friday, November 14, when dawn broke in Big Bear, the sun didn't provide much warmth. Clouds continued to gather, taunting Marlow and Coffman with the threat of a downpour.

"We've gotta try to get out of here," Marlow moaned. "But we'd better not wear these clothes.

The cops might have a description of them, so we'd better change."

"Into what?" Cyndi asked with an incredulous frown.

"The bathing suits we bought," he blithely announced, oblivious to the weather and the probability that they would look a little peculiar.

While he trotted down to the portable toilet, she stripped naked in the cold culvert. She stuffed her white panties and bra into Corinna's purse, wiggled into the bikini she had acquired at the Alpine Sports Center, and pulled a sweater on over the tiny garments.

Greg, too, put on the new bathing suit, leaving the trousers of the suit he had been wearing, with a pair of handcuffs in a pocket, lying on the toilet floor. He climbed back up the hill, looking ridiculous in the dress shirt, bathing suit, and boots. Cyndi's appearance was just as startling, with high heels, bare legs, bikini bottom, and bulky white sweater. She carried only the bulging, black, shoulder strap purse. Leaving the clothing they had worn and some of the things they had bought in the cave, they headed down the hill to the main road, Highway 38, and turned east.

At the first pay telephone they found, Greg asked Cyndi to try to get in touch with Coral to see if she could help them. He knew that his half sister was staying temporarily with the woman for whom she worked at the Redlands Mall. Cyndi called the woman's home and asked if Coral was there. No, she was told, Coral was being held for questioning by the Redlands police.

When Cyndi hung up and told Greg what she had learned, they were upset. Yesterday morning they had learned that Coral was being questioned, but were alarmed that she was still in police custody. They would have been even more concerned if they had known that the woman they had just phoned, immediately after talking to Cyndi, called the police to report the contact with them.

Shivering, hungry, and exhausted, Cyndi and Greg trudged eastward, looking nervously at each car that passed them. They didn't notice when a Dial-a-Ride driver, who was carefully watching pedestrians, glanced in the rearview mirror toward them and immediately picked up the two-way radio to call headquarters.

Deputy Frank Tossetti and Det. Gale Duffy, of the San Bernardino County Sheriff's Office, worked out of the Big Bear substation. With the veteran Duffy at the wheel of an unmarked car, they were cruising eastbound along Highway 38, near Maple Lane, on Friday, November 14. They were on the lookout for a couple, of whom they had only a general description, with just a couple of specific characteristics. The man had a full mustache, and the woman, they had been told, had a very short haircut.

Tom Dorsey's suggestions were in full effect; all three exit roads were swarming with officers.

At three P.M., Tossetti and Duffy saw Cynthia Lynn Coffman and James Gregory Marlow, wearing bathing suits, walking along the south side of the highway. The couple had also been spotted by two officers in another patrol unit, who had passed the two, made a quick U-turn, and arrived back simultaneously with Tossetti and Duffy. Marlow and Coffman were pinned from both directions.

The four lawmen leaped from the two vehicles with weapons drawn, assumed the positions of security that they had been taught, and shouted "Freeze." When they were sure that they had control, they ordered Greg and Cyndi to lean forward and put their hands on the hood of one of the cars. The two suspects meekly complied. Tossetti approached Cyndi while two of the other men handcuffed Greg.

Tossetti reached for the purse Cyndi was carrying, but she didn't want him to take it.

"I need that purse," she defiantly told him.

The deputy was in no mood for games. He pulled the purse from her grasp, handcuffed her wrists behind her back, and handed the purse to Duffy. The two suspects were placed in the backseat of one of the cars and locked in. When Duffy started to place the purse in his car, he looked into it and saw the butt of a handgun.

Eleven

The cubicle that served as an interview room in the Redlands Police Department headquarters was just large enough to hold three chairs and a small table. James Gregory Marlow sat in one of the chairs six hours after he had been arrested in Big Bear. Sergeant Tom Fitzmaurice from Redlands and Detective Odie Lockhart from Huntington Beach occupied the other two chairs.

"You have the right to remain silent," Fitzmaurice read to Marlow, reciting the Miranda warning known to every cop, felon, and television fan. "Anything you say can and will be used against you in a court of law. You have the right to talk to a lawyer and to have him present with you before and during questioning. If you cannot afford to hire a lawyer, one will be appointed to represent you before any questioning, if you wish one. Do you understand the rights I have just explained to you?"

Marlow said that he did.

"And with these rights in mind, are you willing to talk with us about the charges against you?"

A tape machine continued to roll, recording the

silence in the room. Fitzmaurice and Lockhart stared intently at Marlow as he adjusted his position in the chair and returned their gaze. If he demanded a lawyer, they realized, they faced a serious decision that could affect the outcome of a trial. More than one criminal has walked because his Miranda rights were violated.

"I want an attorney," Marlow calmly announced.

The two lawmen didn't even hesitate. They launched into a series of questions without obtaining the services of a lawyer. If Corinna Novis were still alive, they were not going to let a technicality of law prevent them from getting the information from Marlow that might lead to the rescue of a terrified, possibly injured, captive girl.

First, they convinced the prisoner that they knew that he and Coffman had abducted Corinna Novis, and were suspects in the death of Lynel Murray.

After several minutes of questioning, Fitzmaurice asked Marlow if he would tell them or show them where the Novis girl was. "I know you can do it, and really think you want to do it," he cajoled.

"Yeah, I want to tell, yeah. Believe it or not. But I can't," Marlow mumbled.

Fitzmaurice continued, "Look, Greg. I've done things wrong in my life. I've never killed anybody, but I've done things that were wrong." He was prompting Marlow in a gambit to get him to tell whether he had killed the girl or not.

"I've never killed anybody either," Marlow told them.

Lockhart picked up the conversation, trying to gain Marlow's confidence and yet convey that he was in serious trouble. "It's over and done with, Greg. And it ain't gonna be easy from here on out."

"I know it ain't," Marlow agreed.

The wheedling and cajoling continued as the hours passed. The two cops could visualize the captive girl, whose life might be slowly draining away, while this stubborn prisoner refused to reveal her location.

They brought up Cyndi's participation in the disappearance of the victim. Marlow seemed to be making vague hints about her involvement.

Lockhart said, "I don't know what you're trying to say because you don't come out and tell me what you're trying . . . are you trying to tell me this is all Cyndi's fault?"

"No, no."

"Is that what you're trying to tell me?"

"I'm trying to say it's a fifty-fifty deal," Marlow admitted.

The word games continued for almost three hours. Finally, the detectives persuaded Marlow to take a ride with them to search for the girl. With Marlow giving directions, the trio traveled along the I-10 freeway for several miles, turned up the off-ramp to Sierra Avenue, and parked in a gas station. They were less than two miles from the shallow grave site in the vineyard.

The detectives sensed that they were close, but Marlow suddenly withdrew into a sullen silence.

Fitzmaurice and Lockhart coaxed him, but he informed them that he wouldn't go any farther unless Cyndi Coffman joined them. She was still back in the Redlands police station being interviewed by Detectives Scotty Smith and Richard Hooper. By the time telephone connections were made, Marlow had changed his mind. The sullen captive rode back to Redlands in silence and later refused to cooperate in any way.

Hooper and Smith had started their questioning of Coffman at 5:30 P.M. on the day of the arrest. They, too, read the Miranda warnings to their prisoner.

"Now that you know your rights, will you talk to us?" Hooper asked Coffman.

"No, I don't want to. I want a lawyer," she promptly responded.

Faced with the same barrier that had been broken by Fitzmaurice and Lockhart, Hooper and Smith also charged forward. They wanted to find Corinna Novis, and if saving her life meant violating Cyndi Coffman's Miranda rights, so be it.

After listening to a few inquiries from the detectives, designed to test her resolve, Coffman said, "I messed up last time. I'm not dumb, just should have kept my mouth shut like I'm doing this time." She was apparently referring to her arrest in Barstow with her ex-boyfriend.

Despite her obstinacy, Hooper and Smith continued to probe. Hooper asked, "If you were going

to look for her (Novis), where would you start looking?"

"I don't know where she is. I don't. I have no
idea."

Sometime during the session, Coffman mentioned Lytle Creek.

"How long has it been since you've been up
there?" Hooper asked.

"I don't know. It was a long time ago. About a
year ago," Coffman lied, concealing the visit of six
days ago.

Scotty wanted to know if Marlow had made
Cyndi carry the gun that had been found in the
purse she was carrying.

"Oh, no," she disavowed. "I put it in my purse."

They wondered if Cyndi would show any emotional response to a photo of Lynel Murray, so
Hooper brought out a picture that the dead girl's
family had given him. He could see no visible reaction by the prisoner. Her cold detachment struck
the officers.

Cyndi asked if she could have a cigarette.
Hooper's bronchial infection had not improved
and he was having difficulty controlling his cough-
ing even without the irritation of cigarette smoke.
He refused to let her smoke, but as the hours
dragged by, he finally left the room and let her
have her cigarette and some food.

When they resumed, the discussion centered on
Lytle Creek again. Cyndi interpreted one of their
comments to mean that Marlow had suggested to

his interrogators that they look for Novis at Lytle Creek.

"That's what he told those guys already?" Cyndi asked.

Smith and Hooper did nothing to dissuade her notion that Marlow had talked.

Coffman told them that her feet were cold. She had spent the night in a cave, had been arrested wearing a bathing suit and open high heels, and her feet had been freezing ever since. The detectives arranged for some jail-issue slippers to be brought in for her.

"Cyndi, he ran your life," Scotty sympathized, referring to Marlow. "Okay, I never met you before in my life but I've done enough work and I've talked to enough people that I know he controlled you just like he controlled other people. . . . People get in over their heads. It's like a snowball rolling down hill. Just keeps getting bigger and bigger, and you get deeper and deeper, and I believe that's what happened to you. Something you couldn't control because of him."

Cyndi's expression softened.

Hooper picked up Scotty's theme. "Cyndi, you're not a slave any more. You don't do what he tells you any more. You're a human being. . . . You never have to be intimidated by him again. He'll never cut your hair again. He'll never put handcuffs on you again, or beat you. . . . He'll never gag you again. He'll never put a blindfold on you again, and he'll never urinate on you again."

Hooper's litany and instincts were remarkable.

At that point, he did not know that Marlow had urinated on the body of Lynel Murray.

Slowly, after several hours of applying the ingratiation strategy, their persistence began to pay off. A little after midnight, Cyndi relaxed visibly and started dropping bits of information about the abduction. The crack in her initial reticence grew larger, and she began filling in details of the capture of Novis and the killing of Murray.

Hooper asked who had taped Lynel Murray's mouth.

"Greg held her head up by the hair, and I put the tape on her mouth."

"Did she give you the PIN number for her bankcard?" Scotty asked.

"She told me it at the store (cleaners) and at the hotel."

"Did you have to threaten her?"

"Yeah, sure did."

Scotty turned the questioning back to Corinna Novis, and Coffman told how she and Marlow had approached the girl at the mall and asked for a ride, how they had taken her to the Drinkhouse apartment, and about the episode in the shower.

"How did she get undressed?"

"He (Marlow) started to help her and . . . he took the cuffs off. She undressed herself."

"How long were they in the shower?"

"Five, ten minutes at the most. . . . He was in the shower (with Novis) and she was standing against the wall like this." Cyndi stood and leaned against the wall to demonstrate.

"Did you take your clothes off?" Scotty asked. Cyndi nodded.

"I took my dress off while they . . . and I put my jeans and T-shirt on . . . I had a dress on and I wanted to change clothes. Didn't take a shower, though."

Taking a cue from Hooper's showing Cyndi a photo of Murray, Scotty held a picture of Corinna Novis up to Cyndi's face to observe her reaction. He later described it. "She just stared at the picture and showed no outward visible signs."

Because of the several references to Lytle Creek, the two detectives were beginning to suspect that Marlow and Coffman had taken Corinna up there. They told Cyndi that they were going to go for a ride to Lytle Creek and that she was going with them. They hoped that she would continue to talk during the ride and reveal where Corinna was.

The trip to Lytle Creek was a wild-goose chase that wasted time and effort. They arrived back at one A.M., but did not give up trying to get Coffman to reveal where Corinna was.

She did talk following the trip, but she told them a story that she later recanted. She said that after they left the Drinkhouse apartment, Greg had dropped her off at a convenience store, left with Novis, and returned nearly two hours later without the victim.

Like poker players in a high-stakes game, the two detectives knew that Cyndi was holding a pat hand, but they continued to bluff and bet, still trying to find a way to get her to fold and reveal where

Corinna Novis was. According to Cyndi's subsequent account of that night, they found her weakness when they brought up the subject of her son.

"How would you feel if he was missing and you
didn't know where he was?" she quoted one of the
detectives. "Wouldn't you want to know if he was
dead or alive, one or the other?"

That question, she said, combined with their
claim that Marlow had confessed, caused her to
cave in.

She later explained, "They said that he had already confessed and that he told them generally
where it (the body) was, but I had been driving so
that I would be able to show them better and that
I should show them."

She made a bid for Marlow to accompany them
if she led the detectives to the grave site in the
vineyard. "They said they couldn't take him because he'd try to run and they'd have to shoot
him."

It was past three A.M., Saturday, November 15,
when the detectives escorted Cyndi to a car. With
Richard Hooper in the driver's seat, Odie Lockhart
beside him, Cyndi Coffman in the backseat beside
Scotty Smith, and followed in another car by Det.
Joe Bodnar, the group once again made the trip
along I-10 to Sierra Avenue. Cyndi told them to turn
left at the top of the off-ramp and drive south on
Sierra toward the dark hills. When they reached the
intersection where Jurupa Street dead-ended
against Sierra, from the right, they turned left,
bounced along a dirt road in the vineyard, and

parked where Cyndi told them to. Hooper, Scott, and Bodnar left Lockhart to guard the prisoner while they began to search for a grave site in the vineyard.

Odie Lockhart, with Cyndi giving him directions, aimed the beam of a handheld spotlight to guide the other three men where to search.

Lockhart later described in a written police report the conversation that he and Cyndi had in the car:

"What happened that night?" Lockhart asked.

"I drove and when we got here, James got the girl out of the car and took the handcuffs off her and walked her out into the field," Coffman replied.

"Did the girl seem scared or was she pleading?"

"No, she just told us to be careful with her car and not wreck it."

"What was the girl wearing?"

"Black pants and a green-and-white striped blouse, or something like that."

"Did you hear the girl scream or a shot or anything like that while he was killing her?"

"No, the only thing I heard was him digging. When he got out of the car with the girl, he carried a shovel out into the field with him."

"How do you think he killed her?"

"I guess he strangled her."

"Did he say anything when he came back to the car?"

"He told me the ground was very hard where he buried her, and he didn't bury her very deep."

"Do you think he had sex with her in the field?"

"No, he wouldn't do anything like that."

Lockhart switched the conversation to the Huntington Beach girl, Lynel Murray.

"Was she scared or anything like that?"

"No, she just talked all the time and wouldn't shut up. James had to put tape over her mouth in the car to shut her up."

Lockhart asked one final question. "Why did the girls have to be killed for just a little money, a car, and some credit cards?"

Coffman's reply caused Lockhart to shiver, and it wasn't from the chill night air.

"So there'd be no witnesses."

Out in the dark, cold vineyard, where Lockhart bounced the spotlight beam, Joe Bodnar shouted, "Over here! I think I've found it." Lockhart could see Hooper and Scott break into a run to reach Bodnar, and Hooper dropped quickly to his knees. After a couple of minutes, Hooper stood, and with sloped shoulders, stepped away while the other two men continued to dig. They had found the brutally violated body of Corinna Novis.

Bill and Donna Novis, Corinna's parents, glanced for the thousandth time at the telephone in the Glendale home of Bill's cousin Tom Keaton. Each time it rang, their nerves tightened and their hearts pounded, and they prayed for good news. A few miles north of downtown Los Angeles, and sixty miles west of Redlands, the two families huddled in the living room and tried to reassure each other that Corinna Novis would be found alive, and that life would return to normal. But none of them sounded very convincing. The anguish in the house was as thick as the smog outside.

The telephone rang again.

Tom Keaton answered the phone, listened for a few moments, then stepped into the living room, his face gray and drawn, his eyes moist, and quietly asked Bill Novis to come into the other room with him.

"We knew right then what it was, y'know," Bill recalled. "Everybody broke into hysterics."

Twelve

James Gregory Marlow was still verbally fencing with Det. Tom Fitzmaurice. Fitzmaurice finally became weary of his evasiveness, and asked, "Why did that girl die?"

Marlow's eyes became vacant, with the thousand-yard stare of a combat-weary soldier. He sighed and whispered, "I didn't really want to kill that girl. . . ."

"Was it just to keep her from being a witness? Is that the idea?"

"Yeah. She (Coffman) can say whether . . . it's been pretty much fifty-fifty."

"She was into it?" Fitzmaurice wanted the details of Coffman's involvement.

"Yeah," Marlow admitted. "She was. She got the ball rollin'. I never done anything like (that) ever before with anybody else."

"How did she die?"

"Strangulation."

"Where?"

"Out there," Marlow slurred, waving his arm in the general direction of Fontana.

"In the field? Was she alive when you took her there?"

"Yeah."

"Handcuffed and taped—her mouth taped?" the detective asked in disgust.

"It was, but then I took the tape off of her."

"Who strangled her?"

"I did, some," Marlow slurred, cryptically admitting and yet denying his involvement in Corinna's death.

"What did you use?"

"Uh, used a tie or something."

"A what?"

"A tie."

"What did you do with it?"

"I threw it away somewhere. There should be some tape around there somewhere."

Over the next hour, shifting in his seat, avoiding eye contact with the detectives, Marlow also told a horrifying story of the death of Lynel Murray, and described the bungled attempt to escape in Big Bear.

When the interview finally concluded, Marlow had confessed to his and Coffman's involvement in the crimes against Corinna Novis and Lynel Murray. But, despite the fact that Coffman had also confessed, the detectives were painfully aware that the admissions would be useless in a court of law because their Miranda rights had been violated. They could, and did, arrest the pair on suspicion of murder, rape, and robbery, but acknowledged that they would need a great deal of corroborating evidence to make the charges stick.

Marlow would later deny remembering any of the answers he gave to Tom Fitzmaurice, and would say that he had only used his arm to choke the girl, but didn't kill her. "I never strangled Corinna Novis," he would say. "I did a little bit, but she was alive when I left her." He also recanted his admissions regarding Lynel Murray.

Richard Drinkhouse was arrested and, along with Coral Willoughby, who was already in custody, was booked for aiding in the kidnapping of Novis.

Coffman's confession, even though virtually useless for conviction, at least gave the detectives a foundation from which to build a case. If they were to have any chance of bringing the pair to trial—and having a jury believe that Marlow and Coffman were both guilty of murder—they were facing a mountain of investigative work.

Kentucky Trooper-Detective Colan Harrell received a call from Redlands Detective Scott Smith. Smith was sending a map drawn by Cynthia Coffman depicting the location of a killing in which she had participated last July. Were there any unsolved homicides in that region? Smith wanted to know.

There certainly was, Harrell replied. The murder of Greg "Wildman" Hill had been a real thorn in the side of the local law enforcement community. A relative of Hill had claimed he was in Greg's cabin when the killing took place, and falsely pointed a finger at several local young men. They had been arrested, then subsequently released when no real evidence turned up.

Now, Colan Harrell could breathe a sigh of relief. The Kentucky State Police would be able to wipe the unsolved mystery from their books.

Detective Joe Bodnar, Redlands Police Department, who had discovered the poorly camouflaged grave site in the vineyard, drew the sad duty, two days later, of attending the autopsy of Corinna Novis. He watched as Dr. Joseph Reiber, forensic pathologist, examined the external features of the girl's body in minute detail, then performed surgical procedures to complete the internal examination.

There were injuries to her wrists and neck, including broken cartilage, that Reiber described as "antemortem," meaning sustained before death. There were "postmortem" injuries to the face and right hand. Her middle-finger nail had been torn off. Her face had dirt ground into the skin, and "a fair amount of dirt in the mouth."

In Dr. Reiber's words, "Most of the dirt was trapped between the inside of the lips and the front teeth. There was also a smaller amount of

dirt which was deposited over the top surface of
the tongue and over the hard palate or roof of the
mouth."

The savage treatment she had suffered didn't
correlate very well with Marlow's admission that
he had choked her "a little" with his arm, but left
her alive.

Joe Bodnar observed something else that he
found especially interesting during the autopsy. In
Corinna's left ear, he noticed, was a post earring
with a yellow stone. The right ear had been
pierced, but the earring was missing! He knew that
Lynel Murray, the Huntington Beach victim, also
had been missing one earring.

The purse that Deputy Tossetti and Detective
Duffy had taken from Cynthia Coffman when they
arrested her in Big Bear was bulging with items
that fascinated the investigators, including the
handgun that Duffy had seen. Just a few minutes
before midnight on Saturday, November 15, Det.
Michael Nakama arrived back in Huntington Beach
from his trip to Big Bear where he had gone to pick
up the purse.

Nakama and a property officer inventoried the
contents and found an astounding thirty-eight
items. Among them were:

- piece of stationery from the Compri Hotel,
  with the name Lynel Murray written on it
  several times

- Phoenix, Arizona, street map
- gray vinyl woman's wallet containing Lynel Murray's driver's license, social security card, student ID card from Golden West College, and eleven other cards and documents
- Smith and Wesson two-inch, .22 caliber blue steel revolver, loaded with six rounds of ammunition
- cigarette box containing seventeen cigarettes and one hundred and four dollars
- receipts from the Compri Hotel and Denny's restaurant
- pair of blue designer sunglasses with mirrored tint, and two felt drawstring bags for the glasses, one containing two rounds of .22 caliber ammunition
- white bra and pair of white panties decorated with little red hearts
- black vinyl credit card holder containing Lynel Murray's BankAmericard and Versatel card
- some cosmetic items
- wrench
- calculator
- clear plastic wallet credit card holder containing Cynthia Coffman's California driver's license, some photos, and a check-cashing card in her name
- snake-bite kit
- roll of toilet paper, inside of which was

wrapped two plastic syringes and plungers
and an orange plastic needle cap
- small flashlight
- silver metal earring for pierced ears, with
no backing device on it. It was a distinctive
elongated leaf shape.

On his inventory list, Nakama entered a notation
beside the earring description. "** Make special
note of this: The mate to this earring was found
on the ear of victim Lynel Murray."

In the shadows of the tall ponderosa pines, near
the east end of Big Bear Lake, the owner of the
unfinished chalet-style house, Frank Moulton, was
helping his neighbors with some chores. He was
in the front of his new home, near the outhouse,
when he noticed that a rock, that was strategically
placed to signify if the facility was in use or not,
had been "kicked away from the door."

"I looked inside," he told police, "and found
some gray pants. And as I picked them up, some
handcuffs fell out. I thought it was illegal to have
handcuffs, so I went to a neighbor lady's house to
use the phone. Her boy works for the Sheriff's Department, so she called them."

Later, Coffman's fingernail, broken off at the
Huntington Inn, was found in the pants pocket.

While Moulton waited for the police to arrive,
he thought it would be a good idea to search
around a little more. At the top of a rise, among

some big boulders, he saw a man's gray coat, same color as the pants, a black-and-white dress, and a white knit scarf. He left everything intact in the crevice so the sheriff's deputy could personally recover the clothing.

Jeff Thompson, the Huntington Beach criminalist who had found the earring post clip in the room where Lynel Murray had been killed, took a trip to Redlands where Scotty Smith gave him some evidence that had been transported from Big Bear. The deputy sheriffs up there had searched the cave where Marlow and Coffman spent their last night of freedom, the area around the Honda, and the Bavarian Lodge motel room. They had also found the stuffed pillowcase Marlow disposed of when he and Coffman deserted the Honda.

Among the dozens of things that Thompson brought back with him were the clothing that Marlow and Coffman had left in the cave, Marlow's duffel bag, and a large red paper bag containing a maroon bra, panty hose, and checks and receipts from the Prime Cleaners. Thompson was especially interested in a makeup kit found in the motel room. It contained five single earrings.

Thirteen

Hopalong Cassidy "died" on Friday, May 11, 1956. More specifically, Clarence E. Mulford, the author who created the perennial Western hero, died on that day.

On that same day, in Cincinnati, Ohio, Doris Walls Marlow, age seventeen, gave birth to a son. The infant arrived two months early, with a mild case of jaundice, at St. Mary's Hospital. Doris named her baby James Gregory Marlow. The father, Jeffrey, who was nine years older than his young wife, didn't show much interest in the event.

Jeffrey Marlow had married Doris in Southeastern Kentucky in the fourth month of her pregnancy. McCreary County, where they lived, wallowed in poverty and unemployment. A family man just couldn't earn a decent living, so Jeffrey decided to move his swelling bride to the industrial opportunities of Ohio. A steady job helped, but after James Gregory was born, Doris became agitated, bored, and homesick. She and Jeffery fought constantly over her refusal to work, her use of drugs, and her love of wild parties. The marriage fell apart before the little boy was two years old. Doris left Jeffrey and returned to her hometown.

In Stearns, Kentucky, Doris was able to survive by living with her mother, Lena Walls, and spending time with anyone except her child. Frequently, she strayed five miles up the road to Whitley City, the home of Donald Bender, a part-time preacher. Donald was only too happy to catch Doris on the rebound. She was quite a catch, too, with her shiny, shoulder-length brown hair, long red fingernails, and sensual beauty. Toward the end of 1958, she married Donald, and on April 17, 1959, produced a daughter, Coral.

Donald treated his new daughter fairly well, but didn't care much for his stepson, James Gregory Marlow, who was called Greg by his family. He frequently berated the youngster, yelled at him any time the boy's path crossed the man's, and generously dished out physical punishment. He wasn't so generous with other things. When he would give his daughter treats, such as cookies, milk, or candy, he would forbid them to the little boy. Instead, he would cram him into the space beneath the sink, and force him to stay there for hours at a time.

Poverty was still common in McCreary County, and sometimes the barefooted, ragamuffin children got up from meager dinner tables, in dilapidated shacks, with their stomachs unsatisfied. Greg and Coral, like many of their peers, were usually dirty, ragged, and hungry. Sores formed on the mouths and limbs of both children, and Coral developed chronic kidney problems that doctors eventually attributed to malnutrition.

Jobs in the region were scarce and the few to be found paid pitifully small wages. Some of the folks, in desperation, others due to shiftlessness, turned to sources of income that were on the shady side of the law. Kentucky was a "dry" state, which provided the opportunity for a cottage industry in bootleg booze.

The rolling hills and hidden gullies in McCreary County were ideal to cultivate a crop that was considerably more valuable than the booze or tobacco grown farther north. Marijuana supplemented several family incomes and drew customers into the area who rode motorcycles, sported beards and tattoos, and liked to "party."

Doris liked to "party," too. Her interests and activities left little time for attending to children. Once, she took Coral and Greg to a friend's house to leave them for a little while. She even left a quart of milk for them to drink to avoid being a burden on their host. She came back for them two weeks later. That event set a precedent that Doris would repeat many times. Her choices of entertainment, friends, and methods of child care bred discontent and friction between Doris and Donald.

If Doris had fought with her first husband, she went to war with Donald Bender. By 1963, he had shot her once, and she had stabbed him seven times. Doris's sister also attempted to shoot Donald, and he fought back by trying to run over her with his car.

By the time Greg was six, and Coral was three, that marriage, too, disintegrated.

Doris took her two kids back to her mother's house to try to make it without her husband. But there simply was not enough money to support both of them, and Lena Walls, Doris's mother, was hard-pressed just to take care of herself. Doris felt that her first husband, Jeffrey, should share some of the burden.

Jeffrey Marlow had also remarried, and moved to Vermilion, Ohio, with his wife, Anita. In the fall of 1962, Jeffrey and Anita received a letter from Doris's uncle, Justus Walls, asking if they would take Greg. The letter told a tale of hard times in Kentucky, and described the filthy conditions in which the child was living, such as human and animal waste on the floors of the house. The boy, Justus stated, was in terrible shape.

On November 13, 1962, Greg got off the Greyhound bus in Vermilion, Ohio.

Jeffrey Marlow drove to the station to pick up his oldest son. Anita, Jeffrey's wife, could not go. She was in the hospital, delivering a daughter on that very day.

Jeffrey took his son directly to the hospital to see his stepmother and new half sister. The baby had arrived several hours before Jeffrey and Greg, and Anita had recovered enough strength to receive them at her bedside. She was stunned when she saw the boy. He was wearing ragged, filthy clothes that Anita had sent to him the previous Christmas. The sweater was threadbare, his blue jeans and shirt were shredded at the knees and elbows, and the soles on his worn-out shoes flapped when he walked. His mouth had sores all around it, and most of his teeth were rotten. He looked much older than his six and one-half years. Her heart melted, and she later described him as "a lonely, lost little boy wanting somebody to love him."

At Jeffrey's home, Greg met his younger siblings, a half sister and half brother. When Anita was able to leave the hospital three days later, she was faced with the formidable task of taking care of her three children, including the infant, and rehabilitating the health and appearance of Greg. Weekly visits to the dentist did wonders for his rotten teeth, and the new clothing she acquired was like a coat of paint on a weather-beaten house. She arranged for medical treatments that put the gaunt lad on a health-recovery program, and she enrolled him in school.

In the first two or three days after Jeffrey was reunited with his son, he seemed agreeable to the arrangement. "Oh, this is going to be great. We are really a good family now. We've got all the kids together," he declared. The happy glow of family bliss dimmed in less than one week. Jeffrey was at first irritated, then angry at everything Greg did. If Greg didn't eat the way Jeffrey wanted him to, he was sent away from the table. If he didn't speak to Jeffrey in an acceptable manner, he was promptly spanked. Other infractions would earn him a slap or an early retirement to bed without a meal. The punishment Jeffrey administered was usually in direct proportion to the amount of liquor he had consumed, and he was frequently drunk.

"That man should never have been a father," Anita later proclaimed.

Despite the discipline dished out by Jeffrey, conditions for Greg were better than they had ever been before. His stepmother, Anita, was treating him like he was one of her own children. He was eating enough, his medical needs were met, and he was in school.

Some people can't stand prosperity, and Greg's real mother, Doris, was one of those people.

In early February 1963, Doris walked into the school where her son was preparing to leave early for a visit to the dentist. Greg had told her about the appointment and Doris convinced the teacher that she was there to take the boy to the dentist. Instead, she took him with her back to Kentucky.

Anita and Jeffrey called the police when they learned that Doris had kidnapped her son. But in 1963, the local cops did not regard it as a high-priority crime when one parent took custody of a child from the other parent.

Greg Marlow attended Stearns Elementary School, a few blocks from Grandma Walls's house, from February 5 until May 27, 1963, then suddenly dropped out.

Doris Bender was fed up with the deprivation of Southeast Kentucky. She decided it was time to move her family, including Greg, to the golden opportunities out West.

Doris and one of her relatives stole Donald Bender's car, drove it to a ledge overlooking the Cumberland River, and stripped the tires from it before pushing it into the deep green water. They mounted the tires on the relative's old Ford, and left Kentucky. Doris, her two children, her mother, Lena, and two nephews piled into one car. Justus Walls, Lena's brother, crammed his wife and remaining three children into his Ford, and with the vehicles in tandem, headed to California.

The caravan from Kentucky first headed south, then trundled west and eventually onto Route 66 in St. Louis, Missouri. Three days later, the travelers passed through Barstow, California, watched the temperature gauges on their dashboards soar as they traversed the Mojave Desert, and then dropped down out of the Cajon Pass into San Bernardino. There, Route 66 made a big, looping right turn and took the weary travelers along Foothill Boulevard. James Gregory Marlow would become all too familiar with the communities along the route. Barstow, Fontana, Upland, Ontario. They would draw him like a magnet, again and again.

The two families landed in East Los Angeles, a largely Hispanic community where rent was cheap and few questions were asked by landlords. After a few weeks of living in motels and crumbling apartments, Doris, with her mother and two children, left Uncle Justus and his clan, and moved a few miles eastward to El Monte where they found an affordable house. They were able to qualify for welfare payments for the children, and that, combined with Lena Walls's Social Security pension, provided beans and potatoes.

Doris found a whole new social structure where she could satisfy her insatiable appetite for partying. Her many new friends in the Hispanic population generously shared booze and pot with the gorgeous young woman who spoke with a cute Kentucky drawl. She drifted into a pattern of sharing her body and sexual favors in return for drugs that graduated from pot to LSD, cocaine, and heroin. Her social life took her away from her mother and children for days at a time.

The moves continued throughout Eastern Los Angeles County. Grandma, Doris, and the two children lived for a few months in El Monte, then Azusa, and San Dimas. Greg and Coral spent most of the time with Grandmother Lena Walls, until the social welfare agents stepped in. Because Doris was usually absent, and the grandmother could barely manage, Greg was sent to a series of foster homes. Few of them worked out, and before long, he would find his way back to his "Gram" and sister. Now and then, Doris would have temporary use of an apartment, and the two kids would be able to spend a few days with her. They were treated to a real education.

Doris would require silence during the mornings that Greg and Coral were with her, because she needed to sleep off the effects of wild nights. Then, when she pried herself from the bed, she would spend most of the remaining part of the day getting ready for the next party, picking the right clothes and applying makeup. She usually left before dark, but would occasionally host the party. The men, mostly Hispanic, would arrive, break out the booze and drugs, and focus lusty attention on Doris. They did not hide their pleasures from the children.

Occasionally, the kids were useful to Doris. During a drug bust by police, officers were searching Doris's apartment for her stash. Little Coral sat on a shoe box watching the entire hunt, her eyes round in fear. She knew the shoe box contained the marijuana the officers sought. They did not find it.

Grandma Walls found a home in San Dimas, and decided it was time to stop moving around endlessly. That provided Greg and Coral with a place to stay when Doris was unavailable to be with them, which was most of the time. The 1960s, for the two youngsters, was a nightmare of changing homes, changing schools, and watching their mother sink into a vortex of drugs, men, sex, and degradation.

While most children Greg Marlow's age were participating in Little League, learning social niceties, and starting school, Greg's cultivation was entirely different.

Asked, in later years, about his relationship with his mother, Marlow answered, "I loved my mother. When I was just a little guy, we did robberies and burglaries and stuff. She used to take me to these big parties. I mean East L.A. and Hollywood, and, man, everybody would go in these big rooms and do heroin and stuff, and I would pretend like I was sick until they were gone, and then I'd get up and I'd hit the purses and grab jewelry and money, and I'd run out to the car and put it in my mom's stash spot. We had an old car and I'd put it in the trunk.

"They (Doris and male friends) used to put me through holes in the roof of stores and stuff. I used to go through little windows in houses, and get a chair so I could unlock the door. They showed me how to unlock the doors, and they'd come in and steal everything.

"I just wanted to do good," Marlow recalled. "And every time my mom left, I thought it was because I didn't do good enough. I tried to figure out what I did wrong. . . . If I could just do better the next time, maybe she'll stay or maybe she'll take me with her. So I always tried to do better, and I'd practice and I did real good on robbing and stealing.

"We didn't necessarily hurt anybody. We survived. She had to have her drugs, and we had to have food, pay rent, and other things. That's just the way it was."

* * *

When Greg was approaching his thirteenth birthday, welfare workers were convinced that something different must be done to provide for the boy. They contacted Jeffrey and Anita Marlow in Ohio to see if they would take him again. With a certain amount of trepidation, Jeffrey and Anita discussed it and agreed to give it another try. Anita was privately concerned because she remembered how Jeffrey had treated his son seven years earlier, and because her marriage was on shaky ground.

This time, dressed in cheap but clean clothes provided by the welfare agency, Greg flew to Cincinnati. He was welcomed by Anita, Jeffrey, and their three children, then taken to a barber shop to cut his shoulder-length hair.

The reunion started well, but sputtered and backfired almost immediately.

Anita was working at the RCA Company in Norwood, and Jeffrey was employed by the Fisher Plant where bodies for General Motors cars were manufactured. Financially, things had been pretty good for them, but Greg arrived at an unfortunate time. There were problems between some union factions and the Fisher management which resulted in strikes. And when he wasn't on strike, Jeffrey tended to take all of his available sick leave. He used the time off to enjoy his favorite hobby, drinking.

In exact repetition of Greg's previous stay with his father, the period of welcome lasted about three days. Greg then found that once again, he couldn't do anything right. Minor infractions of the house rules resulted in whippings with a belt, a switch, a yardstick, or whatever else was handy. The punishment was usually carried out in the garage, where Anita, when she was home, could not hear it. Jeffrey preferred it that way because Anita would usually try to intercede on behalf of the children and prevent a harsh whipping.

She was later asked if she had ever seen any bruises, welts, cuts, or other marks on Greg.

"Yes," she replied. "His little behind would look like somebody had beat it really good. And it would go down his legs and toes where he (Jeffrey) would use a belt."

Greg was not the only one of the siblings subjected to punishment. His younger half brother, who was eight years old when Greg returned, also remembered the abuse. "My father," he would recall, "was an alcoholic. An abusive man with a temper, very unstable. Selfish. I can tell you all kinds of things about my father. He wasn't a father to me or my sisters nor to Greg."

The sisters were not exempted, either, from Jeffrey's treatment. The youngest daughter, who was born the day Greg arrived for his previous stay, had nightmarish recollections. "He raped me when I was ten. He also molested my sister. He used to beat us, too, with a belt and a switch and a brush."

For Greg, just as it had been before, life was pretty good in Ohio except for the abuse he withstood from his father. In addition to his family members, there were neighborhood kids to play with, and a stepmother who really seemed to care about him and did everything she could to provide for his needs.

In school, Greg struggled to make up for the lost time that resulted from so many moves and school changes. He was behind in his reading level, which made it difficult to make progress in the other disciplines. But he tried. Anita recalled, "He was a little slow, but they always gave him an 'E' for effort." Anita would try to help him with his homework, and he responded by trying to help her around the house and doing what she asked.

The abominable behavior of Jeffrey Marlow was as painful to Anita as a dentist's drilling after the anesthetic has worn off. She finally decided to take her children and leave. She knew, however, that she could not get legal custody of Greg, and she did not want to desert him in the abusive atmosphere with his father. She sought counsel from a social services agency, who arranged to place Greg in yet another foster home.

It wasn't the ideal solution for Anita, but she could think of no other alternatives. She waited until Greg had been moved to the foster home, then left Jeffrey Marlow. Greg, after nine months in a stable home, albeit an abusive one, had once again been sent packing.

A few weeks later, Anita received a telephone call. It was the social services group who had placed Greg with a guardian family. The message

Anita received was confusing, but the gist of it was that someone, possibly Doris or someone acting for her, had taken Greg from his newest foster home. He was once again in California.

Fourteen

Cynthia Lynn Haskin screamed in agony each time she was lifted or moved during the first five weeks of her life. The frail infant had been born in St. Louis, Missouri, on January 19, 1962, with a bilateral inguinal hernia. Her crying and kicking only served to aggravate the malady, creating a vicious cycle of pain that caused crying that caused pain.

The pain was just as intense, if only empathetic, for Sally Haskin. "Poor little thing," the baby's mother lamented. "This protruding bump comes out down in her groin, on both sides. It hurts her something terrible. And I have to take it and push it back in every time it comes out. That just makes it hurt her worse."

The doctor advised Sally that the infant could not have an operation to correct the hernias because she was "too tiny." It would be necessary to wait until she was at least one month old. So, on February 28, at the end of the baby's fifth week, Sally drove the five miles to Children's Hospital at the Washington University Medical Center in St. Louis. She placed her daughter in the hands of a reassuring nurse and waited. Two days later, the delicate surgery was completed and the doctors informed the worried mother that her baby would be fine. Cynthia could begin, six weeks late, to experience life without constant, searing pain.

Sally brought Cynthia home from the hospital to the little three-room, second-floor apartment in central St. Louis, and relaxed for the first time in weeks. Now she could pay equal attention to both of her babies. Her first child, Robby, was fourteen months old, and two babies, she thought, were almost more than she could handle, even without the health problem. She loved the children, but wondered what had happened to her hopes and dreams.

Just eighteen when she met Bob Haskin at the USO club in St. Louis, Sally Kreasky hadn't intended to become serious about anyone so soon, but he, at age twenty-two, had something that excited her. He combed his well-oiled dark brown hair back on the sides into a fashionable ducktail and let a lock tumble down from the pompadour onto his forehead. His face, with brown eyes and high cheekbones, radiated confidence. He wasn't exceptionally tall, about five-ten, so he didn't have to bend far to kiss her.

With her slim figure encased in a popular angora sweater and full skirt with several petticoats, Sally had no trouble attracting young men. Her auburn hair was long enough to wear in a ponytail, and her full lips, dark blue eyes, and high cheek-bones were aesthetically proportioned. She and Bob looked and felt good together. The physical attraction, combined with his "sweet nature" and thoughtful attentiveness made him irresistible to her.

Marriage to Haskin, Sally realized, would probably interfere with her most cherished goal. She wanted, more than anything else she could imagine, to be a singer. In high school, she had been encouraged and applauded. Following that, she had experienced the thrill of being a professional entertainer by singing at a few local clubs and civic celebrations.

Bob Haskin's charm had derailed her ambitions but she was sure that it would be just a temporary delay. In February 1960, they were married in a civil ceremony; he was divorced and she was Catholic, which precluded a church ceremony. He thought she was a virgin on their wedding night, but she later revealed that he was wrong. They moved into a small basement apartment.

Exactly nine months later, in the same month that John F. Kennedy was elected to be President of the United States, their son, Robby, was born, postponing her singing career even longer. The young father had left the military and was employed by the post office; Sally took part-time clerical jobs to supplement their income. It was a struggle, but they managed. In April 1961, her dream seemed even more elusive when she discovered that she was pregnant again.

By cutting corners on all expenses, and borrowing to help with the down payment, Bob and Sally invested in a small home. The financial strain of mortgage payments caused one of the first discordant notes in their relationship.

Even though Cynthia's health had improved, her disposition hadn't kept pace. She was increasingly moody and emotional with her mother. By contrast, she cooed and giggled when her father played with her. But the distinct friction between mother and daughter gradually flared into overt antagonism. As soon as Cynthia learned to talk, she began to "sass" Sally and resist anything the frustrated mother wanted the defiant girl to do.

The relationship with her older brother was the same. "Robby was a delightful child, but Cynthia couldn't get along with him, either," Sally said. She hoped that it was just normal brother-sister antagonism, but worried that something far worse was wrong.

Intense pressures of coping with noisy, arguing children, Cynthia's intransigence, money problems, and a battery of daily crises typical for young couples who have shouldered too much responsibility, too soon, tore at the seams of the marriage. Screaming arguments let off some of the steam, but ultimately, only made the problems worse. Anger boiled, then ebbed into hours of sullen silence and acrimonious glares.

Bob dealt with the conflict by the age-old technique of avoidance. He found excuses to be late returning home from his job every day. Evenings out with "the boys" became more frequent.

The first eruption of physical violence between Bob and Sally took the form of exchanging slaps just to punctuate an argument. Gradually, the ferocity and force of the blows grew, until terrified screams from the children would embarrass the couple into a simmering armistice.

Little Robby endured the turmoil better than his baby sister. Cynthia, by the time she was two, screeched and bellowed during her parents' angry battles. Her screaming and belligerence toward her mother occasionally earned her a slap. After a while, though, she began to withdraw into her own protective shell, and just watched with an empty stare when Sally and Bob fought.

As the strain on the matrimonial bonds stretched tighter and threatened to rip the marriage apart, in September 1964, Sally once again began to feel nausea and morning sickness. Robby was almost four, and Cynthia was a few months away from her third birthday. Sally was less than elated when her doctor confirmed that she was pregnant again. A few weeks later, the news was even worse.

Nearly exhausted from working a late shift, Sally trudged into the apartment desperately needing some rest. As usual, before attending to her own needs, she gathered enough energy to spend some time with the two children. Little Robby, like most four-year-old children, was observant and loquacious. Sally noticed that he was pouting and babbling, bursting to let her know why he was very upset. "Tell Mommy what's wrong," she murmured, attempting to pacify him.

"Daddy made us go to bed early," he wailed. Sally smiled, but her expression froze when the youngster continued. "Him and the lady wanted to go to sleep, so he made me and Cyndi go to bed early."

Sally was stunned and then furious. She had fought off some suspicions that Bob might be interested in other women, telling herself that she was just being petty and jealous. But her child's innocent description was like a slap in the face. She didn't know who the woman was, but she had no trouble developing a mental picture of what happened. She couldn't decide what made her angrier, his indiscretion or the idea that he had cheated on her while the children were in the house.

Confrontation with her husband resulted in denials, tears, shouts, and ultimately, angry silence. Sally was pragmatic, though. She realized that she could not support the children by herself and that problem was magnified by her swelling belly. She decided she would tough it out for a while longer.

Just when Sally thought things couldn't get any worse, they did. The straw was added that literally broke her back. In a freak accident, she was knocked unconscious. When Sally woke up, she was in a hospital, completely immobilized. She had a fractured vertebrae. It wasn't life-threatening, nor would it cause paralysis. But it would cause her immeasurable discomfort during her pregnancy, limit her ability to deal with the children, and prevent her from working for several months.

Upon the arrival of their third child, Jeff, on June 7, 1965, Bob and Sally realized at last that the marriage was beyond repair. They separated.

Cynthia was devastated. Despite the traumatic fights she had observed and endured, the little girl dearly loved her father. She had delighted in sitting on his lap, being tickled and sharing little secrets with him. Early in life, she had learned that she bonded easily to the opposite sex. His absence created a void, both physical and emotional, that would exacerbate the growing disturbance harbored deep in the psyche of Cynthia Lynn.

One bright light in her life was her baby brother. "Cyndi and Robby constantly fought and argued and played one against the other," Sally complained. "But there was a real bond between Cyndi and the baby. Jeff was probably the most loving child I've ever seen. When he reached out to you with his little arms, you couldn't have anything to do but love him. Cyndi was never that way. She didn't like to be held and loved. And it was hard to love a child that doesn't want to be loved."

Sally's secretarial job did not pay enough to support her and the three children. She scanned classified ads daily for a part-time job that would at least provide enough money to pay a baby-sitter. An appeal to her parents for help had been answered with a stinging rebuff. "You made your bed, now lay in it," her father had firmly told her.

Opportunities for part-time employment in traditional jobs continued to elude Sally. The old dreams of a professional singing career had not been entirely extinguished, so she began to look longingly at nightclubs and bars. Finally, she worked up enough nerve to answer an ad for a cocktail waitress in a club where the revealing barmaid costume included a push-up bra and a cotton ball attached to the derriere, in imitation of the classier Playboy Clubs. It was not a singing career, but if the tips were good enough, it would help pay the bills.

Cynthia Lynn, now called Cyndi by most everyone, missed her father, and took out her hostility on her mother. Some of her aggression was directed at the various baby-sitters, most of whom did not wish to make a career of tending the three children. But Sally was the main focus of the four-year-old child's distress.

Perhaps more frustrating than anything else, for Sally, was that she knew that Cyndi could behave nicely. The child was polite around most people, especially males. Even to her little brother, Jeff, she was attentive and loving. But with her big brother and mom, the friction was constant. Sally found herself anticipating the relative peace and

Don Lasseter

quiet of her secretarial job and the bar where she worked at night.

Even though it meant squeezing into her brief costume six nights a week, constantly smiling at customers, and maintaining her composure despite amorous or belligerent drunks, Sally didn't mind working two jobs. Her tips and wages were enough to balance her budget, pay for baby-sitters and keep up mortgage payments on the house she and Bob Haskin had purchased. The work hours were long; time with her children was short. But she couldn't see any alternatives.

Sitting at the desk of her day job, Sally was typing a letter when her boss asked her into his office. She sensed that something was wrong. There was. Someone had whispered a rumor to him. He wanted to know if it was true that she worked as a cocktail waitress at night. She couldn't deny it. He didn't mince words. He fired her, effective immediately.

Sally had made some contacts in the bar, people who dropped some hints about her going on the road and using her talents as a singer. She hadn't recently given it much serious thought, but this new crisis forced her to make a decision.

Sally wasn't especially close to her family, but decided that she had better contact them to discuss what she was doing. She telephoned her sister, Janet. "Jan, I just can't take care of my kids anymore. I lost my daytime job, and I just don't have enough money to make ends meet. I don't want to put them in a foster home, but I don't know what else to do."

Janet called her parents and relayed to them the plan to place the children in foster homes. Then she called her sister back.

"Sally, Mom said that she and Dad would look after Robby, temporarily. They picked him because he's the oldest and least likely to disturb Dad with a lot of noise. Mom is pretty sure that Aunt Florence and Uncle Conny will take Cyndi. And if it's okay with you, Sally, Jim and I will take the baby, Jeff."

It was the only reasonable solution to her problems, so Sally agreed to place her children in the respective homes until she could re-establish her financial stability. Each child, tearfully resisting, was bundled off to live with a relative. Sally, at last, in May 1967, was going to pursue her dream of a singing career.

Show business, Sally soon found, was not all fun, fame, and big money as she had imagined. For a few weeks, she happily traveled to various nightclubs, in several cities, even to Nashville. Each night she warbled through her repertoire then sang numbers requested by rude, noisy, intoxicated customers. Before long, though, the glamour tarnished and faded like dime-store jewelry. The pay wasn't nearly what she had hoped for.

Cyndi Lynn Haskin wasn't happy in her great-aunt's home, and the feeling was mutual with her benefactors. The middle-aged couple began to fear that Cyndi was going to be left with them indefinitely and such prospects did not fit into their plans for the future. She didn't behave terribly, but they felt that she belonged with her mother. By the middle of summer, when Sally called, they tactfully suggested that she retrieve her daughter before school started in September.

The opinion that Sally should take her children back was shared by her father. When she telephoned her parents, to see how Robby was doing, Pop pulled no punches. "Why don't you get a legitimate job," he bellowed. "Come back, and take care of your own kids."

Mediocrity in her singing "career" and the pressure she felt from her father and aunt to take Cyndi and Robby convinced Sally to return to St. Louis. She picked up Cyndi in July. When school started in September, Sally's parents delivered Robby back to the little house that she and Bob Haskin had bought five years earlier.

Janet agreed to keep the baby, Jeff, a little while longer to help Sally. They had grown very fond of the child. The "little while" would last much longer than they thought.

By the time Cynthia Lynn Haskin was six, she had been estranged from her beloved father, farmed out to live with relatives who rejected her, left by her mother, and separated from her brothers. The reunion with her mother and Robby did little to alleviate the disturbance that had taken root within her and flourished. She missed little Jeff, whose stay with Aunt Janet had extended well past the September beginning of school, and into 1968. Cyndi had not even seen her baby brother since he went away.

Too young to understand her mother's financial difficulties, Cyndi was still aware of the effects of it. Sometimes, Sally slept with the two children in order for all three of them to stay warm and save heating costs. Sally had finally been forced to give up her small home and move into an apartment. She still worked long hours to support her children, and pay for baby-sitters. In addition, she had enrolled in school to obtain a degree in accounting so she could find a higher paying job. Sally had also started dating.

Cyndi found someone she truly liked. The man who came to the apartment to see her mother really seemed to care for Cyndi and Robby. He played with them and bought toys for them. He even took them to ball games, sometimes leaving Sally at home. He pressured her to get Jeff back from her sister. Sally wasn't yet ready to do that.

Sally later explained her breakup with the man. "I guess the main reason I didn't marry him was because I felt he loved the kids more than he loved me."

The end of the relationship left Cyndi feeling deserted again. The emptiness would soon be filled, though, with a new man in Sally's life.

Carl Anderson was perfect for Sally. Six-feet, four-inches, wearing a blazer and dark slacks, which flared fashionably over his black loafers, he looked very sophisticated sitting next to her in the cafeteria at school. His blond hair was well-groomed, unlike most of the other men, whose long, unkempt manes, tie-dyed shirts, and patched jeans reflected the fading era of hippies and flower children.

Serious feelings grew quickly. Carl's gentle strength and confidence was like a balm in Sally's frazzled life. He had a future, too. He was attending law school while working as a controller in the accounting department of a large machine company in St. Louis. His frugal respect for money and his financial skills, Sally knew, would be a great influence on her. She was always in debt, but Carl didn't believe in credit. He told her that the only smart way to buy anything was to save the money first, then pay cash for it. He practiced what he preached.

The children immediately liked Carl Anderson, and he liked them. Cyndi, Sally eventually concluded, had actually competed with her for the affection of her earlier boyfriend. But, with Carl, it was different. She genuinely liked him.

Another one of Sally's burdens about which Carl offered advice was the status of baby Jeff, who was still living with Sally's sister. "Look, Sally," he said, "he's been with Jan now for all this time. You can't disrupt him. You can't take him back because he's settled. He's happy, and they're giving him a good home." He very clearly thought that Sally should let Jan and her husband adopt Jeff.

That opinion was shared by someone else. Sally's father urged, "You can have children so easily. Your sister can't have them. The least you can do is let her keep Jeff." Internal conflict gnawed at Sally, but she let Jeff continue to stay with her sister.

Fiscal prudence was not the only positive influence Carl had on Sally. She, too, had been raised in the Catholic religion, but had not loyally practiced it or regularly attended church. Carl changed that. "Carl is a very devout religious person," said Sally. "Once he and I got serious about each other, we started going to church all the time."

Did that include the children? she was later asked.

"Everything always included the children. We never did anything without the kids."

When Cyndi was enrolled in school in September 1968, it was in St. Margaret's Parochial School, a coeducational institution where Catholic discipline was taught by nuns. Her grades were passable but her teachers detected an incipient tendency to fudge a little on the truth. When confronted with an accusation of some misbehavior, Cyndi would invent any lie she could imagine.

While she was still in elementary school, one of the brightest experiences for Cyndi was joining the Girl Scouts. "She loved it," Sally recalled. "That was her big thing. She loved the camping, doing the projects, doing everything." Sally hoped that the scout training might relax some of the tension between Cyndi and her, but there was no change. On one occasion, when Cyndi refused to stay in the house while Sally went shopping, the mother was determined to have her way. She simply tied her daughter's legs to the bedpost, securely enough that Cyndi was still there when she returned.

As with everything in Cyndi's life, happiness ebbed and flowed with dizzying extremes. Sally and Carl Anderson were married in August 1972, and he quickly adopted her two children. Her youngest child, Jeff, was still with his aunt Jan, who would eventually adopt him. Cyndi was very fond of her new stepfather. She adjusted easily to calling him "Dad," and gradually began to confide in him about her problems. But there was one problem she could tell no one.

Robby first observed what was going on. Cyndi, he thought, was spending far too much time with someone who lived in the same apartment complex. The man, known to Robby and Cyndi only as Joe, frequently came to visit the children, sometimes accompanied by his brother, especially when no other adult was there. Robby didn't like him because he "seemed rough and smoked too much." Cyndi seemed to welcome his affections and demonstrated it by allowing him to kiss her. Distressed by the man's attention to his prepubescent sister, Robby told his mother about Joe. Sally had no proof to support a confrontation with the man, but worried that either Joe or his brother was sexually molesting Cyndi. She promptly decided it would be better to move her children to another location.

By the time Cyndi reached her twelfth birthday, Cyndi's fights with Sally escalated. Bickering and nasty insults turned to physical struggles. If Sally slapped her daughter, the slap was promptly returned.

Cyndi finished the eighth grade then announced to her parents that she no longer wanted to go to parochial schools. The timing was agreeable to Carl and Sally, because they were preparing to move to a new two-story home he purchased. Carl had changed jobs, to a large electronics firm, where he had vaulted up the corporate ladder to an executive position. The commensurate salary increase improved his family's standard of living, and the new home reflected that. Sally had ceased working since her marriage to Carl. On their wedding day he had firmly stated that he did not want her to work outside the home anymore.

As a freshman in high school, Cyndi discovered that she was a reasonably good athlete. She lettered in two sports, softball and field hockey. The glowing feeling of achievement dimmed, though, when her family didn't bother to attend any of the games, and flickered out the next year.

In the tenth grade, Cyndi's grades and attendance were average. Having never established camaraderie with fellow athletes, she found friends among a different social level. The student smoking lounge was a "cool" place to spend time. There, she met kids who liked to smoke cigarettes at school and something a little stronger off campus. Years later, she explained, "I got acceptance from, you know, the pot smokers. That's all I used, marijuana. But they're the ones who accepted me."

Cyndi cut classes perhaps a half-dozen times that year, but never skipped an entire day. After school, she rushed to a Burger Chef fast-food restaurant where she had her first job, working behind the counter and cleaning up. That summer, Cyndi found more exciting employment, driving a tram at the Six Flags amusement park.

Her attendance deteriorated the next school year; she was frequently late or absent from classes and failed to show up six times. Carl and Sally were concerned with the truancy, but they were far more worried about a new problem with Cyndi.

"When I discovered them, I about went through the roof," Sally remembered. "First, I found a small handful of red pills. Then, I went through her room with a fine-tooth comb and found some kind of a little burner thing and several different kinds of pills and things like that."

In 1978, drug rehabilitation clinics were not as readily available as they would eventually become in Missouri and the entire country. Sally said, "I didn't know about those things then. So we just sat her down and talked to her. She told us that she had taken drugs only once or twice and promised us she would not do it anymore. We watched her like a hawk for the next couple of months, and she seemed to be fine."

Toward the end of her junior year in high school, Cyndi's social life kept her out increasingly late at night. When she came home at two or three o'clock in the morning, Sally would confront her and, in frustration, grab her shoulders and shake her as hard as she could. Cyndi's reaction was often equally violent; slapping her mother, running out the door, and staying away the rest of the night. After one such incident, Cyndi disappeared for three days. Frantic, Sally and Carl called the police and searched everywhere for her. When she returned, she didn't bother to explain her activities or her whereabouts. She repeated the disappearing act twice more within the next three months, staying away two days each time. She never did divulge where she had been.

To prevent some of the strain between Robby and her, their parents arranged for them to attend separate high schools. Robby was a stand-out athlete in baseball and basketball, and asked to go to Parkway West School because of an attractive sports program there. Carl Anderson "pulled some strings" and Robby attended the school of his choice. That suited Cyndi just fine. She went to Parkway Central where she would not have to live up to her brother's academic excellence.

Working again at Six Flags in the early part of

the summer, Cyndi felt a growing sense of dissatisfaction. She quit and found another job with a Walgreen's store. It was during that time she met a youth, two months her junior, who had dropped out of school at fifteen to become a fry cook. He wasn't especially handsome, and stood no taller than Cyndi, but she was attracted to him. Perhaps it was because Ron Coffman, too, found escape in a world of pot and pills.

Ron Coffman became one of the main subjects of conflict between Cyndi and her parents. Truancy was another sore point, and her late hours incited arguments. A variety of other disagreements caused constant unrest between Cyndi and her family until finally, in early November, the tug-of-war rope unraveled and separated.

Sally and Cyndi had been continually exchanging accusations, slaps, and furious insults. Both of them were screaming and crying one evening after an emotional argument over Cyndi's behavior, which Sally thought was outrageous for a girl of seventeen. Fed up, Carl stepped in and told Cyndi, "If you're going to live under this roof, you're going to abide by the rules."

Continuing to sob, Cyndi howled, "All right, if that's the way you want it . . ." and ran upstairs. Carl and Sally could hear her slamming doors and stomping the floor for about twenty minutes. She emerged from her bedroom carrying a suitcase and a purse, hurried down the stairs, and headed for the front door. Carl stepped to the door with her. He courteously opened it, and said, "Go ahead if you think you can do it."

Cyndi strode out the door and disappeared into the night. She would be gone for more than three months.

Fifteen

Greg Marlow was consumed with an aching desire for his mother, Doris, to return the unconditional love he gave to her. The still sensuously beautiful woman finally did return it, but Doris never did anything according to social convention. She found the most forbidden way to respond to Greg's affection and loyalty.

In a dark bedroom, vile with the odors of unwashed sheets and blankets, and stained with years of tobacco smoke and grime, Doris came to her son. Her logic burned out by booze, her inhibitions eroded by dancing topless in bars, her morals destroyed by snorting coke or LSD, and her blood boiling with injected heroin, she came to her son. Sex wasn't sacred, it was nothing but pleasure for Doris; she had been selling her body for longer than she could remember. There were no rules anymore. She taught him all she knew, and more.

Years later, Marlow talked about it to a journalist. "I had sex with my mom. I was about thirteen, something like that."

"Did she initiate it?"

"Yeah. I didn't even know it was sex with my

mother. It was . . . it seemed so normal. It seemed so normal to me. I didn't know that anybody else didn't do that. I didn't know it was wrong."

Tracing his finger on a stainless-steel counter in front of him, as if scribing a route on a road map, Marlow continued. "I'm just from another area. We have this area out here, and people in this area have certain ways of doing things, and these people out here have other ways. It even happens with kids. Put kids in certain areas, and they grow and act certain ways."

According to Marlow, Doris "educated" him in carnal knowledge more than once.

A man with whom Doris lived, on and off over a five-year period, known by her two children as Pinky, recalled Doris's effect on Greg Marlow. "I didn't even know she had kids for the first year. She kept that from me. When I found out, I thought, man . . . why did you have to be such an influence like that on that young man? He was an innocent child. And he didn't ask to grow up that way in an abnormal home. He never had a father to show him the right way to throw a ball, or take him out on a wagon, or, you know, fix his bike. I don't even know if he had a bike. He grew up around nothing but dope fiends all his life."

One night, Pinky said, he saw Greg lying beside Doris on her bed. She sent him to his own bed, and confided in Pinky that Greg was always afraid that she was going to leave him and never return. From then on, Pinky understood when he saw

Greg slip into Doris's room at night and sleep on the floor as close as he could to his mother.

The man spoke from experience. He had been Doris's connection, keeping her seventy-dollar-per-day habit supplied. Before straightening out his own life, and becoming deeply religious, he had floundered in the depths of a thirty-year drug dependency that had ended in painful withdrawal during a ten-year prison term. He and Doris had shared needles on many occasions.

Doris shared her heroin needle like she shared her sex. In the same year that she taught her son the forbidden pleasures of her body, Doris injected him with heroin.

The daughter of a woman with whom Doris often "hung out," remembered: "I had a little trouble with my mom when I was thirteen, and I didn't know where to go. So I got a hold of Doris in San Gabriel and I went to ask if I could stay there. When I got there, I saw Coral, and she let me in. I had to go to the bathroom real bad, and you had to go through the bedroom to get to the bathroom. I opened the door, and I saw Jim—Greg and Doris. And Greg had this band around his (arm) and his mother injected him. She had a needle, like this [gesturing] in his arm. And she came to block the door because they didn't want me to go in no more. But it was too late. I was in there."

Asked how Doris Bender earned money to supply the habit, the young woman responded, "(By) stealing. Burning people. Taking it from people. Trying to work out a deal. She would tell them she

would do a trick with them. Take them behind the
bar (or) in a car, and steal their money." The girl
added that she, at age thirteen, had personally witnessed Doris engaging in acts of prostitution.

Coral had troubling memories of those years. In
addition to witnessing Doris injecting Greg with
heroin, the little girl felt an overwhelming sense
of loneliness. "There were times that she (Doris)
would go out for the night and not come back for
months."

Greg Marlow's life continued much like that of
a stray dog. His uncle, Justus Walls, was living in
Fontana, the old steel-mill town near San Bernardino, California. When juvenile authorities,
who had been bouncing Greg from one foster
home to another, discovered that a relative was in
the region, they arranged to place the boy with his
uncle in early 1970. It lasted eight months, until
August. Greg's behavior was settling into a negative
pattern. The tenure with Uncle Justus ended when
he could no longer tolerate his nephew's intransigence. Greg was placed in the California Military
Academy in Cherry Valley, but his early training
certainly had not prepared him for a tight regimen
of disciplined activities, so the experiment lasted
only three months.

Once more, Grandma Lena Walls shouldered
the load. She and Coral had been forced to move
again, landing in a small house in Muscoy, also
near San Bernardino. Ironically, the move provided

James Gregory Marlow with his first real chance for a normal life. Across the street from Granny Walls's new residence lived Terry and Joanne Sydnes, with their brood of four children.

Joanne Sydnes was an angel of mercy, a Good Samaritan of the first order. While her husband, Terry, worked two jobs, sometimes three, to make ends meet, Joanne spent most of her time trying to help people. When she met Lena Walls, Coral, and Greg, it was immediately obvious to Joanne that the elderly woman was unable to cope with the kids or the expenses.

Several times during the ensuing weeks, when Doris visited Granny and the children, the Sydnes family heard angry, profane screaming. Doris could be overheard calling the kids filthy names and wishing that she didn't have them. She demanded money from Lena because she "needed a fix." When Joanne and Terry saw Doris, who was thirty-one at the time, they thought she looked much older than her age and "all used up."

Greg got into a minor scrape that brought out the juvenile authorities again, so Joanne contacted a probation officer to offer the boy a place in the Sydnes home. In February 1971, Greg moved in with them. Not long afterwards, Joanne made a request for the probation department to provide some counseling or psychological help for Greg to get him started on the right path. The department refused, saying that it wasn't necessary. Their decision would be a mistake of monumental proportions.

Restless, feeling out of place and rejected by his mother, Greg Marlow didn't know how to play the good hand he had been dealt by the Sydnes family. He was often rebellious, didn't relate well to the other children, and frequently skipped school. Marlow ran away on May 4, and again on June 28. Finally, in the fall of 1971, Joanne and Terry had to admit failure when they discovered drugs in Greg's room. It had taken him only eight months to wreck a golden opportunity. It was time for the fifteen-year-old nomad to move again.

New drug charges forced Doris to cool her ardors in prison once more. Greg stayed temporarily with Uncle Justus and with Granny Walls. In February 1972, Doris was paroled and Greg was again officially placed with her. In May, on his sixteenth birthday, the juvenile court washed their hands of him, having heard that Greg and Doris had moved to Kentucky. But they hadn't. The mendacious pair had lied to remove themselves from the scrutiny of any authority.

Late that summer, Greg Marlow was arrested twice—once for involvement in a burglary, and a second time for selling drugs to minor children. "I'm innocent," Greg protested, and Doris came to his rescue. Appealing personally to a probation officer, Doris said all the right things, ostensibly accepting responsibility for any mistakes by her son. She blamed her own drug problems. In a clever bit of manipulation, she pointed out that she hadn't been able to help her son avoid trouble because she had been incarcerated. No, she demurred, blinking innocently, she didn't know that her boy used drugs. She promised that she would take care of that right away.

The probation officer, in a written report, characterized Doris and her errant son as honest, candid, and motivated. Greg was granted probation.

Months later, the embarrassed probation officer was searching for the "honest, candid, motivated" youth who had failed to report as scheduled. A warrant was issued for Marlow's arrest.

While Greg was still living in Muscoy, with Granny Walls and later the Sydnes family, a tall, big-boned, young mother settled on the same street. Her ebony hair accentuated tawny skin and features that the teenager down the street, Greg Marlow, found attractive. He didn't seem to mind that she was five years older than he, or that she had two infant children.

Among the things that Connie Tysen and Greg Marlow found in common was a mutual taste for drugs. They often used crystal methamphetamine, and a couple of times shared it with Doris before dropping her off at a bar. Doris didn't try to hide the fact that she danced topless and bottomless at the garish dive.

The forbidden encounters Greg had shared with his mother were now replaced by an active sexual relationship with Connie. For the next few months, they lived together periodically at Granny Walls's house. On the last day of December 1973, their first son was born.

A few weeks prior to the birth, Greg was arrested on suspicion of burglary and for the warrant stemming from his failure to report to a probation officer. Doris faced the same official she had fooled earlier. He was leery this time, inclined to throw the book at the young man. Doris told the officer that Greg had married Connie and really wanted to support the expected child. It worked. Greg was released for "humanitarian" reasons.

After so many years of dissolute life, brushes with the law, the constraints of parole supervision, and her unhappy environments, Doris wanted a change. She asked Coral to join her in a move back to Kentucky. Coral was reluctant, but Doris persuaded her to go by promising to withdraw from drugs and never to use them again. For the first time in years, Coral believed her mother. On the day before Coral's fifteenth birthday in April 1974, mother and daughter departed for Kentucky. Neither of them bothered to tell Greg they were leaving.

One month later, just after Greg's eighteenth birthday, he and Connie were married in Las Vegas.

For a few months, the newlyweds lived in a small apartment with the baby and Connie's two children, but when money ran out, they called on Granny Walls again, and moved in with her. Connie was the primary breadwinner but most of her income went for speed, Seconal, tuinal, marijuana, cocaine, and heroin. Greg's laziness, regular unemployment, and failure to accept any responsibility irritated Connie. She threatened that if he didn't get a haircut, find a job, and clean up his act, she would leave him. He complied with her wishes, and tried working as a shoe store salesclerk. His newfound profession lasted three weeks.

As Christmas approached in 1974, Connie was furious. Greg had been arrested twice for drug possession, and had committed a burglary. Pregnant again, Connie wanted to withdraw from drugs and live a clean life. She moved back in with her parents in San Bernardino.

While waiting for sentencing in January 1975, Greg wrote a letter to probation officer Robert Jetsen. "Please let me out because I want to support and take care of my family," he begged. He described the "pure hell" he would experience without his wife and children. "And I hope to God you believe me, without my family I am lost."

Robert Jetsen was moved by the plea. He recommended leniency probation and drug counseling, and convinced a judge to deliver that sentence.

Greg Marlow was elated that he had once again avoided prison time. But his joy was short-lived. Two weeks later, he received the most devastating news of his life. His mother, Doris, the focus of his deep love, was dead.

Doris and Coral had stayed in Kentucky a short time before migrating north to Ohio. The small trailer house where they were living had mysteriously caught fire, and Doris, alone inside, had died of smoke inhalation before fire ravaged her body. A nasty rumor circulated that Coral, in a fit of rage, had touched off the fire because her sixteen-year-old boyfriend had been intimate with Doris. No evidence ever surfaced to support the whispered allegations, and no charges were ever filed.

Doris's charred body was transported back to California for burial. At the funeral home, Greg hysterically demanded that the casket be opened to allow him to verify that his mother had really died.

Distraught and aimless, Greg walked away from his marriage to Connie. He was absent—committing a burglary—when their twin sons were born on April Fools' Day, 1975.

In that period, Marlow started spending time with a friend he had known for several years, Richard Drinkhouse. Portly, olive-skinned, and well-acquainted with drugs, Richard invited his buddy Greg to stay with him at his mother's house.

Marlow remembered: "Richard was okay. His sister was my girlfriend. I was her first . . . I guess, I was her first lay. I was great with their mother. Used to smoke pot with her and bring her pot. Got along great with them. I was a member of the family for a while. They lived next door to Darlene Miller."

Darlene was the girlfriend of one of Marlow's cousins. A few days after the burglary, Darlene was sitting outside, on a pretty spring day, chatting with Richard Drinkhouse, Richard's mother, Marlow, and her own parents. Greg announced that he was going to the store to buy some beer and invited Darlene to go along. In Richard's car, he drove with Darlene toward a convenience store, but part-way there, Greg pulled to the curb in front of an old house.

"I've got to go in there and talk to someone," he told his passenger. "Want to come in with me?"

"No, I don't think so. I'll wait out here."

"C'mon," Greg insisted. "It's warm out here. C'mon in."

Darlene agreed to go in. She would later report what happened: "I made it to the front door, and I felt there was something wrong with the house. It didn't seem to be lived in. And I turned to (ask) him, 'What's going on?' He hit me in the back of the head. Then he pushed me in the house and started beating me. I passed out. When I woke up, I was tied, my hands together behind my back and tied to my feet. I was in a closet." She had been stripped naked and hog-tied before being locked in the closet, she said.

Continuing her account, Darlene told how she was sexually assaulted several times and sodomized. She remembered being struck repeatedly on her face, upper body, and her back. The rapes and beat-ings lasted for three days while she was held captive in the house. Marlow would disappear, return, rape her again, and disappear once more.

Darlene described what happened between at-tacks: "He'd be very apologetic, tell me that he was going to let me go. But then he would turn and just be mean all over again." At last, Marlow untied her and told her to get cleaned up because he was going to take her home. "I didn't think he was going to take me home, so I kicked him in the groin and I ran to my friend's house."

The sanctuary Darlene sought was the same house Greg Marlow had burglarized a few days earlier on April 1. Darlene had been a childhood friend of the resident, and had lived in her home at various times, including the previous few weeks.

When interviewed, the resident reported, "(Darlene) came to my door . . . she was very beat up. She had bruises on her arms and her face and her back, on her chest, and she was very upset. She had a black eye and a swollen lip, and one side of her face was swollen."

Asked how she knew about the bruises on Darlene's body, the resident replied, "When she showed up at my door, I took her into the bedroom. She undressed and showed me her body."

Greg Marlow was no stranger to the burglary victim. She and her husband had met him on previous occasions through Darlene, and had accused him of being the burglar. Darlene was too embarrassed to report the rape, but her brutal treatment galvanized her friends into action. The woman telephoned the police to complain that Greg Marlow had burglarized her home and threatened her husband with a gun to demand that he not press charges.

That night, Fontana police officers found Greg Marlow at the home of Richard Drinkhouse. Following the arrest, the probation officer who had once recommended leniency, Robert Jetsen, prepared a new report. He noted that Marlow blamed his criminal conduct on the death of his mother. "Everything went wrong," Marlow told Jetsen. This time, he recommended that Marlow be remanded to the custody of the California Youth Authority.

In CYA custody, Greg Marlow was examined by a psychiatrist. In between outbursts of crying, he told the psychiatrist how his mother had turned him on to dope and was promiscuous. He seemed to be blaming his mother for his problems, but ambiguously expressed his love for her. Greg claimed that he had borrowed sixteen hundred dollars to fly Doris's body back to California from Ohio for burial. (Granny Lena Walls had actually borne that expense.) Regarding his drug addiction, Marlow expressed remorse and a desire to "break away" from the world of dope. "I believe him," the examiner wrote.

As a result, authorities placed Marlow in a drug rehab program, in a halfway house not far from the scene of his crimes. Seven months later, they released him. In 1976, Marlow was arrested again. He served ninety days in jail for being under the influence of drugs. Not long afterward, he walked away again, released on bail after being charged with carrying a concealed weapon. Afraid that the latest rap would result in some serious jail time, he fled to Kentucky in May 1977. That same month, his wife, Connie, filed for divorce.

* * *

McCreary County, Kentucky, seemed more homelike to Greg than the pandemonium of Southern California. He stayed with relatives and began circulating with people on the outer fringes of the law like Lardo, Automatic, and Duce.

Hanging out at one of the men's apartments was a favorite pastime of several young women. One evening, among them, was nineteen-year-old Jennifer Williams, pretty, tall, blonde, blue-eyed, and buxom. Jenni was impressed when the stranger from Los Angeles named Greg entered the room. She thought he was very attractive and sexy with his "pumped" physique. Marlow knew that she was interested, so he took off his shirt to give the circle of girls the full impact of his pecs and dorsals. Jenni and her girlfriends began giggling and nudging each other.

Even though she didn't see Marlow for nearly two weeks, the arousal he stirred in her lingered. She and two other young women were joyriding late one evening when they spotted Marlow walking. They offered him a ride. She later succinctly summarized the night: "We partied, and Greg and I went to bed together." He was a "very good lovemaker and it blew my mind away." She added that he could "go for hours" and that when the lovemaking was over, he whispered to her, "Now you are pregnant."

Marlow came close to destroying the budding relationship a few days later at a gathering of teenagers. While he and Jenni were talking within earshot of the others, Greg made a crude reference to performing oral sex on her. She was furious, and thought she would never speak to him again.

Two months passed before Jenni saw the muscular Mr. Marlow in the mobile home of Duce and his girlfriend, where a dozen people had assembled to share speed and pot. Greg's rude transgression had eased in her mind, and the electric attraction was just as strong. Jenni found Greg "very gallant, a Prince Charming." She agreed to go to a party with him.

The unlikely venue for the party was a graveyard where music and reveling lasted into the wee hours. As Jenni drove Greg away from the gathering, another motorist, whom Jenni recognized as an acquaintance named Jeff, flagged them down to ask for drugs. Marlow undiplomatically told Jeff they didn't have any drugs, and insulting words were exchanged. Greg covertly withdrew his pistol from its hiding place in Jenni's purse. When the interloper assaulted Jenni's windshield with a bumper jack, sending glass splinters into her face, Greg leaped from the passenger's seat, vaulted over the car, and ripped the jack from the stunned man's grip. No shooting was necessary because Jeff capitulated after Greg "slapped him around a couple of times."

Laughing about it an hour later, and snuggling alone on the couch in Duce's trailer, Jenni and Greg were interrupted again. The trailer door eased open and the barrel of a shotgun poked quietly in, leveled directly at Greg's head. Jeff stepped in behind the gun. Jenni screamed, "If you kill him you are going to have to kill me." Marlow charged from his seat, lunged forward to grab the shotgun barrel, and wrenched it from Jeff's hands. The assailant tumbled out the door and sprinted away into the darkness, while Greg fired a shot into the air to punctuate his dominance.

Jenni's bold knight had saved her twice. They made love several times that night. Nothing could separate them now.

The following afternoon, Marlow was arrested on theft charges by Tennessee authorities. Jenni wasn't going to let that interfere with the new romance, though. She visited Greg in jail, brought him money, cigarettes, and other small gifts, and volunteered to do his laundry. Greg seized the opportunity to cement their relationship by confiding his past hardships to her, gambling that her sympathy would turn to love.

"He told me," Jenni remembered, "that both of his parents were dead, that his mother had died in a fire, that he was raised in California, that his mother had affiliations with the Hell's Angels, and that when he was a small child, there (were) bowls of pills around the house."

Intimate secrets Greg shared with Jenni enchanted her. This brawny, powerful man had an appealing vulnerability, she thought. It was a potent combination that melted away any resistance to falling in love. Jenni's parents, responsible middle-class folks, were troubled by the romance, but would do anything for their daughter. Against his better instincts, her father gave in to Jenni's plea to bail Marlow out of jail.

Jenni became the second Mrs. Marlow on the following day, December 14, 1977, in Huntsville, Tennessee.

In order to make a fresh start, away from the impoverished McCreary County, Jenni arranged for friends to drive to Indianapolis with her and her new husband, where she knew of a job opportunity for Greg. In early January, Greg finally went to work, installing dry walls in new buildings.

Maybe it was employment that made him irritable or maybe something else. "Greg started being mean to me," Jenni later lamented. "He would accuse me of things like going out on him or flirting with other people. He would question me about my friends, if I'd ever had sex with them. Just continually tormenting kind of stuff." Greg began to physically abuse her. "At times, for nothing at all, no concrete reason, he would get real angry and slap me or hit me with his fist."

She described how Marlow developed an unreasonable jealousy over a man named Glen who was living with them, and was pestering her about it one night. "He was accusing me of wanting to be with Glen instead of him. I was fully clothed and I was sitting on the commode. Greg was real angry and he hit me a few times. And he had his pocketknife open. He would always threaten to cut me and he just slashed . . . me. I held my arm up to protect myself, and he cut my arm, too."

Doctors worked four hours in the emergency hospital to repair and suture the gaping wounds in Jenni's arm and shoulder. Their heroic efforts saved her from being permanently crippled.

Marlow, in the typical pattern of abusers, was remorseful. Jenni could stay in bed and he would cook breakfast for her and pet her like a child or worship her like a queen. He would tenderly wash her in the shower as a prelude to having sex.

When her injuries were healing, and Greg had lost his job after only six weeks in Indianapolis, the couple returned to Kentucky. In the Cumberland region, her grandparents offered a bedroom because Jenni was pregnant.

Attempts at employment by Greg, pumping gas, collecting coal samples to be analyzed at a mine, were short-lived. He argued violently with Jenni, smashed a TV, pitched a clock through a window, and choked her with a telephone cord until she passed out. Pinning her on the bed one night, he hissed, "I am the Devil and I own you. I can look into your eyes and read your mind." Resistance to his battering, he told her, "would only make it worse." He was always apologetic afterwards, offering to leave because she "deserved better than that." Sex often followed the apologies. Greg seemed to particularly enjoy making love in the shower.

Abuse and torment can have a cumulative effect, working on the mind's stability. "I was kind of a docile little puppy," Jenni said. "I wasn't a person anymore, didn't have any spirit. I couldn't talk to other people, or make eye contact with them. It was a real small town and I was always afraid that someone I knew in school would speak to me and get me in trouble." She lost over fifty pounds.

Pine Knot and Stearns were more appealing to Marlow than the Cumberland area, but Jenni opposed his campaign to move back there. She realized that he wanted to be among the drug-using bikers again.

Behind closed doors of the bathroom in her parents' home, Greg was needling Jenni, wanting her to agree to move, threatening to make her go. In desperation, she groaned, "You're not going to make me do anything because whatever you can do to me, I can do to myself." To prove it, she plunged a pair of scissors into her thigh nearly two-inches deep. Greg departed immediately. When Jenni limped out of the bathroom, bleeding profusely, her father exploded. A huge man, six-four and nearly three-hundred pounds, he grabbed a pistol from the top of the refrigerator and lumbered out the door.

No one witnessed it, but Greg Marlow suffered a gunshot wound that day. It wasn't a life-threatening injury, so he survived. But when he tried to approach Jenni a few days later, at her parents' home, her father menacingly filled the doorway. Marlow retreated, by himself, on April Fools' day, 1978, all the way to his old stomping grounds, McCreary County. The following December, Jenni gave birth to Greg Marlow's fourth child. Greg was in McCreary County jail at the time.

Soon after leaving Jenni, Marlow embarked on a series of crimes including drug possession, car theft, and forgery. He even tried working sporadically, once as a carpet-mill machine operator in Dalton, Georgia. But that just didn't suit him. He was arrested on April 22 in McCreary County for possessing drugs. Released after simply paying a fine, he forged several checks in the name of Jenni's father. In July, police snapped cuffs on him again, this time for receiving stolen property, a car that had disappeared from Dalton, Georgia. While being held in custody in the courthouse, he simply walked out. He was picked up again, two days later, and was subsequently indicted for forgery, receiving stolen property, and escape.

While waiting for the sentence hearing, Marlow applied for admission to a St. Louis drug rehabilitation program. The McCreary County judge, believing a probation report that cited Marlow's problems as "drugs and association with certain peers," was convinced to hand down four concurrent five-year sentences, all to be probated on the condition Marlow would enter, and successfully complete, the drug program. Greg gleefully agreed to enter a Methodist Seminary halfway house in Wilmore, Kentucky.

A minister telephoned Jenni in the spring of 1979 to ask her if she would come to visit Greg and allow him to see the baby. Jenni's father reluctantly drove her and the baby to Wilmore. Marlow,

at first, seemed fascinated by the infant. He told
Jenni that his previous behavior had been the
Devil's doing and begged for a reconciliation, all
the while quoting Bible verses. She was swayed
enough to have sex with him that night. The visit
extended for a full week, during which Marlow
seemed to grow increasingly calloused. Jenni
thought his concern for the baby's welfare was also
shallow.

After Jenni returned home, Marlow contacted
her, insisting that she visit him again, alone. His
strategy backfired. She was finally convinced that
they had no future together. There would be no
more visits and no reconciliation.

Bored with drug rehabilitation, Greg Marlow decided that the halfway house was not his choice of
fun. Not long after Jenni's visit, he slipped away
and headed for California. By December, 1979,
they were divorced.

Sixteen

Cynthia Lynn Anderson was still crying thirty minutes after she had hightailed it out of her parents' home on a chilly November night in 1979. When she found her boyfriend, Ron Coffman, she wailed that her parents had kicked her out, and she really didn't have any place to go. They both knew what she really meant—she and Ron could now be together.

Ron took her home with him and informed his parents of her plight.

Coffman's father, a retired police officer, offered his recollection of the event: "Cyndi and my son came to me and she told me that her mother had kicked her out of the house. . . . She was crying at the time and my son asked me if it would be possible for her to stay at our house for a while until they could get the matter straightened out. I agreed. I don't like to see anyone out in the cold."

Mrs. Coffman recalled, "We didn't want to let her, but we felt sorry for her because she was crying."

The "overnight" stay stretched out to three months.

Still attending school sporadically, Cyndi also worked at Walgreen's and at Things Remembered, the gift store. Evenings and nights, she and Ron Coffman took full advantage of her freedom from parental control, indulging in drugs, sex, and fun. There were no restrictions.

There was time for her to pay attention to herself, without interference from annoying siblings or a mother who didn't understand. Cyndi could spend hours, if she wished, manicuring her long red fingernails or pampering her luxuriant hair.

In spite of all the freedom, life was far from perfect. She and Ron bickered, and she missed some of the comforts she had taken for granted at her parents' home. In January, Cyndi asked Carl and Sally if she could move back in and go to school full-time. They welcomed her back.

When Cyndi discovered that she was pregnant, she first admitted it to her stepfather, Carl, blurting it out as he drove her home from school. He later described his reaction: "It was something I didn't like, but I couldn't change it. So, basically, after we talked for a while, I felt the best thing for her to do would be give the baby up for adoption . . . she was young. She had a life ahead of her. She wasn't married. You know, it's a difficult thing to do, but I felt that was the way to go."

Cyndi's mother heard the news that evening. A bitter instant replay ran through her mind: From the time Cyndi was ten years old, she had insisted, "Mom, I'm not going to be like you. I'm going to wait until I'm twenty-five to have my babies. I'm going to see the world. I'm going to have fun. I'm going to enjoy life. Then, I'm going to get married and have a baby." Now, Cyndi celebrated her eighteenth birthday with a child growing inside her.

Mother and daughter both agreed there would be no abortion. They had been raised under the doctrines of the Catholic Church which precluded such action. Anyway, Cyndi wanted the baby. They also decided that the first order of business, during the pregnancy, would be for Cyndi to complete high school. (She managed to do it, earning a 1.977 grade point average.)

During the ensuing summer, Cyndi and Ron wrangled about the possibility of getting married for the baby's sake, but he procrastinated, waffled, and delayed. He finally agreed to marry her, and her family arranged for a wedding shower in July. Ron backed out on the day before the shower.

At Sally's urging, Cyndi entered a Catholic home for unwed mothers and agreed to consider putting the child up for adoption. But when her little boy was born on August 31, all thoughts of giving him away quickly faded.

Perhaps because of the baby, and heavy pressure from two sets of grandparents, Ron Coffman and Cynthia Anderson were married on October 18, 1980. They moved initially into an apartment known as "the Whitehouse," a favorite residence and hangout for drug users. Cyndi and Ron happily joined in the illicit activity, but couldn't afford

Don Lasseter

both drugs and rent. Within a short time, they moved to a small bungalow behind the Coffmans' home, virtually rent free. Even at that, it wasn't a great bargain, with no indoor bathrooms.

Cyndi confided to her mother that things weren't going very well. Sally later related what she'd heard: "He (Ron) beat her and they argued a lot. And I held my tongue. I didn't say 'I told you so.' It's . . . it's like you see two fires and eventually they are going to join and just explode."

Ron Coffman worked part-time as a cook, and Cyndi resumed her old position at Things Remembered, until March 1981 when she took a better paying job as a cocktail waitress. When the bar closed in mid-summer, Cyndi found work as a housekeeper in a retirement home, but the constant illness and smell of death sickened her. She resigned when a resident whom she particularly liked suddenly died.

The baby was often left with Ron's parents while Cyndi and Ron were working, or arguing, or partying. The paternal grandmother would later remember that the infant was usually "soiled" when Cyndi was around. "He was never clean and cared for," she grumbled. But she did acknowledge that, "(Cynthia) played with him, and read a lot of books to him. They had a lot of fun together like kids would."

Dissension between Cyndi and Ron erupted into a physical fight in January 1982, near her twentieth birthday, resulting in the end of their sex life together. Ron struck Cyndi, she said, and consequently she had to lie on the couch three full days to recuperate.

By March, their marriage in serious trouble, Cyndi walked out with the baby in her arms. She rented an apartment, and found a job on an assembly line making kits for carburetors at the Ballwin-Washington company. Later, she would be assigned to the shipping-receiving department, interrupted temporarily by a futile attempt to be a machinist. "I hated that," she would complain. "It was a very noisy, dirty job." She was relieved to return to the cleaner, quieter environment of shipping-receiving.

Cyndi's work schedule and social activities forced a need for a baby-sitter, and no one was more reliable than Ron's parents. The infant once again spent a great deal of time with his paternal grandparents.

Shortly after Cyndi left Ron Coffman, she met and fell immediately in love with a fireman, John Lorentz, twenty-six, who remembered:

"I was visiting my cousin in the (Whitehouse apartment) building where Cyndi lived. She was either leaving or coming in when I met her." He took her for a ride, then to a bar where he asked her out the following night. Cyndi was infatuated with him, and on their second date, she went to bed with him. On the third date, Cyndi told John that she loved him. John was considerably more reserved; he had a live-in girlfriend at the time.

Later, John candidly admitted that his primary relationship with Cyndi was for sex, adding that she never refused him sexually in any way. She would do anything he asked, in bed or out.

"For instance," he said, "if I would be at work, the guys and I would want to pitch in and buy a pizza or something . . . it wouldn't make any difference what time of the day or night it was, I could call Cyndi and she would go pick it up, tacos or pizza, whatever." The guys in the station house were "impressed" with her.

The relationship lasted six months, with Cyndi repeatedly telephoning him to ask when they could be together. "Can I see you tomorrow? No? How about the next day? Please?" Gradually, John found more reasons to avoid her, telling her to wait for his calls. Cyndi knew of the other girl, and showed up at John's home once when his housemate wasn't there. The frustrated fireman tried to shoo her away, but Cyndi insisted on waiting until the other woman returned. When she did, Cyndi created no scene, and pretended to be visiting on a work-related matter. Her behavior did nothing to endear Cyndi to John.

Announcing that he wanted to break up, John rationalized that he was upset with Cyndi because she would go out drinking with her girlfriends at midnight, at the end of her work shift, and he would wonder where she was.

Cyndi pleaded with him to reconsider and promised that she would do whatever he asked. If he wanted her to quit drinking or stop going to bars, she would. Through a flood of tears, she said that she would do anything to avoid ending the relationship. John felt compassion for her: "She was pathetic. I would put it that way . . . like if you'd beat a dog, (it would) just kind of whimper and whine, and still want you to pet it."

What John didn't tell Cyndi was that her child was a large factor in his decision. He wasn't interested in being a father figure. He didn't want to see Cyndi any more.

Struggling through the heartbreak of rejection by the man she thought she loved, Cyndi endured an emotional low for months, into the beginning of 1983. The major stability in her life was her job at Ballwin-Washington, which provided a regular income that finally allowed her to splurge on a decent car. With the help of her parents' cosigning, Cyndi bought a sleek, silver 1977 Pontiac Trans-Am. Zipping around her usual haunts in the sporty car lifted her spirits. Also, an old girlfriend reappeared in her life.

Kelly had been one of Cyndi's female pals in high school, but had vanished after graduation. Soon after Cyndi bought the Trans-Am, she was having an after-work drink in her favorite bar, when she spotted Kelly. They hugged, laughed, reminisced, and filled each other in on their current lives. Kelly had spent some time in Page, Arizona, on Lake Powell, she said, and enthusiastically praised the area and her experiences there. She thought she might return soon.

The reunion temporarily cheered Cyndi, but it wasn't long before the doldrums took hold again. "It was really a hard time for me. I felt very unwanted, and wanted to start over . . . a new life in a new place."

Spring brought the buds out on trees and sprouts of fresh green grass all around St. Louis. But to Cyndi, life was still as gray as winter. In April, Kelly suggested they pack their clothes, load the Trans-Am, and take off for Arizona.

"She just hit me at the right time. She knew this place where I could get a good job and it was nice. So I left the baby with the Coffmans and asked them to please keep him and I'd be back before his birthday (August 31) to pick him up, and they told me okay. And then I left."

Seventeen

Everyone at the party was drunk, loaded, when James Gregory Marlow walked in, accompanied by Coral. The whispered word, on the street in Montclair, California, had been that there would be an ample supply of speed and coke. Bearded men with red bandannas, denim jackets, and bleached, tattooed blondes straddling behind them on roaring motorcycles, rode east from Los Angeles and west from San Bernardino, to party and ingest or inject whatever was available.

George Tinnly, a thirty-five-year-old ex-con and heroin addict, noticed Marlow and his sister. He had recently been dating Coral. Tinnly eased away from a noisy group of carousing bikers, and welcomed the couple. Over the din, they somehow managed a conversation.

Tinnly learned that Marlow, too, was hooked on heroin, to the tune of about three hundred dollars each day, and chuckled. His own habit took nearly five hundred bucks, every day, to support. Neither man had a legitimate source of income.

As the evening progressed, Marlow and Tinnly

found themselves isolated, discussing the possibility of stealing some drugs.

"I was talking to somebody about it a little earlier," the older addict confided to Marlow. "He told me that there was maybe a half a pound of coke at a certain location."

Marlow was interested. He severely dreaded the inevitable bone-racking pain and sickness that would infiltrate his body when the drug-induced high melted away. George Tinnly had his undivided attention.

"I heard that the guy who has the stuff is a police snitch," Tinnly continued. "Don't know the dude's name, but he's a construction worker and lives in an upstairs apartment over in Upland. He's supposed to have about ten grand of coke money, too." The convincing addict told Marlow that he wanted to pay a visit to the apartment, but he didn't have anyone to back him up. Marlow enthusiastically agreed to help out his new buddy.

A loud knock at the door startled Jodie Kilson. He glanced out his bedroom window and squinted at the bright Southern California sunrise, then had trouble focusing on his watch. It was 6:45 A.M., much too early for strangers to visit, and Jodie was certainly not expecting any friends at that hour. Opening the upstairs apartment door a crack, he peeked out, saw two crusty strangers standing on the landing of the stairwell.

George Tinnly, skinny, slightly shorter than six feet, dressed in a sleeveless denim jacket, jeans, and boots, was closest to the door. Expressionless blue eyes stared from his thin pockmarked face, and his long, greasy brown hair was pulled back into a ponytail.

The second man crowded close to his partner. James Marlow, at twenty-three, matched Tinnly's height, but was more muscular. His high, wide forehead was creased with a half-dozen horizontal lines, and his long hair was beginning to recede on either side of the prominent widow's peak. A full mustache drooped over the corners of his mouth, exaggerating his grim countenance.

The expressions on both men scared the hell out of Jodie, who thought that they resembled outlaw bikers.

"Are you a construction worker?" Tinnly demanded of Kilson. Nervous and frightened, the young man told them that he was, convincing the intruders that they had found their target. Before Jodie could even attempt to block them, they pushed forward into the apartment and kicked the door shut. Without warning, the skinny man slammed his fist into Jodie Kilson's face, stunning him with pain and sending him crashing awkwardly to the floor.

"Okay, where are the drugs?" Tinnly snarled at Jodie. Shocked and disoriented, Jodie struggled to his hands and knees. Then, as he later recalled, the second man struck him with a drive chain from a motorcycle. The stinging blows on his back and head drove him flat against the floor again. His nose started to bleed.

While Tinnly hovered over the injured man, who choked out denials of any drugs being there, Marlow started ransacking the apartment. He found a sword that Jodie had used to decorate a wall, and gave it to Tinnly, who waved it around threateningly before snatching a butcher knife from the kitchen. With the menacing blade in his face, Jodie felt like he was going into shock. Marlow, who had wrapped the chain around his waist like a belt, continued to trash the apartment while searching for drugs. "Where the hell is the cocaine?" both men continued to question Jodie Kilson, who repeated his denials of any drug possession.

"Jeez . . . damn," Tinnly muttered. "Maybe it's in the apartment downstairs." He barked at Jodie, "Put some shoes on, we're going downstairs." With Tinnly pressing the knife into Jodie's back, and Marlow following close behind, the three men descended the stairwell, stepped outside, and crowded around the door of Apartment B. Tinnly twisted the knob and pushed. It was not locked.

Ann Moon had heard the alarm clock, but was still half asleep. She didn't know whether her sister, Pat, who occupied the other bedroom, was awake yet or not. It would be considerate, Ann thought, to wake her sister who planned to give her boyfriend a ride to work. Ann hadn't yet made up her groggy mind when she heard the front door squeak open.

She couldn't believe it when her upstairs neighbor marched right into her bedroom. "What are you doing here?" she yelled. Then, fear flooded her when she saw two men following Jodie, whose nose was dripping blood. Ann grabbed at her bedcovers and tugged them up around her neck. She was suddenly very sorry that she slept nude.

The skinny man, Tinnly, ordered Ann to get out of the bed. "I can't, I don't have any clothes on," she begged.

Ann's heart somersaulted into her throat when the muscular man, with "long, wild, curly-looking hair" lunged toward the bed and grabbed at the sheet she was clutching under her chin. Tears welled in her eyes as she screamed. She felt a rush of gratitude partially replace the fear when the thin man told her attacker to stop. Marlow obeyed.

Tinnly seemed to be in command. He told his captive, Jodie Kilson, to get on the queen-size bed with Ann and lie facedown. "You, too," he barked at the trembling girl. "Turn over and lay facedown."

"Can I please stay under the covers?" she requested, her voice breaking. Tinnly allowed her to remain on her back, with the covers tightly pulled up, but ordered her to keep her arms out next to her body so he could see her hands. Jodie complied with Tinnly's order, and lay prostrate atop the covers to the left of Ann Moon.

"Okay, where the hell are you hiding the drugs?" Tinnly now demanded of Ann. Between sobs, she managed to tell him that she didn't have any drugs. "Check the other rooms," he directed Marlow, who launched into a repeat of the rampaging search he had conducted upstairs. Ann noticed that he was carrying a thick "biker chain" in his hands. He was also wearing a gold nugget earring. Tinnly, she could see, was armed with a knife, which he held while he ransacked the drawers in Ann's room.

For the first time since the trio had entered the apartment, Ann's terror shifted from herself to thoughts of safety for her sister in the other bedroom. She didn't know that Pat Moon had, indeed, left earlier. Her sister's good fortune, however, was short-lived.

As the two men searched, their heads suddenly jerked toward the apartment entrance where they heard the door being opened. Tinnly yelled at Marlow to see who it was. By the time Pat Moon heard him, she was too far inside the room to escape. She saw a "biker-type," who was carrying a chain, step toward her. "Get into the bedroom," Marlow demanded, as he grabbed her arm, and led the astonished young woman into Ann's room. Pat Moon, too, was ordered to lie facedown on the bed next to Jodie.

Tinnly was trying to ask the girls where the cocaine was, but they were crying and noisily trying to comfort each other. "Shut up," the frustrated intruder shouted.

Marlow took two steps toward the bed with his hand cupping his crotch, and growled, "I've got something to shut her up with." Pat appealed to her hysterical sister to be quiet, and Marlow backed away.

Once more, but this time halfheartedly, Tinnly demanded to know where the drugs were. When Pat protested that there were no drugs, confirming the stories told by Ann and Jodie, the intruders wilted.

"Damn, we must have the wrong place," Tinnly spit through clenched teeth.

Marlow nodded. "Let's get the hell out of here."

The two men stepped toward the living room, but Marlow hesitated, then retreated toward the bed. Ann could see that he had her driver's license and credit card in his hand.

"Please don't take my credit card," she pleaded. "Take whatever else you want, but don't take the card."

Marlow smirked, rejecting her appeal. He would keep the card and the license, he warned, just in case he needed to find her and the other two frightened victims. They understood his implied threat that they had better not call the police or try to identify him or his partner.

"We'd better go out the back door so nobody will see us," Tinnly told Marlow. "And we'd better tie them up." He grabbed the cord of Ann's electric blanket, jerked it loose, and told the trio to lie facedown on the bed with their hands behind their backs. When they complied, the two men used the electric wire and a long telephone cord to wrap tight loops around the wrists of the two girls and Jodie Kilson.

"Don't move," Tinnly warned. "Don't call the police or we'll be back. We've got your address and your cards."

The two men fled the bedroom through the sliding door, vaulted over the fence of a small patio area, and disappeared into the bright Southern California morning.

Easily managing to free themselves, the Moon sisters and Jodie Kilson called the police, and reported their terrifying experiences. Officer Daniel Milakovich, Upland Police Department, arrived at the scene and listed the net haul the two thieves had taken. In addition to the credit card, driver's license, and some keys, they had taken less than thirty-five dollars from the girls. Jodie Kilson reported that he had lost one hundred and eighty-five dollars in cash and a kitchen knife. No drugs, they said, had been found or stolen. Officer Milakovich filled out his police report, signed it, and dated it. It was November 5, 1979.

On the day following the robbery, Greg Marlow still felt an unsatisfied urge.

There is a small shopping center, or strip mall, in Upland just two miles east of the apartment where Kilson and the Moon girls lived. The mall is on Foothill Boulevard, old Route 66, one-quarter mile west of the major north-south thorough-fare, Euclid Avenue.

In mid-afternoon, Marlow glanced up and down the row of a dozen stores in the outdoor mall. He stood next to a brick pillar with his back toward a walkway that led to a rear parking area. To his left was a yogurt cafe where three women were enjoying their favorite dietary dessert. To his right was the entrance to the Leathermart, a store that offered various coats, jackets, shoes, and other products made from animal skins. At 3:30 P.M., Marlow entered the Leathermart.

The store owner, Lynn Black, was attending to a customer, Vickie Ibison, who was sitting down, trying on shoes. Mrs. Ibison glanced up and noticed the young man, whom she later described as about five-ten, thin, with brown shaggy hair, wearing a blue sweatshirt with side-slash pockets, and an earring in his left ear. Lynn Black observed that the sweatshirt was a zipper-type worn over a white T-shirt, and that the man wore jeans and a red bandanna wrapped tightly around his head.

"Yes, may I help you?" Black courteously asked the potential new customer. Ibison rose from her chair.

"Yeah, you can both get down on the floor," Marlow barked at the two women. "I've got a gun." Both of his hands were stuffed into the sweatshirt pockets, and something, perhaps a gun, was causing the cloth to protrude from the right pocket. The women froze and just stared at the man. Black weakly asked, "What was that? I didn't hear you."

Marlow repeated his order for them to get down
on the floor. In a menacing voice, he warned, "I'm
serious."

The shop owner leaned over to her customer
and softly advised her, "You'd better do what he
says." While Lynn Black lowered herself to a fully
reclined position, facedown, Vickie Ibison just sank
to her knees and crouched as low as she could.

Marlow quickly attacked the cash register and
stuffed about seventy-five dollars into his pockets.
Whirling around, he reached for a wall display
and removed a rabbit-fur coat. Glancing quickly
at the motionless women, he strode deliberately
toward the front entrance, paused to grab a
leather coat, then stepped outside. The frightened women remained still for a few moments,
afraid that he might return but grateful that he
hadn't harmed them. They didn't know how
lucky they were.

In the yogurt shop, across the walkway from the
Leathermart, three women were sitting at a small
table, chatting and finishing their desserts. Glancing out the large windows toward the walkway, they
saw a man leave the front entrance of the Leathermart. He was carrying a leather coat and another
garment on "several hangers." The witnesses
thought it was peculiar that the merchandise items
he was carrying still bore tags, as if they had just
been taken off the rack.

One of the women later told the police, "He was
acting very nervous, pacing back and forth and
kind of looking back in the window . . . the idea

he gave me was that he was looking for somebody to come get him." She watched as he walked rapidly through the walkway between the buildings and disappeared toward the rear parking lot.

Lynn Black and Vickie Ibison, inside the Leathermart, nervously rose high enough to peek through the side window and see Marlow hurry through the passageway. Black told Ibison to run to the back of the store and try to see where the thief went, while she called the police. Ibison complied, and saw Marlow get into the passenger's side of a "silver-looking small car." The driver was a male "with dark brown hair." It all happened too fast for her to remember any other details about the second man.

When the Upland police arrived, five women excitedly described the robbery and the flight of Marlow. The descriptions of him given by the three yogurt patrons exactly matched those given by the two women in the Leathermart store.

Greg Marlow had escaped after committing robberies on two consecutive days. But he had left vivid memories etched into the minds of several victims and witnesses who provided law enforcement officials with detailed accounts of his crimes along with accurate verbal portraits of him.

Two weeks after Marlow and Tinnly had robbed Jodie Kilson and the Moon sisters at their apartments, and Marlow had robbed the Leathermart with an unknown accomplice, the two thieves were suffering. The drug-withdrawal symptoms that Marlow had dreaded were ripping holes in them. Both men were staggering through hot and cold sweats, back pain, joint pain, teeth pain, pain all over. Their noses were running and their eyes were watering. Their nauseous stomachs threatened violent upheavals. They desperately needed to feed the demons that occupied their bodies.

Another inspiration came to George Tinnly, and it was immediately very appealing to Marlow. There was a methadone clinic in Ontario, south of Upland, where the chemical was administered to addicts as a substitute for heroin, to help them through the horrors of withdrawal. "It's right over there by the big Sunkist plant, next to the railroad tracks," Tinnly said. "I took a buddy over there the other day. I found out when the truck delivers the methadone. We could rob the truck when the driver makes the delivery." Once again, Marlow was ready to try anything to alleviate the sickness.

Hurrying across town, the two men drove past the sprawling Sunkist plant, where the tangy citric aroma of crushed oranges and lemons teases the nostrils of passing motorists. As they approached the tracks and turned toward the yellow one-story clinic, which looked like an ordinary house, they were disappointed.

"Damn," muttered Marlow, as they watched the delivery truck pull away from the building. "Well, it's too late. They're leavin'. I guess we might as well call it off."

"Naw, man," said Tinnly. "They just delivered some. We don't have to take it off the truck. I know they have it inside. We can just go in and take it."

The senior drug counselor, Wilson Lee, Jr., was standing next to the coffeepot inside the methadone clinic, at about 10:30 A.M., November 20, 1979. He had stopped in the receptionist area, to get a cup of coffee, and was in the process of pouring it when he saw two men walk through the entrance door. Instead of pausing in the waiting room, the men barged through the Dutch door leading to the clinic, turned sharply, and entered the receptionist's office where Lee stood. That's when Lee saw that they were both carrying guns.

At first, Lee wasn't frightened. "I thought they were police officers coming to arrest a client for some reason or another." Lee realized his error when Tinnly poked the barrel of a handgun into his ribs, while Marlow stood guard in the hallway with a sawed-off shotgun.

"We want the methadone," Tinnly demanded. He then motioned for Lee to move toward the dispensary and ordered him to get the methadone.

"It's locked in the vault," explained the counselor. "The dosing hour is over." Tinnly didn't believe him, and prodded the man to the cabinet where the chemical was ordinarily kept during dosing hours. The cabinet was empty.

Tinnly, his face reddening in anger, forced Lee to lead the way to the vault and ordered him to open it. Lee said, "I don't have the combination."

"Who has it?"

"The nurse," said Lee, trying not to volunteer too much, and faintly hoping that the men would get discouraged and leave. But it was a futile attempt. Tinnly, by threatening to shoot him in the legs, convinced Lee to summon the nurse. She nervously opened the safe and withdrew a bottle of liquid, approximately the size of a fifth of whiskey. Reluctantly, she handed it to the pistol-wielding man.

Holding the bottle up, Tinnly quickly examined it to assure himself that it contained the desired liquid. He recognized the label, which indicated ten thousand milligrams of methadone. The street value, the addict knew, was about the same figure in dollars.

Ordering Lee and the nurse to stay at the vault, Tinnly ran toward the Dutch door, joined Marlow, and the two men fled the way they had entered. As soon as they were gone, Lee punched a silent-alarm button, then telephoned the police.

Back in Tinnly's dingy apartment, he and Marlow couldn't wait to use the methadone. At first, to satisfy the demon, they drank it, in small quantities, straight. Then they would vary the ingestion, sometimes mixing it with water or orange juice, as it is done in clinics. Later, a small amount was put into a baby bottle, and drops from the rubber nipple would be applied to their tongues.

The methadone was half gone a few days before the two men were arrested. Local police were familiar with Marlow and Tinnly. The latter had a long record of felony convictions.

A few days after the arrests, the two suspects were easily identified in police lineups by the Moon sisters, Jodie Kilson, and Wilson Lee, Jr. Marlow was recognized by the women in the Leathermart store and the adjacent yogurt cafe.

To avoid a trial, George Tinnly entered into a plea bargain and was ordered to serve five years in Folsom, one of California's toughest prisons.

Following the lead of his crime partner, Greg Marlow also agreed to plead guilty to armed robbery. He had been in jail since the December arrest, and the legal process lasted until June 12, 1980, when he, too, was sentenced to serve five years. He was handcuffed and transported to Deuel Vocational Institute, near Tracy, California, fifty miles east of San Francisco Bay. Five years seemed like an eternity to the young man, who had just turned twenty-four the previous month.

Sweating it out in the San Bernardino County jail, while waiting to be processed into prison, Marlow met the woman who would become his third wife. Beverly Ryan was visiting another inmate when she met Greg Marlow. A tall, buxom, somewhat muscular native Californian, with long brown hair, big eyes, and ivory skin, and four years older than Marlow, Beverly was also in trouble. She faced felony charges for shooting another woman with a handgun.

Years later, she described how she met Marlow: "Well, it was like a game there (in the jail visiting area) to get as many prisoners out as you can and visit with them. You could fill out a paper and get anybody you want, so the friend I went there to see asked me to get Marlow out with some other guys."

Beverly began visiting the jail as often as possible to see Marlow. Greg told her the story of his childhood, and she felt sympathy. He told her how he had loved his mother, and that she had shot him up with heroin, and had brought men into the house and prostituted herself in his presence. Beverly's pity mixed with a growing sexual tension. Greg described how his mother had died, and Beverly cried for him. She would one day write that his strongest qualities were "honesty and the ability to stand up for what he believes in."

She fell in love with him.

On July 9, 1980, Beverly brought a man to the jail visiting room with her. The Reverend Payson Gregory, from the Grace Bible Church in San Bernardino, performed the ceremony, through a wire grille, that made Beverly the third Mrs. James G. Marlow.

The newlyweds were soon parted by the State of California. Greg Marlow was sent to the California Institution for Men at Chino for evaluation and processing, then to Deuel Vocational Institution (DVI), sixty miles east of San Francisco, to continue serving his sentence. Beverly served six months in San Bernardino County jail for assault with a deadly weapon, and was given three years of supervised probation following her release on March

17, 1981. She had been excitedly counting the days until she could have "contact" visits with her husband.

At DVI, a corrections officer conducting a routine search of the cell Marlow shared with another inmate reported finding "what appeared to be a prison-made marijuana/hashish pipe secreted in the top shelf of a locker." He confiscated the pipe and sent it to a laboratory for testing, where it was found to contain residue of marijuana. Marlow was charged with a violation of Section 115 of the California Department of Corrections Rules, being in possession of contraband. It was his second infraction of that rule. Shortly after his arrival at DVI, he had been charged with having stimulants/sedatives in his cell. He said that he thought it was "toothpowder."

Marlow had an excuse, too, for the pipe being in his cell. Someone left it there, he rationalized, so he could make one like it. No, he had never used it.

After a hearing, the punishment committee voted to restrict him to "booth" visits with no physical contact. He would have to wait until October to request a change of that ruling. Greg's cellmate tried to rescue Marlow by scribbling a note to the warden. "I and James Marlow got a 115 for having a crudely made hash pipe and Mr. Marlow did not know anything about it. It was mine. Therefore, I feel Mr. Marlow's 115 should be dropped."

Since his cellmate was willing to take the fall,

Marlow wrote a letter to rescind his original admission of knowing that the pipe was in the cell. He was trying desperately to preserve contact status for Beverly's pending visit. It didn't work. His appeal was denied in the warden's written decision: "Your hearing officer states that your cellmate agreed to responsibility for the item to preserve your pending family visit. Your cellmate did not accept responsibility at the time of the hearing. Your appeal is denied as you are both responsible for the items in your cell."

Furious at the "injustice," Beverly wrote to the Board of Prison Terms in the state capital, Sacramento, and to a congressman, protesting the decisions. By October, she filed a lawsuit, claiming cruel and unusual punishment. A San Joaquin County Superior Court judge read the charge, noted that it was Marlow's second offense, and found that the "disciplinary action taken appears to be reasonable and justified, and not cruel and unusual punishment."

Administrators at the prison must have had a change of heart. Marlow was allowed to have a contact visit with Beverly on November 7. On that same day, he was slammed with a new charge of possessing contraband. The documentation noted that, "while conducting an unclothed body search of inmate Marlow, after a contact visit with his wife, the officer found two five dollar bills in Marlow's socks." Institution policy prohibited inmates from accepting money from a visitor for any reason.

Marlow freely admitted that his wife gave him the money, but claimed that he "inadvertently" stuck it in his sock, and forgot about it. Since this was the first contact visit he had been allowed, he pleaded, his mind must have been "elsewhere." He was given another disciplinary period allowing booth-only visits.

In 1982, Marlow's prison problems became far more serious than lost visitation rights. He had several altercations with other inmates. He later commented:

"In prison, I was a victim, twice. I was a victim at Tracy (DVI). I got stabbed nine times. And 'cause I wouldn't testify on the guy, they took all my property, and sent me to Folsom." Wounds to his neck and stomach healed, and, indeed, he was transferred to one of California's toughest prisons.

Within his first few months at Folsom, Marlow accepted the de rigueur tattooing that seemed to be a requirement among hardened convicts everywhere. First came a flaming swastika inscribed on his chest, then dramatic drawings of vikings on both shoulders. Several more pictures decorated various parts of his body, including the name of Marlow's third wife needled in blue ink on the end of his penis. All counted, he wound up with fourteen tattoos. Marlow's crowning glory, though, was the artistic depiction of a snarling wolf tattooed on his left side. Admiring fellow inmates used that symbol to christen Greg with his prison nickname, Folsom Wolf.

Friendship with an inmate everyone called "Buzzard," and the swastika on Marlow's chest, gave the impression that he was associated with a white supremacy gang, the Aryan Brotherhood. Marlow neither confirmed nor denied the rumor, for years. Sometimes it worked to his advantage and, more often, to his disadvantage.

"I was sitting in the chow hall. I worked on kitchen row, and there was A.B.s (Aryan Brotherhood) over there, and black guys and Mexicans, and I had nothing to do with them. But you sell sandwiches to people, you have your little hustles, you inter-relate with people. I was in the chow hall, eating, when a black guy dropped his tray. WHAM! I don't know what he hit me with, but he hit me a good one. They all jumped up right by the table. The guard up there cracked that mini-14, he was ready. All I could do is grab this guy and pull him down on the floor. They took me up to the infirmary."

Ten days before his twenty-seventh birthday, on May 1, 1983, Marlow was released on parole. His wife Beverly was there to take him home to Barstow, where they would live with her mother. Beverly was happy:

"The first few months it was . . . everything was fine. He didn't do any drugs, he wanted a real chance at a real life, you know with a family and everything. He always had a job, he worked, no drugs, no alcohol. He spent a lot of his time lifting weights."

Within six months of freedom, the descent began again. Halloween was a major turning point. "We went trick-or-treating," Beverly said. They had purchased a double-handled broadsword at a flea market, and Marlow carried it as part of his costume. "Greg dressed up like Conan the Barbarian to show off all his muscles. I was a clown. I got mad because he was going to go out half naked, and I didn't like that, so I hit him. He hit me right back in the ribs, and knocked me to the floor. Had to go to the doctor the next day."

November was not a good month for Greg Marlow. November 1983 saw the beginning of the "death walks" with Beverly. She told of them:

"That was when he was lifting weights, and he would get mad all of a sudden for nothing. He would take my hand behind my back and he would wrap his arm around me as if walking down the street in a loving way. And he would walk me down my mom's street, take a left, and the desert's there. He was going to stab me and kill me and leave me in the desert. He always carried a knife hidden under an army jacket."

Beverly trembled nervously as she described her terror:

"He'd pull the knife out and put it to my kidneys, and put it in enough to go through my clothes but not break the skin. We went on those death walks fifteen or twenty times. He said I was a bitch and I deserved to die."

One night, Beverly said, Marlow tied her to her bed. "He was like . . . in the twilight zone again.

Real weird, mumbling and crazy. He slapped me a little bit in the bedroom, and I escaped, went into the living room, thinking with my mom there I would be safe. But he just picked me up and took me back in the bedroom and said he was going to kill me, because I was a bitch, I was a prude, I was Miss Goody Two-shoes, I was conceited."

Beverly recalled that she stalled by telling Marlow, "If I'm going to die, I want to take a bath first. Then, after I got in the tub, I went, God, how stupid, now I could get drowned, so I got out of the water and went back in the bedroom. He took his weight-lifting belt and tied my hands to my body real tight, so tight I thought I was going to faint. I couldn't move at all. Then he took the Conan sword and shoved it right next to my body where I could feel the steel. He said, 'This is how I'm going to kill you,' and he shoved it in and out between my legs. All over my whole body."

Choking back tears, Beverly continued the horrifying narrative. "He set the sword down and took a razor knife. We had a four-by-five oil painting on the wall, and he cut the entire oil painting up to show me what he was going to do to me. He was going to cut my face up to make me so ugly no one would ever want me. He drug (sic) the knife along my face, arm, and leg just enough to make the blood come out."

After what seemed like hours of torture to Beverly, Greg stopped, stared at her as if in a trance, and started crying. Untying her, he told her that she didn't deserve that, he was sorry, and that he should die. He pulled a gun from a drawer, loaded it, pointed it at his head, and told her to pull the trigger. When she refused, he handed the weapon to her, and ordered her to shoot him. "Kill me," he demanded. She couldn't do it.

The beatings and harassment lasted all through November and stretched periodically over the next thirty months. Beverly estimated that Greg battered her at least fifty times. Sometimes, she said, he would become "The Monster." This meant that his eyes would dilate, and he became deadly calm, mumbling, talking to himself. Beverly was terrified of The Monster and tired of the abuse. But she wasn't ready to end the marriage.

For part of the three years with Beverly in Barstow, Marlow was employed by a subcontractor who helped build microwave towers with Elmer Lutz, whom he would meet again in Utah and Atlanta in the near future. He also worked for a butcher, a freight company, and for Chuck's Rent-A-Throne.

Beverly was expecting Greg home one night after work in March 1986, but he was late. "He was supposed to be home at nine-thirty. About ten o'clock, I went to find him, because I'd had enough of the whole thing. I was tired of lies and being beat up."

She went to a Barstow bar where she knew Greg sometimes stopped. Seeing the orange Dodge pickup, Marlow's company truck, parked outside, she went in and found him there drinking with his boss.

"I turned him around and told him, 'You were supposed to be home by nine-thirty. What are you doing?' He tried to introduce his boss to me, and I told his boss, 'Fuck you, I don't want to meet you.' Greg got a little irritated because I wouldn't shake his boss's hand. I told him, 'I'm sick of this shit,' and I turned around and started walking out of the bar.

"I didn't know he was behind me. I opened the door to the back of the bar and he knocked me down the cement stairs. When I got to the bottom, he kicked me in the head, the ribs, and the kidneys with steel-toed boots. He dragged me, and threw me in my car, and he held my mouth. There were keys in his hand, and a key went up my nose and blood was pouring out. I tried to scream and he slugged me in the head." She managed to kick the door open, tumble out, and run away.

Beverly entered a battered women's shelter that night and stayed for two weeks. Working up her courage, she went home and started packing a rental van to move out of Barstow and away from her husband. As she pulled out of the driveway, she spotted Greg parked in the orange company pickup. Beverly accelerated the big van and raced away, with Marlow in hot, bumper-to-bumper pursuit. She had no choice but to return to her mother's house, where she sprinted inside and called the police.

Marlow slammed his fist against the locked front door repeatedly before climbing into the limo, starting it, and squealing out of the driveway. He

Corinna Novis.

Lynel Murray.

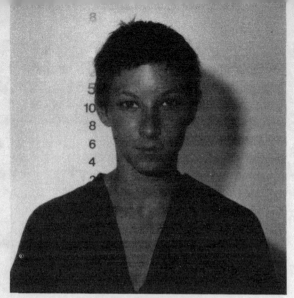

Cynthia Lynn Coffman
at the time of her 1986 arrest.

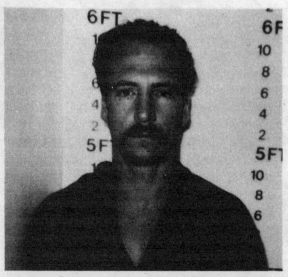

James Gregory Marlow a.k.a. "Folsom Wolf"
at the time of his 1986 arrest.

Marlow and Hoffman confessed to California authorities their role in the murder of their first victim, Greg Hill. *(Courtesy of the Hill Family)*

Old Main Street of Pine Knot, Kentucky, Marlow's hometown near the location of Hill murder.

The rocky cave near Big Bear Lake where Marlow and Coffman spent their last night of freedom.

Corinna Novis as found by police investigators buried in a shallow grave in a local vineyard.

Kentucky state trooper Detective Colan Harrell
(left) and Chief Deputy Sheriff Jim Brim.

Detective L. Scott "Scotty" Smith, head of the investigation into the murder of Corinna Novis.

Detective Richard "Hoop" Hooper, head of the investigation into the murder of Lynel Murray.

Corinna's Honda CRX as it was found near
Mountain Village.

Apartment where Corinna was taken and
sexually abused.

Marlow shortly after his arrest.
(© *San Bernardino Sun*)

Marlow in court surrounded by security officers.
(© *San Bernardino Sun*)

Marlow testifying.
(*Courtesy of
Redlands
Daily Facts*)

Cynthia Lynn
Coffman
testifying.
(*Courtesy of
Redlands
Daily Facts*)

Coffman and attorney Alan Spears as the verdict is
announced at first trial. (© *San Bernardino Sun*)

Orange County prosecutor Robert Gannon.

Coffman with paralegal Kristen Widmann and attorney Leonard Gumlia (back).

had conveniently taken the keys and the ownership certificate (still in Beverly's name) from her purse while she was in the battered women's shelter.

When the police arrived at 3:15 P.M., April 5, 1986, Beverly told them that her limo had been stolen by Marlow, and gave them a detailed report including the information that he was staying at the Stardust Inn Motel. As soon as they left, so did she. Beverly drove the rental van away from Barstow, leaving Greg Marlow and all of her troubles behind her as she headed to a new city and a new life.

One hour after taking the report, sheriff's deputies cruised through the Stardust Inn parking lot, and saw the orange pickup, but no limo. At 5:05 P.M., they received a report that Marlow was again banging on the door at the home of Beverly's mother. Within two minutes, the deputies arrived and saw Marlow leaning casually against a fence outside the house. He quietly complied with their request to extend his hands behind him. They snapped handcuffs on his wrists, and transported him to jail.

After being booked, fingerprinted, and photographed, James Gregory Marlow was led to a cell, and the hollow, metallic clang of barred doors slamming behind him echoed in his mind. He sat on the bunk, looked around, then started a conversation with his cellmate, Sam Keam. The conversation eventually got around to Keam's girlfriend, Cyndi "Cynful" Coffman, who had been arrested, along with Sam, just one hour before Marlow.

Eighteen

Warm April winds caressed Cyndi's body, tossed her long brown hair, and brought smiles to her lips when she stepped from the Trans-Am. She felt better than she had in months. Page, Arizona, she thought, certainly had the potential for starting a whole new life.

After drinking in the pollution-free mountain air, and touring the small town of Page, Arizona, which took about five minutes, Cyndi and Kelly set about looking for a place to stay. They settled on an inexpensive motel until they could establish more permanent residence, then began the search for jobs.

Cyndi thought the marinas along Lake Powell looked like attractive, fun places to work. She drove north into Utah, then started working her way back, applying for employment. She heard the same story repeatedly: they weren't hiring just now.

Tired, she returned to Page, and walked into a rectangular cinder block building near the edge of town, a bar known as the Windy Mesa. Yes, the owner nodded, he could use a bartender.

Cyndi's experience mixing cocktails back in St. Louis landed her the job.

Windy Mesa was built during the construction era of the Glen Canyon dam, and had developed a reputation for serving roughneck men, bikers, and rowdies. Since Page had grown respectable, the bar's old image had faded, but not vanished. Live rock 'n' roll music and dancing remained, but the bar still attracted customers who were well acquainted with the local jail. None of that mattered to Cyndi Coffman. She needed the job, which offered three-fifty an hour plus tips.

Cyndi's traveling companion, Kelly, drifted on, but among the Windy Mesa crowd, and at the recreation centers around the lake, there were plenty of new friends to be found. That's where she met Sam Keam. Thin, not quite six-feet, blue eyes, with brown hair down to his shoulders, and a Roman nose, Keam impressed Cyndi with his strong independence. He was just a year older than Cyndi.

"About a month after I got there," Cindy recalled, "I met him at a party, at the lake actually. See, you go to the lake . . . weekends at the lake there would be a bunch of people who would go and camp out for the whole weekend. I worked at night, so I would go out there in the day, then back to work that afternoon, then back out to party for the rest of the night. That's where I met Sam."

Cyndi and Sam found time for each other before and after her working hours. They shared some booze, his high-grade pot, and then his bed. He later described her as an "experienced lover" who was "pretty active, sexually." She would soon learn more about him, that he had a long arrest record for drug possession, disorderly conduct, and a series of motor vehicle violations. He was also paying child support but missed the payments now and then.

Spring winds gave way to dry summer heat, with temperatures climbing into the nineties, but the high altitude kept the Page climate quite comfortable. Cyndi continued her nights behind the bar at the Windy Mesa while living in a mobile home she shared with three college students who were working in Page for the summer. She spent very little time in the crowded cubicle as she was generally at the bar or with Sam Keam.

The bar owner hired another new employee who became a close buddy to Cyndi. Cyndi later fondly remembered that first summer in Page:

"It's a beautiful place. Judy bought a four-wheel drive, and we'd go all over . . . all around the lake, where ordinary cars couldn't go. Some people would try it, but they'd really tear up their cars and trucks. . . . You could lay in the sun, get lots of sun. I was very tan. I wish I had never left."

Because they spent so much time together, Sam and Cyndi figured they might as well share living quarters. She moved out of the college kids' trailer house, and into his. It, too, was crowded because Sam already shared the place with a man and a woman. No one minded, though. It made for good parties.

The relationship between Cyndi and Sam filled

most of their mutual needs—sexual, emotional, and the desire for companionship. But something was missing and they argued. Sometimes, their bickering expanded to shouting matches accompanied by exchanged slaps. On the last day of July, Cyndi tried to run over Sam with her car.

Cyndi's busy schedule did not preclude an occasional call to St. Louis to her son, now four years old. She told him that she would come and get him soon. In mid-August, she tried to keep her promise. Cyndi and Sam drove to St. Louis where she planned to retrieve her son and take him to Page. She was in for a serious disappointment.

What Cyndi didn't know is that her name had been in the back pages of a St. Louis newspaper for four consecutive weeks from June 15 to July 6, 1984. The announcement read: "The State of Missouri to respondent Cynthia Coffman: You are hereby notified that an action has been commenced against you . . . the object and general nature of which is the Dissolution of Marriage and Child Custody." The petitioner was listed as Ronald Coffman. Cyndi had until June 15 to respond, or a judgement by default would be rendered against her.

She had missed the deadline by two months. Her marriage was dissolved, and the child was in the legal custody of her ex-husband. Cyndi was given visitation rights at the Coffman home, with specific limitations on days and hours and with a firm proviso that the child would not leave the Coffman premises.

But Cyndi was unaware of all this as she excitedly traveled toward her parents' home, anxious to see her son and take him back to Page. When she arrived, she introduced Sam to her parents. "He was very nice," Sally observed. She liked him much better than Ron Coffman. Later, Cyndi and Sam drove over to the Coffman home. Their reception was chilly.

Ron Coffman's mother was irritated by the abrupt way in which the couple arrived with no advance warning. She recalled what happened on answering the doorbell: "We opened the door and she (Cynthia) pushed it open, came in, and grabbed (the child) out of the high chair. She just said, 'I'm taking him.'"

"No, you're not!" Mr. Coffman growled, in the firm voice of an ex-cop. According to the senior Mrs. Coffman, her son, Ron, took the child away from Cyndi. Furiously cursing, Cyndi ran outside to seek Sam's assistance, and started to reenter the house with her boyfriend in tow. Mr. Coffman stopped them.

Asked if Sam tried to intimidate him, the elder Coffman replied, "Well, we had a few words. I just told him, 'You'd better back off.' Then they went back out to the car and I called the County Police."

Within minutes, county patrolman George Ice pulled into the driveway, talked to Cynthia, Sam, and the Coffmans, and ended the confrontation peacefully by escorting Sam and Cyndi off the property.

It was a long ride back to Page, Arizona, for Sam and Cyndi. A few days after she arrived there, she received official notification of the divorce and custody award.

By immersing herself in work and social activities, Cyndi was able to alleviate some of the anger and pain from the disappointing trip to St. Louis. In addition to her bartending job at the Windy Mesa, she took a job at the Holiday Inn, two blocks away, as a cocktail waitress. In September, she quit the Windy Mesa and worked full-time at the hotel. Cyndi also had a little sideline for income, selling marijuana.

Drug usage between the couple also escalated. Now, in addition to pot and speed, they did cocaine.

Restlessness overcame Cyndi and she began arguing with Sam almost daily. Fed up, she grabbed her clothes, and moved into another trailer house with a girlfriend, Sherry, and her housemate, and then to another trailer with a platonic couple. Cyndi thought the man, Mike Hamblin, was attractive. His narrow face, close-set eyes, prominent nose, and long brown hair parted in the middle were features Cyndi found pleasant enough. He was only two inches taller than her own five-feet six-inches. She felt relaxed and cozy with him in the few hours she had away from her two jobs.

Still working at the Holiday Inn, Cyndi also served cocktails at a country club, but eventually dropped both jobs to return to bartending duties at the Windy Mesa. She knew more people there, and was contented in the surroundings. The comfort level with Mike Hamblin grew, too, and they became lovers.

Mike worked seven days a week at the power plant down at the dam. His income allowed Cyndi to taper off her working hours until she reported only sporadically to the Windy Mesa.

The daily routine of serving booze in the bar and sitting around in Mike Hamblin's trailer house began to wear thin with Cyndi. She seemed bored to Mike:

"She was a little younger than me. I had lived a full life by the time I was twenty-nine. She wanted to live, and it just wasn't going to work out. I went to work, seven days a week, came home, that was it. It was hard to give her enough attention. She had her friends, and I wasn't much of a partyer . . . I'd gotten it out of my system before that. I understood why she wanted to break up, but we were still good friends afterwards."

Amicably leaving Mike, Cyndi boarded with Judy, the fellow employee at the Windy Mesa with whom Cyndi enjoyed four-wheeling.

After their breakup, Sam had moved to Barstow, California, a crossroads community in the middle of the Mojave Desert, to work at Fort Irwin, a sprawling military base just south of Death Valley. But he missed Cyndi, and made excuses to travel frequently to Page during October 1985. On November 1, she packed everything she owned, threw

it into his station wagon, and left with him for
Barstow. Her Trans-Am, battered, sick, broken-
down, and still not paid for, was abandoned in
Judy's backyard.

Barstow is considerably larger than Page, and
has some rough-hewn edges. On the east side of
town, across a bridge that spans a wide cluster of
railroad tracks, rows of dusty, squat single-story
cinder block apartments bake in the desert sun
against a backdrop of barren hills. Sam brought
Cyndi home to one of the dreary dwellings. She
found work at a bar named Maya, where the crowd
was tougher than the regulars at Windy Mesa. She
seemed to hold her own among them.

One evening, a customer at the bar decided to
give nicknames to the female employees. Cynthia
Coffman became Cynful. The patron returned the
following day with a banner-type computer print-
out inscribed with the sobriquet. It was promptly
displayed on the bar-room wall, and Cyndi liked
it enough to pull it down later, take it home, and
post it on her wall.

Trips away from the dreary environment were
welcomed by Cyndi. She and Sam spent Thanksgiving at Page with Judy. During the Christmas
holidays, Cyndi and Sam bought skis, boots, and
poles, and drove south into the San Bernardino
Mountains to Big Bear. They learned to ski during
the days, and spent nights making love in the cozy
Bavarian Lodge.

Sam was concerned about Cyndi working late
hours at a tough bar. To provide her with some

element of protection in the Maya and in the east-side apartments, Sam gave her a tiny, .22 caliber, chromeplated, two-shot derringer handgun. She usually kept it in her purse.

On April 5, 1986, Cyndi and Sam left a bar in the wee hours, and stopped on the way home at a 7-Eleven convenience store.

"It was probably three in the morning," Cyndi later described. "We had been out that night . . . and were on the way home. We stopped at the Seven-Eleven to get a soft drink and something to eat. Four guys just started harassing Sam, saying rude things. They were just looking for a fight. And I kept saying, 'Sam, just don't say nothing. Let's just go.' I mean, there were four of them. But Sam is a fighter, anyway, and it was hard to keep him from saying anything back. So we got outside and the four guys followed us, and they circled us. The next thing I knew, they were all about to jump him. He started fighting with one, and the other three started to get into it. I pulled out the derringer, and told them if one of them wanted to fight him, that was okay, but they all weren't going to beat him up. So they just stood there and didn't do anything. He fought this one guy, and then we jumped in the car, and drove toward home." They weren't aware that someone at the store phoned to summon the police.

The report prepared by Officer R.W. Specht indicated that their "vehicle was traveling at a high rate of speed . . . crossed over the double yellow lines . . . swerved back into the traffic lanes, and made an erratic left turn." The patrolman flipped on his flashing red lights and pulled Keam's car over in front of the apartment where he and Cyndi lived.

A strong odor of alcohol assaulted Officer Specht's nostrils when Sam opened his car window, and Sam's "red, watery" eyes convinced Specht that the driver was probably eligible for a DUI. When he asked Keam to exit the vehicle, Sam "started screaming" at him, requiring the deputy and his partner, D.A. Espino, to "contain" the man.

Cyndi stepped out of the car, watched for a few seconds, and heard the patrol-car radio broadcasting a report of "someone brandishing a handgun" at the 7-Eleven store. Immediately, Cyndi grabbed her purse, which contained the derringer, and ran into their apartment. Officer Specht heard the alert, too, and realized that the couple and the car matched the descriptions. His partner radioed for a backup patrol unit. While Specht put Sam Keam through field sobriety tests, a new arrival, Sergeant Lindley, called Cyndi Coffman out of the apartment. She meekly complied.

Looking in the open purse, the sergeant did not see the derringer, which Cyndi had dumped inside the apartment. But she had failed to remove a cigarette package that held "a bundle of white crystalline substance" under the cellophane wrapper and an assortment of pills wrapped in a peanut package. She was arrested for possession and being under the influence of a controlled substance. While searching Keam, the officers found a five-inch knife concealed in his left boot and five .22 caliber bullets in his pocket. He, too, was placed under arrest for driving under the influence, and transported to jail. With permission of the building owner, the officers recovered the loaded derringer from the apartment, along with "scales, bongs, straws, Baggies, and mirrors," all considered to be drug paraphernalia.

Cynthia Coffman was held in jail from the arrest date, April 5, 6:40 A.M., until 2:30 P.M, April 9, then released on the proviso that criminal charges might be filed later.

Sam Keam was detained longer. In addition to the charges filed against him on the morning of April 5, authorities discovered outstanding warrants on Keam from Page, Arizona, for failure to pay child support. While he waited for extradition, Keam cooled his heels in a jail cell along with James Gregory Marlow.

When Cynthia Coffman walked out of the Barstow jail into the afternoon sunshine on April 9, 1986, she wondered how long it would be before Sam Keam could join her. She had been released on her own recognizance, and had promised that she would appear in court in three weeks. The whole incident had infuriated her, and she hoped she would never see the inside of a jail cell again. Cyndi wangled a ride to the apartment, plopped down on the couch, and wondered where she could find enough money to bail Sam out.

Keam, too, was anxious for freedom. To pass the tediously slow hours, he started chatting with his

cellmate, Greg Marlow. They had chuckled together a little earlier because they had heard Cyndi
"yelling and cussing" at the guards before she was
released. Sam proudly mentioned to Greg that the
girl they heard was his honey. "Might even marry
her one of these days," Sam boasted.

After five days in the lockup, Marlow walked out,
leaving his new buddy behind. On the afternoon of
the next day, he knocked on the door of an apartment on Crook Street. Cyndi opened it and looked
over the stranger standing there dressed in jeans
and a T-shirt that stretched over his muscular torso
and tattooed arms. Grinning, Greg said, "I was in
the cell with Sam and I told him I'd check on you,
make sure you're okay."

They stood at the entry, talking for several minutes. Cyndi mentioned that she was having trouble
with the station wagon. Greg offered to help fix
it, impressing her with his courtesy and generosity.
She didn't invite him in, but accepted his invitation to smoke some pot. His stash was over at his
place, the Stardust Inn, he remarked, tilting his
head in that direction. They could go over there
in his orange pickup and he'd get it while she
waited outside. His manner eased her mind, convincing her that he wasn't trying to lure her into
his bedroom, so Cyndi agreed to go. They inhaled
the pungent smoke while sitting in the cab of the
truck, parked in the Stardust lot. A couple of hours
later, he dropped her off back at her place.

Sam, to Cyndi's consternation and confusion,
was transferred to San Bernardino. She didn't un-

derstand the move, but drove seventy miles to the county seat with the intention of bailing Sam out. Her trip was wasted. He was being extradited to Page, she discovered, for failure to pay child support.

Five hundred miles and two days later, Cyndi pulled into Page, exhausted after herding the banged-up, old station wagon across the endless desert. She needed a change of pace, and got it when Sam was released. The couple drove up to Brian Head, Utah, for a few days of skiing in fresh air and a friendly environment, before circling back to Barstow.

When he and Cyndi arrived back in Barstow, they paid Greg Marlow a call in the Stardust motel. Cyndi felt a surge of excitement looking at Greg's rock-solid bare chest with the ornate tattoos, and knew that he was admiring her, as well. The trio continued to get together over the next three weeks. Cyndi even cooked dinner for them one night in the apartment, and smiled when Greg leaned intimately close to her, while Sam was out of the room, and told her what a fine-looking woman she was. When Sam returned, Greg asked to buy a half-ounce of the high-grade pot, and handed over fifty dollars for the purchase.

By procrastinating on the marijuana deal over the next couple of days, Sam pushed Marlow's patience too far. Greg followed him to the apartment, and let him know, in profane and threatening terms, that he didn't tolerate being cheated, and wanted his money back. He got it.

Further conflict between the two men was a-voided when Greg accompanied the microwave installation gang south to Yuma, Arizona, for two weeks. Simultaneously, Sam was arrested again.

Maybe it was Sam's problems with the police, or maybe the rough lifestyle she was living, or just maybe it was Cyndi's attraction to Greg. Whatever it was, Cyndi was dissatisfied and restless. She wanted to leave, but couldn't think where to go; wanted change, but had no idea what it would be. Her dilemma was solved when she opened the apartment door in early June, and Greg Marlow stood there, smiling at her.

"Where's Sam?" he wanted to know.

"In jail again," she said, making a sour face.

"He was trying to burn me on that deal for some grass," Marlow snorted, testing her loyalty to Sam.

Cyndi didn't know what to say. She wasn't sure that Sam really intended to cheat Marlow, but couldn't explain why he had never produced the goods.

"So, what are you going to do now?" Marlow asked.

"Well, I'm sort of in the process of leaving. It's over between me and Sam." She saw Greg glance at the partially packed boxes in the room.

"I been working down in Yuma," Greg volunteered. "And I know a bar down there, where I go a lot, and I might be able to get you a job bartending. Sure would like to help you out." Greg wanted to make it clear that there were no strings attached, he didn't want anything in return. He just felt sorry for her. "I would like to ask a favor, though," he quickly added.

"What's that?" Cyndi asked.

"I wonder if you could drive me over to Fontana, over by San Bernardino? I need to see my cousin about something, and I don't have a driver's license." In his lie, he didn't explain why a thirty-year-old man, who drove a pickup truck on his job, didn't have a license to drive.

Cyndi unhesitatingly agreed to drive him to Fontana, and they left that same evening. On the way, he told her that the reason for the journey was to buy some methamphetamine. That was okay with her. Greg asked questions on the way, wanting to know all about her. He learned of her childhood, her little boy in St. Louis, her life with Sam, and her nickname Cynful.

The transaction in Fontana took only half an hour, and they immediately turned around toward Barstow. But when they reached his vehicle, Marlow asked Cyndi if she would follow him to a buddy's house. She shrugged, and complied with his request. Greg hopped into an El Camino that Cyndi had never seen before, and headed east on the freeway. After tailing him through thirty more miles of dark desert, they turned off to the tiny, remote community of Newberry Springs.

Greg parked, and climbed into the old station wagon with Cyndi. They sat there for hours talking. Several times, Greg hopped out, ran down the street about a block to his pal's house, then returned and talked some more. Cyndi guessed that

Greg was waiting for someone to wake up to collect money for the speed brought from Fontana. She was partially correct. Greg was also arranging to sell the El Camino and to resolve another more pressing matter.

With half of his business transaction completed at dawn, Marlow asked Cyndi if she would take him to Fontana again, to complete the deal. Tired, but infatuated with this powerful, complex man, she agreed to the long drive again. While they traveled, Greg's buddy in Newberry Springs, Paul Donner, took care of a little problem for him.

When Greg had returned from Yuma, he'd brought with him a brassy, tough-talking blonde. He and his new mate needed a place to stay, so he convinced Donner to let him use a spare trailer house, parked in the yard, for a while. The woman was a hard-bitten Yuma taxi driver who spent most of her off-duty hours in a biker bar. She had succumbed to Marlow's charms, and accompanied him out of Yuma with stars in her eyes. But when Marlow saw Cyndi again, he wanted to dump the taxi driver. He managed to hide the blonde from Cyndi by parking a block away from Paul's house, and making several trips to con his pal into helping him. While Greg and Cyndi drove back to Fontana, Paul did Marlow's dirty work; he drove the woman to a bus station and left her there.

The visit in Fontana was short again, but this time Greg and Cyndi were not in the mood to return immediately.

En route back to Barstow, their mutual attraction

turned to sexual arousal. When they reached Victorville, about halfway home, Cyndi pulled into a motel parking lot. Greg suddenly crawled into the backseat, as if resisting the desire to consummate the passion.

"I love you, Cyndi," he whispered. "I've loved you since we first met. Maybe this isn't a good idea." She was shocked when he began crying, but emotionally touched. "There are things about me you don't know," Greg continued. "You deserve better. My past wasn't very good. My mother was a prostitute and she made me steal from her tricks. She shot me up with heroin when I was just a kid. No one, not even my own father, cared anything about me."

Sympathy swelled in Cyndi and her eyes moistened. This tower of strength, this bold brigand, was vulnerable. He was irresistible.

Greg's wives, he sniffled, had not stood by him when he needed them the most. They couldn't hang tough. "My mother wasn't there for me and neither were my wives. No one has ever really loved me. No one." He wondered if she could love him and help him live a good life.

"Let's give it a try," Cyndi cooed, her voice breaking. "It can work." She agreed to go to Yuma with him where he claimed jobs awaited both of them.

Only then did they register for a motel room. Inside, they kissed, fondled, played, and had the passionate, wild, fulfilling sex that can bond lovers forever.

In the grimy Barstow apartment, Cyndi jammed some clothes into a suitcase with a few personal things, and drove with Greg to Newberry Springs where Paul Donner would let them stay in the small trailer house parked in his yard. Their days, at first, were filled with sunshine and fun, lying around the Donners' pool, swimming, and enhancing the euphoria with methamphetamine. Nights were the time to talk and share dreams and fantasies about the future.

One of his main topics of conversation was prison and his experiences as an inmate. He had killed while inside the walls, he told Cyndi. He hinted about an association with the Aryan Brotherhood. His prison name was Folsom Wolf, he disclosed, as if sharing the most important bit of information in the world.

He frequently addressed her, and referred to her, as Cynful.

Her education expanded daily. She had been using methamphetamine for some time, but had never injected it. She learned how. Greg also taught her his sexual techniques.

The sex between them was sensual, exciting, and explosive. Cyndi found that he could perform for hours and bring her to peaks of enjoyment she had never before experienced. He seemed especially fond of sex in the shower, when their bodies were wet, slippery, and clean. Afterwards, he would tenderly dry her off, in slow motion, gently, lovingly. She wanted to please him with equal fervor, and would do anything for him. She cooked, washed his clothes, waited on him, and responded to his wishes.

Many of Cyndi's possessions were still in the Barstow apartment, and after ten days in Newberry Springs, she, Greg, and Paul went after them. After carrying her things to the car, Greg eyed Sam Keam's vacuum cleaner, and mentioned to Cyndi that Paul needed one, commenting that they did owe him something for staying at his place. Cyndi granted Paul the vacuum cleaner and a painting he admired. They also helped themselves to Sam's skis, ski boots, and much of his clothing. Greg kept some of the clothing for himself. He also kept a little black book he had lifted from Cyndi's purse, which contained all of her personal telephone numbers and addresses. Cyndi didn't think much about it at the time.

She didn't think much about her promise to appear in court to settle the gun-brandishing matter, either. She completely ignored it.

The little trailer in which they slept needed a coat of paint. Greg asked Cyndi to help him with the job, and began working while Cyndi finished manicuring her long red fingernails. Her nails and her hair were special to her, and she didn't want to hurry the grooming of either one. About halfway through the job, Marlow yelled at her to hurry up and help him. She said she would, then continued to preen. He stormed into the trailer, grabbed her hand, looked at a nail she had been trying to secure with superglue, and chewed it off with his teeth. After grinding off two more, he snatched her scissors and snipped the rest of her nails almost to the quick. She was stunned. It might be better in the future, she decided, not to provoke him.

Other behavior by Cyndi bothered Marlow: "She used to wear bathing suits up in the desert around my friends, and flirt with everybody all the time. I couldn't tell you half of what I went through because of this dame flirting with people. I didn't know what to do. She was just gonna run me to the ground and drive me nuts."

If Marlow was jealous, he had a strange way of showing it.

Ernie Greene looked like a movie cowboy. He wore his long blond hair, which was thinning on top, in a ponytail. A Fu Manchu mustache drooped over the corner of his mouth and his blue eyes matched the desert sky. Jeans hung on his wiry, six-foot, three-inch frame, and he wore cowboy boots as if he had been born with them.

The big, rangy cowboy had joined a small group of men at Paul's place for beer and drugs. They were laughing and playing guitars and swapping stories on the warm June afternoon. Ernie dropped the comment that he hadn't had a woman for a long time. As the afternoon wore on, the cowboy found himself sitting alone in the house, nursing a beer and watching television, while the other men horsed around outside. Cynful walked into the room, dressed in cutoff jeans and a skimpy T-shirt. She smiled nervously at him.

"Do you want a blow job?" she blurted out.

Astonished, because she had been introduced to him only an hour earlier, he quickly replied, "Yeah, sure."

"Okay, let's get this over with," Cyndi said, as she dropped to her knees, while he fumbled with his zipper.

In Coffman's version of the incident, told later, she said that she orally copulated Greene for maybe two minutes. But it was awkward, she said. "I was crying and he told me, 'Hey, just don't worry about it, and I'll tell him (Greg) everything turned out fine,' and he just did up his pants. Afterward, Greg came in the bathroom where I was and told me that I was a good girl and that I'd done a good job."

Why had she done it?

"Greg told me if I loved him, that I would. And I told him, 'No,' and he kept saying, 'But you will, you will if you love me.' So I did."

Greene, with an embarrassed grin, later corroborated that the event happened, but denied that Cynful was crying. Marlow had made no prior offer of sex with the woman, he said, but afterwards, Marlow did ask Ernie, "Were you taken care of okay?" Ernie also remembered that the entire group, including Cynful, had been using drugs just before the incident.

Paul would eventually reveal that Greene had told him about the encounter, saying that Marlow was offering up the girl for sex, and suggested that Paul should take his turn with Cynful. When asked if Marlow had ever directly offered Cyndi to him sexually, Paul mumbled, "Uh, it seemed like he had mentioned it a couple of times."

The Jekyll and Hyde monster in Marlow, the Folsom Wolf, appeared to Coffman for the first time in Newberry Springs. In a retrospective narrative, Cyndi described it:

"We were watching Paul's house while they were gone for a few days, and we went over to a friend's to do some speed. We shot it up a few times, and then Greg went outside with the guy, and I was in the bedroom with the guy's girlfriend. She showed me how I could shoot up myself, because I didn't know how. I'd done it with cocaine before, but not speed. Finally, she did it for me. I just laid back on the bed to get myself back together. A guy came in and was sitting on the bed, next to me. Then Greg came in and really got pissed. He told me we're going home now.

"As soon as we got back inside Paul's house, Greg grabbed a gun. Paul kept a holstered gun hanging on a coatrack, and Greg grabbed it and told me to get in the bathroom. In there, he ripped my shirt off, a little T-shirt. Then he took his (shirt) off and ripped it up in little strips, and tied my hands up behind my back and tied my legs.

"Then he started talking differently, and his voice was a monotone, and his eyes got strange, different, glossy. He was Wolf.

"He started slapping me and kicking me and calling me all kinds of names. Slut, I'm a whore, things like that because he said I was flirting with that guy on the bed. I was still tied up and he'd leave for a while, then come back in and hit on me for a while. 'I'm going to kill you now,' he'd say. At one time, he came in with a hypodermic needle and said it was filled with something that would kill me. I would be just one dead junkie that they would find out in the desert.

"He left again, and I started trying to get untied, and he came in and caught me and threw me in the shower. Then, all of a sudden, it ended. He became Greg again and untied me, and said, 'We're going to go get some cigarettes,' just like nothing had happened.

"When we went to get the cigarettes, he told me that I deserved better than him and that I should just leave him. He didn't mean to be that way, that it was something else in him, sort of like a monster. It was the monster that beat me, and he was sorry, and if I would just love him a little more, that it wouldn't come out again."

There was no sex in the shower that day, Cyndi said, but sex was quite frequent between them: "Before Greg, I had performed oral sex maybe once or twice on my ex-husband or Sam. And it's something I didn't do and didn't want to do. But he demanded it all the time, and I did what he wanted."

All of her treatment in Newberry Springs wasn't bad, Cyndi admitted. They still talked about having a good life together, about recovering her son from the custody of the Coffman family, going somewhere else, and starting over. Greg could make money again. He'd had lots of it, he told Cyndi, when he and his wife had owned an Appaloosa ranch in Victorville. And he'd had money from some "hits" he had done.

It all seemed to be coming true for her when Greg told her that his father had died in Kentucky, and that he was going to inherit a farm with lots of acreage. They would have to go to Kentucky right away so that they could launch a new beginning.

Nineteen

Wildman Hill, Corinna Novis, and Lynel Murray had been murdered, and the two prime suspects, James Gregory Marlow and Cynthia Lynn Coffman, languished in the San Bernardino County jail, waiting for trial.

In their respective cells, they missed the constant contact with each other. Marlow had learned, during his previous prison experience, how to "kite" letters, that is to have contraband mail secretly delivered by other prisoners. The two inmates also used the U.S. postal service, when they could obtain envelopes and stamps.

During the period of time between their arrest, mid-November 1986 until September 1987, they exchanged more than three hundred pages of letters, most of which were written on 8½" by 14" legal-sized lined pads.

Many of the letters were eventually seized by jail authorities because they had reason to believe that an escape was being engineered and the correspondence might contain details of such a plan.

When investigators read the letters, they were amazed at the variety of subjects and style written

by Marlow, a dropout from the ninth grade, and
Coffman, a high-school graduate. The content
ranged from Kafkaesque parables to romantic
prose and poetry, to legal wrangling, to raw por-
nography. But the majority of them, especially
the early ones, were filled with page after page
of declarations of love for each other. Many of
them were decorated with drawings, using smiling or leering faces with tongues hanging out,
swastikas to dot the letter *i*, and Nazi-like SS sym-
bols. Others had graphic drawings of sex organs.
On one such document, Cyndi had sat on the
legal-size paper and carefully traced the portion
of her anatomy that was in contact with the paper. On another one, she traced the outline of
one of her breasts and wrote, "Now give it a kiss
for me, it misses it a lot."

Some of Marlow's early writing was full of de-
nial: (NOTE: misspelled words are quoted verba-
tim. Some punctuation is added for ease of
reading.)

—CYNFUL—
    Sure do miss your sweet little self [smiling
face with tongue out]. I guess there talking
"gas" for both of us, on shit we really don't
know that much about! I really don't know
how they come up with sex shit & murder?
Someone be saying shit about us that we don't
even know _____. Saying you lead them to a
grave that you or I could know nothing about
is beound me? I love you till the sun don't

shine, Baby Girl. . . . We're all we've got, so
if either can get anything together, let's take
care of the other. I know that goes unsaid
[smiling face] . . . I'll help you, next court.
Are you OK over there? I have my own cell—
how about you? Being apart from you is like
sailing on an outlander ship to an unknown
country. . . .

The letter continues to rhapsodically declare his
undying love for Cyndi, refers to a dream that he
will write about in a subsequent letter, drifts into
sexual content, and contains a "P.S." about Coral,
using his favorite nickname for her, "Wheels":

. . . You're everything I always wanted but
never could find or really have. I love you . . .
I miss you. I'll hang on as long as you want
me to? Are you getting any calls? Any chance
for help? I sure miss them special legs & all
over softness. . . . If you can touch my special
stuff on a letter for me I'll eat it [smiling face
with tongue]. Maybe just a little dip . . . I love
you, Cyn!

Forever, your daddy, Greg

Cyndi's letters were no less devoted, amorous, or
sexual:

My Love,
How's my baby today? Your Mom's ok, fine.
Except one of the Romans got a hold of me

today and made me file my nails way down.
Life's a bitch! . . . You are my King, my
Knight, my hero, my Love . . . I love you. I
could never go! Forever and ever we shall be
as one! You are mine and I am yours, just like
the birds will forever soar. I'm so lost in love
with you. . . .

SS WOLF SS	Mrs. J. G. Marlow
CYNFUL	your loving 100%
PUPS	true honest devoted wife

My Lord,
  I miss thee so. I am so very happy time
grows nearer for me to see you. I can't take
being away from you much more. . . . You are
my life and I am yours. I love you . . . I finally
find you, and then we get stuck in here. I
know you tried to warn me. I just didn't think
it would happen . . . Hope my "Roscoe" ain't
botherin' ya too much. I'd love to kiss him and
make him feel better for you. I ain't talkin'
about no little kiss either. . . .

Cynthia Coffman needed a friend. Her twenty-
fifth birthday, January 19, 1987, had passed in a
jail cell, virtually unnoticed, making her feel terribly sorry for herself and in need of someone with
whom to commiserate. Robin Long filled the bill.
  Dealing from a deck of cards, deftly arranging
them on a metal table in the recreation room of
the San Bernardino County jail, Robin Long announced to anyone within earshot, "Tell your for-

tune. Tell you your past, present, or future." She brushed her stringy, reddish hair back from her protruding forehead, and glanced around the room. Robin's "hustle" had worked frequently during her recently completed nine months in prison. Now that she had violated parole within days after her release, and was back in jail, her scam would probably work again among this crop of caged women. She had found a long time ago that there was always someone gullible enough to pay for her glib, self-taught, fortune-telling, enabling her to keep a solvent commissary fund.

The short, pudgy, thirty-five-year-old con noticed a bone-thin young woman with closely cropped hair, who reminded Robin of her own teenage daughter, taking sidelong glances at the dealt cards, trying not to look interested.

Cyndi managed to hold out two more days, but finally approached Robin to hear what the cards had in store for her, and to talk. Realizing that the cards were of very little importance to Cyndi, but the urge to share her plight with someone was overwhelming, the older woman was a willing listener.

After exchanging names, Cyndi asked Robin, "Have your ever heard of me?"

"No," Robin snorted. "I've been up in the San Diego hills fighting forest fires for the last year. Haven't heard of anyone."

"You haven't heard of Cynthia Coffman or James Marlow?"

"Nope."

Cyndi, Robin Long would later say, then mentioned that she was in jail for abducting a woman from a shopping center in Redlands. After that comment, Cyndi let the conversation drift back to what the cards had to say. On the next day, however, she opened up even more to her willing audience.

And Robin Long was a good listener. She watched Cyndi's eyes range from emotionless to gleeful as the "kid" described her relationship with Wolf Marlow, and told of his association with the Aryan Brotherhood. The A.B., Cyndi hinted, would probably bust her out of jail within a few days.

"My old man's involved in that, too," Robin told Cyndi, gaining even more of her confidence.

During the next few days, before Robin Long was released from custody on February 5, Cyndi expressed total trust in her new friend by revealing a great deal more than she had planned to tell. There was something about Robin Long that inspired Cyndi Coffman to share her most intimate secrets.

Cyndi and Greg did get to see each other occasionally, when they were taken to court for hearings, and later, for the trial. They both eagerly anticipated the periodic transfers from the county jail to holding cells in the court building. En route, they were sometimes able to have brief physical contact in the bus or in elevators, where they could exchange quick comments and touches.

On an upper floor in the courthouse, the four holding cells in the center of a larger room were arranged in a quadrant, with thick concrete walls dividing the two cubicles reserved for women from the two for men.

At the end of one court session, the deputy sheriff, responsible for preparing the prisoners for transfer, busily arranged for several of them to be taken downstairs to the bus. He had already placed waistchains on Cyndi Coffman and connected her handcuffs to the chain at her sides. He watched her obey his order to move to the rear of her cell and sit on the bunk, then, leaving her cell door ajar, he stepped around the corner to waistchain another prisoner. She was out of his sight for just a few minutes, but he knew there was no danger of escape, since the holding cells were surrounded by more wire and bars.

When he returned to Cyndi's cell, she was gone. Instantly, he stepped around the corner where he could see the cell in which James Marlow waited for transfer. Marlow was standing on his bunk with his back to the deputy. His hips were thrust against the bars. Cyndi was stooped low, facing him, with her head "about waist level with Marlow."

As the deputy entered the doorway, Marlow and Coffman heard him. Coffman jerked her head aside to look around Marlow's body, stared directly at the deputy, and "immediately took off the long way around the cells back to her own cell."

As the deputy remembered it, "Marlow also

turned his head and body and looked toward me. As he turned I could see his erect penis and his face turning bright red. At this time I noticed a tattoo at the end of Marlow's penis which I had not known was there."

When Coffman reached her cell, the deputy, in a "sort of lighthearted way," asked, "What are you guys doing back there, engaging in a little oral activity?"

Marlow, while "situating his genitals back into his jumpsuit," said, "Nothing's going on. Nothing happened." Coffman entered her cell, sat down on the bunk, stared at the floor, and refused to respond to the deputy's "lighthearted" question.

Exactly one day after she was released from jail, a frightened, corpulent woman sat in an interview room with a detective who wore a flattop haircut.

"Okay, Robin," he said, "like I told you before, I'm Detective Dick Hooper and I'm with Huntington Beach. I'd like to talk with you about the conversation you had with a gal by the name of Cynthia Coffman. . . . Now, as I understand it, you were in custody at San Bernardino County jail?"

"Yes, sir. I was in PC (protective custody)," Robin Long answered, nervous and hesitant. She was painfully aware of the consequences informants usually face among their peers when the word leaks out on the street. It was risky, but whatever her motives, she chose to do it.

"Did you share a cell with this Coffman girl?" Hooper inquired.

"No, we had single cells. I was in cell two and she was in cell eight." Robin added that she had never met Coffman before being incarcerated with her. They were allowed to intermingle in cells during the daytime.

"Can you describe her to me?"

"She's about five-foot-six. Her eyes are blue but her pupils are sometimes very dark black. She has extremely short, medium-brown hair, weighs about a hundred pounds, real thin, light complexion, few small freckles, kind of long, oval (face)."

Hooper asked if Robin had noticed any tattoos on Coffman. "Yeah, on her bottom," the fidgety woman replied, describing the blue-inked inscription *Property of Folsom Wolf,* and acknowledged that "you have to shower with them, y'know."

Most of the conversations took place, Long said, while the two women sat on the bunk in Robin's cell. "She would talk to me privately. See, I got a little routine thing that I do . . . and I was trying to find out as much as I could, but she's hard to find out from. I have a little card thing I do and they think I can read fortunes . . . I'm a pretty good judge of liars. I been out on the streets a long time, and so I would just tell her, you know, if I didn't believe it, I'd say, 'What really happened, tell me?' "

"Did you know anything about this case before you met her?"

"No," Robin replied, admitting that she didn't read newspapers because she had only a third-grade education, and didn't like watching television.

"So, when she talked about this incident, was she somewhat secretive about it?"

Robin remarked that Coffman had seemed afraid, and wanted to know what the cards were predicting. "Is Greg gonna talk?" or "Does Greg love me?" and "Are we going to go to the gas chamber?"

"I don't even know how to play cards, let alone read them," Robin admitted. "But I'll tell them anything. I said, 'Well, it says something about his mother in these cards.' I figure everybody's got a mother." Robin Long may not have been able to read cards, but her prescience was remarkable. She had stumbled on a subject that would become a central issue in the case.

Long's narrative continued. "So she goes, 'Oh yeah, his mother was a prostitute, his mother was a dope fiend and she got burnt up in a trailer,' and that Greg hated his mother. And I go, 'Did these two women that he killed look like his mother?' and she said, 'No, *the last two didn't.*'"

Dick Hooper's eyebrows shot up. The last two? "Say that again," he nearly shouted.

Robin dutifully repeated her startling statement, but said that Cyndi had only described the details of three killings. If there had been more than

three, she knew nothing about them. Hooper re-
focused back on the murder of Lynel Murray, because that was his case. "Keep in mind," he
cautioned Long, "that I don't want any opinions
or suppositions. I don't want you to tell me anything that didn't come out of her mouth, okay?"

In remarkable detail, Robin described Coffman
and Marlow's wandering search of the Orange
County beach cities, "driving around looking for
someone," how they had slept in Corinna Novis's
car at nights, and "looked for a victim" in daylight.
She stated that they had noticed Lynel Murray at
the dry cleaners on the day before the murder.
Murray was "the one kept coming back to their
mind . . . the girl who was locking up the dry
cleaners."

"Okay, you're saying 'looking for a victim,'"
Hooper reiterated. "What did they want a victim
for?"

"To rob her and take her money. Whether there
was a hundred dollars or fifty dollars, as long as
they could get some speed or get some money for
a room or, you know, they was having a good time
for themselves." Coffman and Marlow returned to
the dry cleaners, Robin said, and using a gun that
had been concealed in Coffman's purse, robbed
the (dry) cleaners of money and clothing, and abducted Lynel Murray.

"This was Coffman and her boyfriend?" Hooper
asked again.

"Yeah. Greg. They call him 'Wolf.' She has his

name tattooed on her finger with little lightning bolts.''

Reminding Long again to be careful with her accuracy, Hooper repeated, "I want to know what she (Coffman) said, not what you think she said."

"Okay," Robin agreed. "Then they, uh, took her out to the car, put her in Novis's car, and drove to a motel just off the freeway. Oh, yeah, they got her purse, I guess (it) had credit cards in it." Long told that Coffman had driven the car, and used Murray's name to rent the room. The captive, she said, was handcuffed. "When they got her in the room, they gagged her and blindfolded her. Then Greg told (Cyndi) to go get some hamburgers and Cokes, and she left. When she came back . . . she knew Greg had sex with this girl. And that made her mad and Greg had already showered. They all ended up gettin' in the shower."

"Did she tell you why she knew that Greg had sex?"

"She just knew 'cause he had taken a shower, and he always takes showers with his victim, too."

"Okay, then what happened?"

". . . She gave the girl her Coke and hamburger. She loosened the tape, drank some of her Coke, and wouldn't eat her hamburger. Then she (Coffman) went into the bathroom, took a bath towel and ripped it . . . in half, dipped it in a tub of water, and started choking the victim with the towel. She said she wasn't strong enough, so then Greg grabbed the other side of the towel and she pulled on one end . . . I asked her, 'Did she cry?'

(Cyndi) said, 'Yeah,' she could hear mumbling or something, but they just kept on. 'Was she kicking or screaming?' She goes, 'Yeah, she kicked a little bit.' "

Dick Hooper had heard detailed accounts of killings before, more than he could remember, but few of them had sent chills up his spine like this one. His professionalism demanded that he keep an impassionate face. He listened as Robin Long continued:

"Cyndi said that she could see the blood come out of the ears to the bandage and the blindfold. Afterwards, they took her in the bathroom, pulled her over the toilet and over the sink, and stuck her head in the water in the tub. And he urinated on her. And she told me that she was shown some pictures by the police, and the face was like all black-and-blue and that she acted like she didn't know."

To be sure that he understood correctly, Hooper asked Robin to repeat the account of strangling the victim. "How did she say *they* choked her? Coffman tried to choke her by herself?"

Robin nodded. "Uh-huh. And when she couldn't . . . wasn't strong enough to do it, then he took one end of the towel, and she took one end of the towel, and they pulled."

Hooper wondered if Robin could distinguish which house the killers had burglarized after the murder, Corinna Novis's or Lynel Murray's. He asked, "Did Coffman talk about going back to this girl's house?"

"Oh, I asked why they went back to the one's house and couldn't go to this one's house, and she said, ' 'Cause this one lived with her parents.' "

"Did Coffman say how she knew that?"

"I guess the girl told her."

The killers had been driving Corinna's car, Hooper commented to Robin. "Weren't they afraid the police were going to identify it?"

"No," Robin answered. "She told me that they didn't think the police were gonna find this body for a long time."

Noting that Robin Long had not used Lynel Murray's name in her narrative, Hooper asked why.

"Cyndi told me her name, but I can't remember. She called the girl their Huntington Beach victim."

Following standard police procedure, Hooper repeated many of his questions, taking Long through the entire story again. At the point where she described Coffman ripping the towel to use it as a ligature, Long gestured to demonstrate how Coffman had dipped it in the bathtub and twisted it.

"How do you know she twisted it?" Hooper interrupted.

" 'Cause she showed me she twisted it," Robin shot back, adding, "she showed me with my bath towel." She expressed relief that Coffman hadn't ripped her towel, during the reenactment, because Long would have been required to pay for it.

Coffman had also demonstrated the actual strangling process, Long said. "I was sitting on the bunk and she showed me with the towel how she did it." Robin had played the role of Lynel Murray in the reconstruction of the murder. Hooper now asked Long to stage the killing, according to what Coffman had told her, and Hooper would be the stand-in for the victim, while Robin played Cynthia Coffman's role.

After the informant took Hooper through additional details, including the flight from the Huntington Inn up to the desertion of Corinna's car, his part of the interview ended. One phrase Long attributed to Cyndi Coffman kept repeating in Dick Hooper's mind. He had asked why Coffman and Marlow had killed the girl.

"Because you can't leave a witness alive."

Now it was Scotty Smith's turn to interrogate Long. The solidly built, smooth-faced, young Redlands detective centered his questions on the murder of Corinna Novis.

Robin took Scotty through a repetition of her hustle in jail, describing how she had gained the confidence of Cyndi Coffman. "She thinks I'm the best friend she ever could have. I hate doing this to her, but I think what they did was very brutal, and I believe they killed more."

Running her words together in rapid succession, Robin told what she had heard about the Novis killing:

"The first murder was a lady . . . in Redlands. They picked her up in a shopping mall and she had a little white car and they abducted her and put handcuffs on her. They put her in her own car and they got her address and burglarized her home."

After Corinna was killed, Robin said, "They made up a story about a man named Jack. Have you heard a story about a man named Jack?"

Scotty said that he hadn't.

"(Jack) was supposed to be with Greg out in the grape vineyard in Fontana. Cyndi broke down and told me there's really no guy named Jack."

Scotty wanted her to slow down and take it step by step. Where did they take Corinna? he asked.

"They took her to a house in Fontana . . . this fat guy's house. And then, after they tried to have sex with her, and tried to get money out of her, and finished burglarizing her home and everything, they took her out to the grape vineyard." That's where the girl was killed and buried, Robin said, then drifted into the particulars of the Huntington Beach murder.

"Let's back up, now," Scotty said. He knew that she had the sequence confused. Corinna's apartment had been ransacked after her death. The detective wanted to be certain that she told the story as accurately as her memory would allow.

For the record, he asked Robin to declare her reasons for giving this statement. She acknowledged that no promises had been made to her and that she just wanted to help the victim's family.

Coffman, Robin added, ". . . acts like she's scared of Greg, but she's not scared. This kid is a genius, she's not scared of Greg or anything. And she's very good at what she tells you. I mean she's so good that . . . she believes herself at the moment."

"Did they tell you how or why they picked this girl out?"

Long explained that she had never talked to Greg, and that when she said "they," she meant Cyndi. "They said that they sat and watched . . . people getting into their cars and . . . when it looked like somebody they could abduct . . . they told her that they needed a ride, that their car was broke down."

"Okay, where did they go?"

"To Fontana, to the fat guy's house. They took the girl in, and they all took a shower together, the three of 'em. . . . He always made the victims take showers."

"Did they say why?"

"He wanted a clean killing."

Shaking his head at the bizarre pun, Scotty asked about any sexual acts in the shower.

"I think he tried to have sex with her . . . and couldn't perform. He would get in the shower and fondle them . . ."

After retracing much of the same ground again, Robin commented on her impressions of Cyndi Coffman.

"My honest opinion is, I believe she is the first one that thought about the money in this. Him? I believe that he thought about the sex. That was his way of getting with a woman and making it

legal so that he could have the affair without . . .
what would you call it . . . without having an affair. . . . He's a sick man."

Nodding his agreement, Scotty opened his mouth to speak, but Robin was on a roll.

"And I believe that she's a lot smarter than she lets on. I believe she's partly the brains of these two murders. The one that was in Kentucky, they did it for five thousand dollars. They would sell their mother(s) . . . I know people, and I know the game and the hustle, and I don't wanna hear it."

Scotty and Robin continued the session for another hour, then called it a day. Robin Long had said plenty.

Radical changes in Cynthia Coffman's outlook were expressed in a memo written a few months later by Dr. Craig Rath, PhD, a prominent clinical psychologist who would testify at the forthcoming trial.

May 17, 1987

TO WHOM IT MAY CONCERN:

Cynthia Coffman was interviewed while in custody at San Bernardino County Jail on the morning of 5-17-87 at the request of Mr. Palacious (her court-appointed attorney). He noted upon talking to her earlier that she seemed depressed and was crying extensively. The defendant indicated she had been upset for the last couple of weeks after talking to (a

clinical psychologist) and two other doctors
about being battered by her codefendant. She
indicated that "reality had set in" and she was
sad about all she had put up with and scared
because she was going to spend a long time
in jail. She has concluded recently that it is
time she started worrying about herself instead of her codefendant. She had heard rumors in jail that the codefendant was going to
marry someone else and if that was true she
felt very betrayed, feeling as if she wouldn't
be in jail if it hadn't been for him since she
never would have done any of this (the offenses) on her own.

Twenty

Detective Scotty Smith felt like he was holding back an avalanche of paperwork, and the Robin Long interview had just added to the pile, when his office phone rang for the umpteenth time. A quaking, high-pitched woman's voice immediately pulled Smith's attention away from the routine forms, memos, and records he was completing.

"This is Darlene Miller," the woman said, "and I have some information about Greg Marlow." She stammered that she had seen the newspaper articles detailing the murders of two young women and the subsequent arrest of Coffman and Marlow. Darlene hoped that she could contribute to the case against Marlow.

"He kidnapped me, and kept me tied up for three days about twelve years ago," the woman told Smith. "And he raped me over and over."

Her story was clearly unrelated to the murders, Scott realized, but he had testified in enough court cases to understand the need for evidence about a defendant's past record, which could be especially useful during the penalty phase of a trial.

Scotty scribbled furiously in his notebook while the caller spoke.

"Greg took me to a house, I don't even know exactly where it is now, and kept me tied up in there the whole time. It was horrible. He took all the money out of my purse, too."

Detective Smith wanted to know if she had filed a police report at the time.

"Yes," Darlene replied, her voice sounding embarrassed. "But I only told them about the robbery. I was too embarrassed to talk about the rape."

After thanking Darlene Miller for the call and assuring her that he would be in touch, Scotty checked with the San Bernardino Sheriff's Office to request a copy of the old report. It was not on file.

Smith arranged for a colleague to visit Ms. Miller and to take a detailed statement from her. It would probably be useful, eventually, in court proceedings. For now, he continued filing routine paperwork and preparing for the massive investigation he faced to gather evidence needed in forthcoming trials. There were hundreds of local witnesses to be interviewed, and later in the year, he would join Dick Hooper from Huntington Beach in a cross-country tour of Arizona, Missouri, and Kentucky.

Eight months of intensive investigation, long hours, cold meals, and monotonous interviews flew by before Scotty Smith and Dick Hooper finally boarded a plane at Los Angeles International airport, headed for Kentucky. When they arrived, Trooper-Detective Colan Harrell of the Kentucky State Police met them, and gave them an eye-opening tour of the rural towns in McCreary and Wayne Counties. Some of the characters they saw reminded them of hillbillies from the motion picture *Deliverance*.

In his slow drawl, Detective Harrell described the lifestyle of some of the local residents, admitting that it wasn't uncommon for them to solve disputes with guns. He pointed out the exact spot where the body of Greg "Wildman" Hill had been discovered over one year ago. Then he accompanied them to the residence of Wayne Lyons, known locally as Automatic.

Lyons wasn't enthusiastic about answering these Yankees' questions, but at least a local lawman was with them. Yeah, he had known Greg Marlow for near-on-to fourteen years. Last time he saw him was the previous autumn. There was a girl named Cynful with him.

"Did Marlow ever shoot you?" Scotty asked.

"Yeah, 'bout a year ago last August," Lyons replied in a nasal twang. "But it was an accident." The .22 caliber revolver had fired when Marlow had tried to cock it while riding in the rear of Automatic's van, and the bullet went right through the backrest of the driver's seat, "right into my butt."

"We was gonna rob a marijuana dealer, but when I was wounded, that ruined our plans."

"How did Marlow behave during the time he was here?"

"He was his usual wild and crazy self and had a quick temper." Lyons described how he had helped Marlow locate and purchase a motorcycle. He had seen both Marlow and Coffman pull "big wads" of cash from their socks to pay for it. Marlow painted the bike red because "it took blood to pay for it." Lyons wasn't positive what Greg meant by that until they were planning to rob the drug dealer.

"I didn't want to kill anybody," Lyons told the detectives. But Marlow had said, "It's no problem. I've killed people before."

Coffman, Lyons said, interrupted and said, "I shot him," or "I finished him." Then she made a statement to the effect, "You killed the last one, let me kill this one." Lyons glanced into the faces of the detectives, and added, "Cynful sure seemed excited when she said that."

Dick Hooper conducted the next interview, standing outside the mobile home of Marlow's uncle Justus Walls, the brother of Greg's dead mother. Walls told Hooper that he had helped raise Marlow. Greg's mother, he said, died in a trailer fire.

Following a few more innocuous statements, Hooper's relaxed way of convincing people to open up, and speak candidly, worked with Walls. He stated, matter-of-factly, that Coral, Greg's half sister, had bragged to several relatives that she had been responsible for the death of her mother, because Doris had stolen her boyfriend. Justus couldn't remember the names of the relatives who had told him the astonishing story.

He could remember the names of Marlow's local buddies, though. They were Shannon Compton, who was known as Killer, and Donald Lyons, nicknamed Lardo. He also recalled Marlow's girlfriend, Cynful, who was "a small woman with a close-shaved head."

"Where can I find Killer?" Hooper asked.

"Down at the cemetery, I guess," Justus grinned. "His girlfriend's father killed him with a shotgun!" Hooper knew that Killer had allegedly arranged for Marlow to kill Wildman Hill. Now, there would never be a way to confirm that.

"How about Marlow's ex-wife Jennifer?"

"She lives over in another town," Walls said. He volunteered that Greg had only married her so that her father would bail him out of jail.

Justus Walls talked on for several minutes about Marlow and Cynful during their stay in Kentucky. "Greg was mad at Lardo. Said that he was gonna kill him, 'cause Lardo had paid him only five thousand dollars instead of the ten thousand dollars that Greg should have received. Don't know what the money was for."

One of Justus's sons joined the conversation and told of fights that Marlow had been in with some of the local boys. "Greg shot one of them, a guy named Tom," the son commented. "But it didn't kill him."

Dick Hooper thanked the two men, and listened as they expressed dismay over Marlow being arrested for multiple murder in California.

It was Scotty Smith's turn to ask questions again when the detectives found Killer's ex-girlfriend, while Dick Hooper listened. She remembered Marlow and Coffman, whom she knew only as Cynful, from the time they stayed in Killer's trailer a few days in the summer of 1986. The woman had once been married to a friend of Marlow's named Tom. Yes, Marlow had shot her ex-husband one time. He had been pointing the .44 caliber handgun at Tom's chest, and he had tried to slap it away. It fired, and struck Tom in his left arm. No police report had ever been made. She hadn't seen any incidents of Marlow abusing Cynful or anyone else. She had seen them smoke marijuana, however.

On the same afternoon, Tom personally confirmed the incident about being shot by Marlow. Greg "was continuously pushing people around and ordering them what to do," which was the cause of the argument when Greg drew the gun. Tom had been hospitalized with the wound.

Hooper reached Marlow's onetime mother-in-law by telephone, and heard the woman's plea to not disrupt the new life Jennifer had made for herself. After the divorce, Jennifer had straightened out all of her problems, and just wanted to forget the horrible marriage with Marlow. Their son didn't even know that his father was facing serial-murder charges. Hooper told the frantic woman that he certainly wouldn't jeopardize Jennifer's privacy, but really did need to talk to her. The woman agreed to meet with the detectives before she would consider revealing her daughter's whereabouts. After their meeting, she agreed.

Jennifer met with Hooper and Harrell during lunch break at her workplace. She painted a word picture for them of a marriage made in hell, that began ten years earlier when Marlow was released from jail.

"Why was he in jail?" Hooper asked.

"For possession of stolen property," said Jennifer. "Greg and some of his friends broke into a senator's house down in Scott County, Tennessee. He bragged to me how he used a screwdriver to take the hinges off of a big gun case in the house, and that he stole the guns and a bunch of silverware. He was real surprised that he went to jail only for possession, and not for the crime itself."

After she gave them a chronology of the relationship, Hooper wanted to know if the injuries Marlow had inflicted on her had been serious. She pulled her blouse down to bare the front of her right shoulder, exposing a vivid six-inch scar, then held up her right forearm to show Hooper another six-inch scar that was three-quarters-of-an-inch wide. The puncture from scissors had also left a scar three-inches above her right knee.

"I had some X-rays of my face not long ago," she added. "They showed that he also broke my nose."

Her shoulder wound, Jennifer said, had been inflicted once when Marlow was in a jealous rage. He had arrived home and ordered her to go upstairs and prepare to give him a bath, and had followed her. Inside the bathroom, he started to beat her with his fists because he thought she had been flirting with a man. "The only reason he stopped is because (Lardo) Lyons came in and took the knife away from Greg."

"Could Lardo Lyons testify to the assault?" Hooper inquired.

"No, he's dead," she solemnly announced. Lardo and Killer were both dead. Being involved in Marlow's circle was definitely hazardous to the health, it appeared.

Jennifer allowed Hooper to photograph her scars, and she pleaded once more for the preservation of her anonymity. Hooper pledged that he would not divulge anything to compromise it.

Nine months after the tour of rural Kentucky, Hooper and Smith found themselves again suffering jet lag and July heat in St. Louis, Missouri. In a suburb, they first visited Cynthia Coffman's former mother-in-law, who now had custody of the eight-year-old child. She filled in a few details about Cynthia's background and the problems she had caused, but expressed a reluctance to say much more. She had already given an investigator from Cyndi's defense team a full statement. Perhaps her husband could answer the detectives' questions. She directed Hooper and Smith to his workplace.

Hooper and Smith made an appointment to visit the husband on the following morning. Before going to dinner, Hooper telephoned Cynthia's mother and explained that he would like to meet with her for an interview. Sally's voice was tight with stress as she told Hooper that her daughter's attorneys had instructed her not to talk with anyone about the case.

"I'm just interested in getting a statement about Cyndi's childhood," the detective explained.

"I think that all you want to do is hurt Cyndi," Sally contended.

"All I want is the truth," Hooper said.

"Well, I'll try to telephone her attorney this evening, and maybe we can talk tomorrow."

Hooper agreed to call the next morning and hung up. He and Scotty trudged off for a coffee-shop dinner and a good night's rest.

Cynthia Coffman was a very poor mother, was "loose," and used drugs during the time he knew her, Cyndi's ex-father-in-law told the two detectives on the morning of July 12, 1988. She was kicked out of her house because she was "uncontrollable" and had a "bad mouth." When Cynthia left for

Arizona, he said, she came by, dropped off his grandson, and left the area, which wasn't uncommon because she didn't care for her son. He recalled the day in August, four years earlier, when she showed up with a man who "tried to intimidate me."

The detectives were unable to reach Cyndi's parents that day, so they tracked down some of her old friends who had lived at the drug-infested "Whitehouse," which had been demolished. From them, Hooper collected descriptions of Cyndi that included such words as "fun-loving person," "partyer," and "dominant personality." One female pal, Hooper heard, had the common sense, but Cyndi was "the planner."

Sitting at a booth in the restaurant where Ron Coffman worked, Scotty Smith heard Cyndi's ex-husband describe how he had met and married her. He had sought the divorce, he said, "because she was sleeping with various other men in the area." She was also a "casual" user of narcotics, and didn't keep house very well. Smith asked if she had ever been involved in robberies or crimes. "She would rob people for their dope and became bolder in doing this just before she left for Arizona," Smith wrote while Coffman talked. ". . . She would go to various bars and pick up guys and take them to motel rooms . . . and steal from these individuals. She was not committing acts of prostitution, just stealing from them."

"Tell me about her personality," Smith requested.

"Very assertive," Coffman said. "She would take control of situations and she usually got what she wanted." Her major flaw was being "devious." Whether these were the comments of retribution by an angry ex-husband or the truth, someone else would have to decide. Scotty just recorded what he heard.

At a fire department station, Smith found Cyndi's former boyfriend, John Lorentz. The firefighter seemed embarrassed about his association with Cyndi and acknowledged that it was purely a sexual relationship. He described her as very "loose" and commented that they never went out to dinner or did anything else other than go to bed. She was "levelheaded," had "common sense," and "never lost her temper." It was "common knowledge," he said, that she used narcotics.

Hooper still hadn't reached Cyndi's mother by telephone again, so he and Scott visited her stepfather at his place of business on the following morning. He gave them a courteous, conservative, uncritical chronology of Cyndi's childhood and marriage, describing her as having "above average intelligence" and as being "responsible." He illustrated this by pointing out how she had acted as a big sister to her siblings.

* * *

For the third consecutive morning Hooper tried to telephone Cyndi's mother. A female voice answered, sounding like a teenager, and told Hooper that there was no one at that location by the name he requested. Maybe he had dialed incorrectly, so he tried again, punching the keypad with meticulous care. The same voice spoke again, saying that Cynthia Coffman's family did not live at that location. Patiently, Hooper asked an operator to dial the number. It was busy.

Forty minutes later, he tried again, and was sure that he recognized Sally's voice this time. The woman refused to identify herself, and denied that any relatives of Cynthia Coffman lived there.

That afternoon, Dick Hooper and Scotty Smith returned to California to give the results of their investigation to the man who would prosecute Coffman and Marlow, Deputy District Attorney Raymond Haight III.

Raymond Haight III, known affectionately among his colleagues and friends as "Chip," had previously sent two murderers to California's Death Row and had successfully prosecuted a third, who was sentenced to serve life imprisonment. Thirty-eight years old, Haight wore his thick, curly, light-brown hair in a tousled style that covered both ears and tumbled over one side of his forehead. Horn-rimmed glasses magnified the intense blue eyes that sparkled in accompaniment to his high-pitched laugh. A bushy mustache seemed to tickle the corners of his mouth.

Chip's wife, Betty, occupied the adjoining office in the District Attorney's building, one block from the county courthouse in San Bernardino. They had met on the job, fallen in love, and were married in September 1985. As second in command to the D.A., she managed case workloads, personnel, and public relations, while Chip worked the courtrooms.

After joining the D.A.'s office in 1978, Chip had quickly established a reputation as a tough and serious courtroom tactician, even though he still maintained a fine sense of humor. Discussing the prosecutor's job, he told a reporter that "We're stuck in between people who have conflicting goals. Victims want vengeance, cops think we're not filing enough cases, and judges think we're filing too many."

Haight's approach to trial work was exceptionally well organized, reflecting his knowledge of military campaigns he studied in his spare time. "But you have to have some light moments," he explained, accounting for his tendency to inject offbeat comments into the dry legalese or to use quotes from Charlie Chan mysteries or *Alice in Wonderland*, while talking to juries.

Preliminary hearings held for James Gregory Marlow and Cynthia Lynn Coffman in 1987 were conducted to determine if there was enough evidence to try the pair for the murder of Corinna

Novis in San Bernardino County. (Lynel Murray's death had occurred in Orange County, where the D.A. would wait for the outcome of the San Bernardino trial to decide whether a second murder trial would be necessary.) Haight successfully hurdled a battery of complex legal motions and judgments before he heard a judge order James Gregory Marlow and Cynthia Lynn Coffman to stand trial for first degree murder, with special circumstances. California law requires proof of certain "special circumstances" before the death penalty can be recommended by a jury. Marlow and Coffman faced four of them, including charges of robbery, kidnapping, burglary, and sodomy in the course of the murder.

Sodomy? Can a woman commit sodomy? The question was whispered in gasping disbelief by observers in the court gallery, when the accusations against Cynthia Coffman were solemnly announced. Laypersons did not realize that she could be convicted of sodomy if the evidence proved that she aided and abetted Marlow in the sexual assault of Novis, either by sharing the shower with him and the victim or by arousing him to help complete the act.

The preliminary hearing had been only the first obstacle. Now Chip Haight would face the main event, in which he would ask for the death penalty for both defendants.

Haight had already grappled with the first major problem related to the evidence he could use. Both Coffman and Marlow had made statements to Detectives Smith, Hooper, and others, virtually confessing the murders. *But nothing they had said could be introduced in court against them!* All of the incriminating tape-recorded words were useless because prior to making the admissions, both Marlow and Coffman had asked for attorneys. The detectives had plowed ahead with a barrage of questions, anyway, completely ignoring their requests. In one sense, it was a violation of Miranda rights, interpreted by the U.S. Supreme Court as Constitutional guarantees. But the officers had used the little known "rescue doctrine," meaning that they had believed there was still a chance to find Corinna Novis and save her life. The bottom-line result was that Haight could not present the admissions as evidence in court unless the defendants testified, in which case he could use their confessions to impeach them. For his case-in-chief, he would have to rely on physical evidence and statements by other witnesses.

There was no question in Haight's mind that both Coffman and Marlow were equally culpable. Coffman's defense team would no doubt use the "battered woman syndrome" defense, claiming that she was the unwilling puppet of Marlow, who beat her and threatened the life of her son to force Coffman into helping him kill Corinna Novis and Lynel Murray. But Chip Haight firmly believed that Coffman was strong-willed, excited by the sexual aspects of her relationship with Marlow, and voluntarily consented to help in the sexual attack and the murder of Novis.

To explain his view, Haight pointed out that there was a "synergistic" effect when Coffman teamed with Marlow. She had certainly never murdered before, and Haight didn't believe that Marlow's boast of having "offed" someone in prison was true, either. But when they came together, it was like two harmless chemicals combining to become caustic, then explosive. The makeup of each of their personalities mixed and fused into an amalgamation of escalating violence, until it culminated in rape and murder.

Haight would have no qualms about asking for the death penalty for both Cynthia Coffman and James Gregory Marlow, *if* he could persuade a jury to convict them.

After months of scrutinizing the whole body of evidence against Marlow and Coffman, Haight still had some questions. He was particularly interested in the personality of Cynthia Coffman. Could he find enough evidence to neutralize the battered woman syndrome defense? Haight wanted to hear the opinions of people who knew her. Dick Hooper and Scotty Smith, along with the teams of detectives they supervised, had exceeded all expectations in building a case against the suspects, and would continue to dig for any new evidence. Now, Haight would add the skills of D.A. investigator Barry Bruins to help fill any gaps in the monumental case he was constructing, block by block, piece by piece.

The trial was scheduled to begin finally on the last day of October 1988, almost two years after the sadistic murders.

On August 2, 1988, Det. Scotty Smith, accompanied by Det. Russ Dalzell, paid a visit to the Arizona State Prison at Winslow, as requested by Chip Haight. They asked to see inmate Sam Keam, who was a temporary guest of the state. The two lawmen heard Sam's account of Cynthia Coffman's trying to run over him with her Trans-Am in Page after a quarrel one night.

"Would you describe Cynthia Coffman to me in more detail?" Smith asked.

Keam thoughtfully rubbed his chin. "Well, she's got average intelligence level and she's very independent. She does just about what she wants to do."

"Did she use narcotics?"

"Yeah, she used pot and 'go' (methamphetamine). She really wasn't strung out on the stuff. She'd get kinda wired, but it didn't make her act aggressive."

"Do you think anyone could dominate Cyndi?"

"No, I don't. I don't think anybody could make her do anything she didn't want to do."

The view from atop Manson Mesa in Page, Arizona, one day later, August 3, impressed Smith and Dalzell, but they didn't have much time to stop and admire it. Several citizens of Page were on the list of interviews they planned to conduct over the next couple of days.

First, the parents of Sam Keam told the detectives that they thought Cynthia Coffman was "a manipulator" who was a "very good talker, sneaky, and would tell you things you wanted to hear." They were sure that Coffman had told Marlow about the safe in their house and that the two of them had stolen it.

Another friend of Coffman's, known as "Boomer," said that she was "flighty and high-strung." Marlow, he disclosed, was "acting weird" when Boomer met him one night in Big Water, Utah, at the time Cyndi's head was shaved.

"What was your impression of the relationship?" asked Smith.

"Cyndi did all the talking. I think she ran the show," Boomer answered, and indicated that Coffman was the dominant personality between the two. From his brief observation, it was Cyndi who decided where they would go and what they would do. He had one more comment about Coffman. Boomer understood that Cyndi had worked as a prostitute for a guy named "Curly" while she was in Page, but, he added, this was only a rumor and he could not provide any additional information about it.

Coffman's onetime roommate in Page, Judy, told the interviewers that Cyndi had used drugs moderately and got along well with people. Judy had also heard rumors about Cyndi acting as a prostitute, but had no definite facts on the matter.

One of Coffman's fellow employees at the country club described her as "hot-tempered with a short fuse," and "would yell at patrons who appeared to be bothered about something."

Another female friend of Coffman's recalled that she and Cyndi had nearly fought over some money one time.

The final interview in Page was with another former roommate, Sherry, who told Smith and Dalzell that Coffman was an intelligent, independent person who could make her own decisions. She felt that Cyndi was a dominant person who controlled Sam Keam and always won their arguments, was devious, and had ways of getting what she wanted.

Sherry said that when Cyndi had passed through Big Water with Marlow at the end of summer in 1986, she had short hair and acted very subdued. Marlow was a strange-acting guy with shifty eyes. They stayed the night with Sherry in Big Water, and when they left, they gave her a silver dollar. Sherry believed that it was one of the dollars taken from the safe stolen from Sam Keam's parents. Her parting comment was, "I know Cyndi, and I think she knew exactly what she was doing."

Twenty-one

On October 31, 1988, the San Bernardino County trial opened on the third floor of the massive sixty-two-year-old white county courthouse. A few of the employees who peeked into Judge Don Turner's courtroom wore Halloween costumes. The jury filed into the box and took their seats, the women sporting carefully styled hair, more makeup than usual, their best perfume, and new dresses. The men, to lesser degree, were also clothed for the occasion.

Cynthia Coffman sat at a long table, eyes down, flanked by defense attorneys Donald Jordan, Jr., and Alan Spears. Greg Marlow occupied a chair at the north end of the same table, with defenders Ray L. Craig and co-defender Cheryl Andre crowded toward the corner.

In the front row of the gallery sat Bill and Donna Novis, looking drawn, pale, and tense. Their pickup truck, with a camper mounted in the bed, was parked outside. They planned to attend the entire trial, no matter how long it took, while living in the truck at a KOA campground on the outskirts of town.

Judge Turner cleared his throat, faced the jury, and spoke, "When we start a trial like this, ladies and gentlemen, one of the first things that happens normally is that the attorneys get a chance to make, if they wish, an opening statement."

Trying to reduce the process to simplest of terms, Judge Turner explained that the statements by the attorneys are not evidence nor are they necessarily the truth, they are summaries of the evidence the lawyers expect to produce during the trial. "You are the ones that have to actually determine what the facts are," he told them.

Following more explanatory comments, the judge scanned each member of the jury, as if his intense gaze could assure that they understood, then turned toward a nattily dressed man who held a sheaf of legal-sized lined paper, and said, "Mr. Haight."

It was an invitation for Deputy District Attorney Chip Haight to make his introductory comments to the jury.

"Thank you, Your Honor," he responded with a nod, then a quick scan of the attentive jurors. "Corinna Novis was an attractive twenty-year-old young woman.

"Corinna, in May of 1986, moved to California from a small Idaho town where she was raised. She moved to Redlands for a couple of reasons. First she wanted to pursue some career opportunities that weren't available in Idaho . . ."

"Objection," Don Jordan, Coffman's lead defense attorney, interrupted. "That (Novis's job pursuits) is not relevant, and I object to it." He was joined by Ray L. Craig, the burly, fifty-one-year-old lead defender for Greg Marlow. The first objection, in a trial that would be marred by hundreds more, had been voiced.

After hearing brief explanations by the defense counsels, Judge Turner sustained the objection.

Haight started again, laying out before the jury how the innocent victim had settled in Redlands, worked two jobs, and coached cheerleaders at Redlands University, utilizing her experiences in Idaho. She had led an exemplary, wholesome life before she disappeared on November 7, 1986, from the Redlands shopping mall.

His voice growing thick with tension, Haight described how he would present evidence and testimony to reveal how Corinna had been abducted, raped, sodomized, murdered, and left facedown in a shallow grave in a deserted vineyard. Two of the jury members visibly winced when Haight revealed some of the details about the method of Corinna's death and the condition of her mouth when her body was discovered in the lonely vineyard. He told the jury that they would hear how Marlow and Coffman were identified as suspects, then pursued, and arrested.

"I'm going . . . to talk about a couple of the witnesses," Haight confided to the jury. "Richard Drinkhouse and Coral Willoughby. You're going to discover pretty early that they were both charged in connection with this case. Coral is the half sister of Mr. Marlow. She was convicted of some charges, went to state prison, and is on parole. Richard Drink-house pled guilty and was in jail four months. You are not going to like either one of them. You are going to find Mr. Drinkhouse's action, or inaction, inexplicable. These witnesses are important to you because they give insights into the case that you normally would not get in a criminal case."

Haight led the jury through an outlined chronology of the events leading to Novis's death, then turned to the subject of the battered woman.

"You'll hear evidence that will suggest that Mr. Marlow was on occasion abusive, physically abusive, toward Miss Coffman," he acknowledged. "I want to put the focus on what the defendants did to Corinna Novis, not what they did to each other," Haight quickly added. "That is why they are here. And that is where I'm going to put the focus in my case."

After admonishing the jurors not to talk about the case among themselves or with anyone else, the judge called for a short recess, after which it would be Don Jordan's turn to speak.

Donald Jordan, Jr., was convinced that his client, Cynthia Lynn Coffman, had been abused and battered by James Gregory Marlow until she was reduced to a state of helpless subservience. Jordan had a solid argument, he felt, and had exhaustively prepared the ammunition and tactics to wage war on the prosecution's case. He was going to lean very heavily on a psychological condition known as the battered woman syndrome.

At age fifty-one, Don Jordan had the inside

knowledge and experience to win. After graduating from the University of California Law School at Berkeley, and a stint in the Peace Corps in the Philippine Islands, he had landed a job as a prosecutor in the San Bernardino District Attorney's Office. His first boss there was Assistant D.A. Don Turner, before Turner had accepted an appointment to wear the robes of a Superior Court judge. That relationship, Jordan knew, would certainly not sway Turner toward any favoritism in court, but it did give the defender an insight into the thinking process and logic of the judge.

Jordan had spent two years convincing juries to send criminals to prison before he switched sides to become a defense counsel.

The big advantage for defense lawyers, Jordan knew, is called "discovery." The law stated that prosecutors must reveal, in advance of trial, specifically what evidence or testimony they have available to present in court. But defense attorneys were, at that time (California law later changed), under no such disadvantage, so the element of surprise was still available to the defense.

Quite aware of the tactics Haight could use to try to convict his client, Don Jordan was confident that the jury would accept the testimony of his chief witness. Dr. Lenore Walker was one of the leading clinical psychologists in the country and appeared regularly on the talk-show circuit as an activist for battered women. Coffman, Jordan was convinced, was a classic example of victimization by an abusive man.

"Ladies and gentlemen," Jordan began in his opening statement to the jury. "As you know, this is the opportunity that we have to lay some things before you in a brief fashion, the general evidence that we expect to present before you.

"There are many facts involved here and they cover a lengthy period of time. I've done my best to be accurate. Obviously, if some of the evidence comes in differently, go by the evidence, not by what I say.

"This very tragic tale commences on May 11, 1956, when Gregory Marlow was born. About six years later, in January 1962, Miss Coffman is born." Jordan described some circumstances of Cyndi's early life, then made a comment about Marlow. ". . . When Mr. Marlow was probably sixteen or seventeen, he went to prison. . . ."

"Objection!" bellowed Ray Craig, Marlow's defense counsel. Craig, full-faced with long sideburns and a brushy mustache, had been a judge in Oklahoma. More recently, he had served as a San Bernardino municipal court commissioner, but was now a defense attorney, who was exceptionally well-acquainted with courtroom procedure, and didn't want Jordan to comment on Marlow's past.

Judge Turner looked perplexed. He asked Don Jordan, "Counsel, I can understand your bringing in experts as to *your* client's background, but is it your intention in your case in chief to put on evidence about Mr. Marlow's background?"

"Yes, it is, Your Honor," Jordan replied, in an

early surprise move. Even novices to legal process knew that defenders for one client, in a joint trial, do not usually present evidence harmful to a co-defendant. In a conference out of the jury's hearing, Jordan explained that he intended to present anything that Coffman knew about Marlow that "would bear on her state of mind," which may have influenced her behavior.

Ray Craig pointed out that he had sought separate trials for the two defendants because he feared that they would "point a finger at one another." He clarified his position: "I assume that even one defendant saying that he or she was coerced or did the crime under duress, certainly that might be something for the jury to weigh. But this (Marlow's being in prison) is totally inadmissible . . . and ultimately prejudicial. . . . I must ask the court to grant a mistrial."

Judge Turner explained to the jury that the objection was sustained, but that Mr. Jordan was going to present a defense wherein, ". . . Coffman was coerced or under the influence of Mr. Marlow and that it was through the fear of him . . . and her belief as to his prior criminal activities . . . which influenced her decisions. Mr. Jordan may go ahead, providing that it's understood that he's not telling you what the facts are, but rather telling you what his client believed the facts were at the time." He would not grant a mistrial.

Don Jordan resumed his opening, telling the jury about Cyndi Coffman's background in St. Louis, her school years, marriage, and the child

she had lost to the custody of her ex-husband. He
told of a decent, crime-free early life, and then
described how she had met James Gregory Marlow,
had been sucked into a disastrous relationship, and
how Greg had gradually started "slapping her
around."

"You'll hear evidence . . . where somebody does
something very terrible and then the next day
apologizes, and it's never going to happen again,
but it does again and again and again."

Each time Jordan mentioned anything negative
about Greg Marlow, Ray Craig objected. The judge
finally answered by acknowledging, "You have a
standing objection, Counsel."

Jordan continued. "Marlow talked to Cyndi
about people that he had killed in prison . . ."

"Objection!" Ray Craig yelled, frowning at Coffman's attorney. "I'd like to be heard, after Mr. Jordan finishes, outside the presence of the jury."
Judge Turner agreed to that.

". . . And Miss Coffman doesn't know what to
think about these kinds of things," Jordan persist-
ed, as if confiding to the jury. "But Marlow none-
theless talked about them. Still, she didn't leave
him at that time."

Jordan hammered the point. "Marlow dwelt almost excessively on the fact that he claimed that
she had sexual hang-ups, and he explained that,
for instance, oral sex, which she had engaged in
almost never, not never, but almost never, prior to
getting together with Marlow, was a normal
thing . . . and he insisted that kind of thing occur

more and more. And as Miss Coffman got caught up more and more in this thing that was Marlow, she yielded to those demands like she did other demands, and like she would later in November to the tragedy that we're about to hear about."

Each step of the terrible downward spiral of Cyndi Coffman's life was described by Don Jordan. "In Atlanta, Georgia," Jordan said, in an accusatory tone, "he so beat up Miss Coffman and attacked her one night that he ended up brutally and forcibly sodomizing her. He assaulted her, and it was then when he shaved her head. She was bald." In Kentucky, he said, Marlow forced her to remove her bra and blouse, wrap a bandanna around her breasts, and lure a young man to his death.

As Don Jordan approached the events surrounding the murder of Corinna Novis, Judge Turner interrupted. Jordan's diatribe about his client, Cyndi Coffman, was threatening to overflow the court's workday. Turner recessed the trial until the following day.

On Tuesday morning, November 1, 1988, just six days short of the second anniversary of Corinna's death, the trial resumed, and Don Jordan continued. He described in detail how Corinna had been murdered. Then, to the discomfort of Marlow and his attorney, Jordan related the events of a second rape and murder, in Huntington Beach, allegedly committed by Greg Marlow and Cyndi Coffman. He told the jury how the couple had eventually been captured and accused.

To drive home his point that she had been dominated by Marlow, Jordan again used sexual terms to illustrate. "The evidence will show," he said, "that Marlow constantly wanted Miss Coffman to be engaged in sexual threesomes, two women and Marlow. Expert testimony will indicate that this is one of Marlow's fantasies, but Miss Coffman refused to do that even though Marlow wanted her to. Now, the evidence will also show that Miss Coffman somehow changed after meeting Marlow.

"Mr. Marlow exercised a perversion, which the expert testimony will show was an eroticized hatred of women. I guess the most dramatic example is urinating over somebody's body who you have just killed. But it was more. The shaving of Miss Coffman. The brutal sodomy that he perpetrated on her. Branding her with his tattoos of Folsom Wolf. The beatings, the rapes of her, the stabbings, the biting, the humiliation, psychological as well as physical."

When Jordan mentioned the tattoos, Cynthia Coffman squirmed in her chair. It was the first time the jury would hear of the tattoo on her left buttock, and she felt embarrassed. Everyone in the courtroom was probably visualizing her naked tattooed derriere.

Jordan at last began to wind down his impassioned speech to the jury. "Bondage was important to Marlow. As well as robbing, raping, murdering, kidnapping. And he used to say to Coffman sometimes, 'Well, you can leave anytime,' but of course, he's sleeping with a .45 pistol. The expert testimony will indicate that probably if she had said, 'Yes, I will leave,' he probably would have killed her then. Marlow's behavior also was wildly fluctuating. And so, sometimes, was Miss Coffman's. And their behavior together mirrored his behavior to her. But overall, the evidence is going to establish that there was a pattern of coercive control shown by Marlow to Coffman.

"Ladies and gentlemen, as the evidence will show, Miss Coffman's crime was weakness. And serious it was, both for herself and for the three people that are now dead. All victims of Marlow's lust."

Don Jordan looked into the eyes of each juror, then sat down.

Ray Craig, Marlow's attorney, informed the court that he would reserve his opening statement until after the prosecution had rested. Then he made another motion for a mistrial, which was promptly denied by Judge Turner.

Chip Haight squared his shoulders and prepared to present his case.

Twenty-two

The first witness to testify in the case for the prosecution was Terry Davis, the manicurist friend of Corinna Novis. She told the jury that Corinna had missed her five o'clock appointment on Friday, November 7, the night she disappeared. Among other things, prosecutor Haight wanted the jury to hear from this witness that Corinna had long, red, manicured nails and always wore earrings. Davis also described her Monday morning visit to Corinna's apartment to discover that her friend had not been home, the bedroom had been ransacked, and the victim's typewriter and telephone answering machine were missing.

In quick succession, Chip Haight called Corinna's employer, Jean Cramer, the ex-boyfriend, Mike McFadden, and two other acquaintances to the stand. They established that Corinna was reliable, punctual, owned the white Honda CRX, and certainly would not have disappeared without notifying someone.

Mike Willoughby, the brother of Coral Willoughby's husband, swaggered to the witness stand next. Slim, with a pockmarked face, mustache, and silver-rimmed glasses, Willoughby spoke with a drawl, revealing a missing upper left incisor. Waving his hands in flailing gestures, scratching his back, and arching his eyebrows, Willoughby complained of the freeloading of Marlow and Coffman during their stay at his house in the first week of November 1986.

Had Marlow and Coffman ever deviated from their usual apparel of fatigues or jeans? Yes, the witness answered, telling of the one day Cynful wore a blue dress while Marlow wore a suit with combat boots, and that they were driving a little white car. They wanted to sell him a telephone answering machine, but he had no interest in it.

On cross-examination, Coffman's attorney Don Jordan began laying some groundwork for his battered woman defense. "Did Marlow talk like a tough guy?" the attorney asked.

"Yes, he did. Male, macho, bullshit attitude. You know, like if you go to a bar, and everybody thinks they're badder than everybody else, and everybody likes to fight. Marlow was like that. There wasn't a guy out there he couldn't take. Just like Rambo." The witness also acknowledged that he had seen a wound on Cynthia Coffman's leg.

Chip Haight, on redirect, quietly asked, "Other than the leg wound, did you ever see her with other injuries; black eyes, bruises, such that she'd been beaten? . . ."

"None that I had noticed." And he had never heard her complain of being mistreated by Marlow.

Prosecutor Haight paraded eleven more witnesses to the stand to establish that Marlow had
borrowed a suit, he and Coffman had been seen
in the Redlands Mall, Corinna had been robbed,
and the loot taken from her apartment had been
sold or traded for drugs.

On Thursday morning, November 3, Chip
Haight called Coral Willoughby to the stand. She
had previously agreed to testify as part of a plea
bargain related to her own complicity in the crime,
and Haight was hoping that she would give the
right answers.

Coral looked like her half brother, Greg Marlow,
and her tough life was evident in her face and over-
weight body. A nervous frown wrinkled her forehead, and she seemed ready to break into a million
pieces if anyone even tapped her.

Responding to Haight's questions with short,
terse, snappish answers, Coral told of her brother's
arrival in Fontana, accompanied by the girl with
very short hair, in late October 1986. She had not
seen Greg for several years prior to that. After a
tempestuous stay at her brother-in-law's house, the
couple left, and Coral left with them.

Beating the defense to the punch, Haight asked
Coral if she had observed Marlow "order Miss
Coffman around like she was a slave or something
like that?"

"No," Willoughby shot back.

"Did she appear to be hypnotized or dazed?"

"Never."

"Did Miss Coffman appear alert and aware of what was going on around her?"

"She did."

Haight drew from Coral the fact that she, Marlow, and Coffman had slept on the floor of Richard Drinkhouse's apartment after leaving the Willoughby's home. Cyndi and Greg, all dressed up, went with her to the mall, where Coral worked, on November 7. Later, the couple had entered the sandwich shop and handed Coral the keys to her Buick, saying that they had a ride and wouldn't need her car.

As Haight questioned Coral, he offered to let her read the transcript of her own trial to refresh her memory regarding statements she had made. She refused, commenting, "I don't want to read it. I'm trying to forget and get on with my life."

When she had finished her work shift, Coral told the court, she dropped by her friend's house where Marlow's duffel bag was stored, picked it up, and went to the Drinkhouse apartment. A small white car was outside, and she went in where Richard Drinkhouse sat in the living room, alone, watching television. Within a few minutes, Greg came out of the bedroom.

At this point, Coral claimed that she couldn't remember any details about the meeting in the living room. Haight was forced to drag out the transcript of Coral's trial, read portions of her testimony, and ask if it refreshed her memory. No, she answered each time. Her negative responses didn't matter, because using the transcripts still allowed Haight to present the desired information to the jury. They learned that Marlow whispered to his sister, "I have someone here," then told her not to freak out.

Coral's memory continued to lose focus. Haight was forced again to rely on transcripts to build the sequence of events: Coral had left the apartment, met Greg and Cyndi later near midnight, and accompanied them on an expedition to profit from Corinna's possessions. Coral continued denying any specific recall of the events of that deadly night.

During a break in her daylong testimony, the attorneys met with the judge at side-bar, out of the presence of the jury and the witness. Don Jordan commented to the judge about Coral's faulty memory. "I'll speak for myself," he said. "I don't believe she doesn't remember."

"She has exhibited a selective loss of memory," Judge Don Turner mused.

"We concur with that judgment," said Jordan. "But the fact is, Your Honor, that Mr. Marlow has been putting out threats since his arrest. He intimidated her before." Jordan described to the judge how Marlow and his sister had been raised in an environment of crime and prostitution by their mother, and said, "Part of the evidence that we intend to bring out is that the hatred that Mr. Marlow seems to have evidenced toward women came from that." This pervasive hostility for women, Jordan suggested, included Coral. Specifically, Jordan wanted to cross-examine Coral to determine if she had been threatened by Marlow.

Judge Turner weighed the proposal, and commented that the witness, with some alleged loss of memory, had testified only to the facts surrounding the night of the crime. "She has not particularly tried to exonerate her brother or Miss Coffman," he noted, and ruled that questions regarding possible threats to Coral by Marlow would not be allowed.

On the morning of November 8, Coral's husband, William Willoughby, was sworn in. He told Haight that he hadn't lived with Coral for two years. When Marlow and Coffman interrupted his life in October 1986, the short-haired woman had been introduced to him as Cynful. He described the last day of their stay, recounting how he had grabbed a rifle from Coral and how Greg had pointed a pistol at him. Cyndi, he said, followed Greg's orders to steal handcuffs from William's truck.

Haight had heard from his investigators that Marlow and Coffman liked to shower together and have sex in the shower. He asked Willoughby, "They took showers together? Is that something they did commonly?"

"Yes, it was."

"Any particular time or after any activities?"

"No. They'd just go in the bathroom together and be in there for an hour, hour and a half."

"And you would hear the shower running and they would come out with wet hair and that sort of stuff?"

"Yes."

At another side-bar, away from the jury, the problem of a single trial for two defendants came to a head again. Don Jordan wanted to introduce some statements by William Willoughby that would show the jury how Marlow mistreated and controlled Coffman, and Jordan hoped, would mitigate her culpability. He told Judge Turner, "This witness will testify that when he came home one night, he went into the living room and saw Miss Coffman apparently unconscious as a result of the beating she had sustained and the stab wound to her leg. Willoughby asked Coral, 'What the fuck is going on?' Mrs. Willoughby indicated to him . . . information that could only have come from Marlow or Coffman . . . that Miss Coffman wanted to turn Greg in to the authorities because they ripped off and buried a dope dealer in Kentucky and Greg beat her up."

Ray Craig, representing Marlow's interests, heatedly objected. "It's totally irrelevant in Mr. Marlow's case. It's extremely prejudicial. We're going back through the same things we've been arguing about ever since this case began. Mr. Jordan has things which he considers, and which may well be relevant to Miss Coffman's defense, but the prejudicial quality far outweighs the probative value to

Mr. Marlow. Talk about the Kentucky matter is completely inadmissible, certainly at this phase. As I advised the court at the beginning of the case . . . it's going to be impossible for Marlow to get a fair hearing from an open-minded jury. I again reiterate that this case should have been severed."

Argument among the prosecutor and two defense teams continued for several minutes, weighing the admissibility of the disputed testimony. Judge Turner wrestled with the issue and finally ruled that the probative value of any evidence Willoughby might offer on the matter was outweighed by the prejudicial damage it would cause. Turner also overruled another motion by Don Jordan to sever the trial, that is try each defendant separately.

If Haight had a key witness in the first segment of the trial, it was Richard Drinkhouse. The portly, round-faced man with an olive complexion, a short, scraggly beard, droopy mustache, squinted eyes, and worried eyebrows, dropped heavily into the witness chair.

He elicited from Drinkhouse that he had known Greg Marlow and his sister since their teen years, and they had suddenly appeared with Cynful at his apartment on Thursday, November 6, 1986, wanting to spend the night. Drinkhouse mistakenly stated that the trio had arrived in a little white car on Thursday night, when they had actually been in Coral's 1976 Buick Skylark.

"Did you see Mr. Marlow or Miss Coffman during the day on Friday?"

"Yes, I did, about two o'clock. Cyndi had on a blue dress and Greg was wearing a suit." The witness also identified the brown tie that Haight held up as the one Marlow wore.

"Did you see a gun at this time?"

"Yes, Greg had it stuck down in his waistband. When he sat down, he put it in his coat pocket."

Cyndi and Greg left, Drinkhouse said, and he didn't see them again until that evening. He described how they had returned, bringing a girl with them, who wore a black-and-green top and had a jacket over her shoulders. Haight showed him a photograph of Corinna Novis, lying in a shallow, sandy grave. Drinkhouse identified her as the girl he had seen.

"Greg said they needed to use the room, and they walked past me toward the bedroom. Then he came back out. He said they needed to talk to her so they could get her Ready Teller number and rob her bank account."

"What did you do?"

"I asked him if he was crazy. Then I asked him to leave, but he said he couldn't leave."

Drinkhouse told how he tried to peek into the room by pretending to get his shoes, and that he could see Corinna only from the knees down. "After I had gotten my shoes and sat back down on the couch, Greg came back out and told me just to stay on the couch and watch TV."

While he was sitting there, he said, Coral arrived. He could hear the water running in the shower for several minutes, then Marlow emerged, wearing the slacks and a towel over his shoulder. Marlow brought a black purse with him, whispered something to Coral, sat down, and pulled some of the contents out of the bag. (Other testimony put the purse in Coffman's hands.) A few minutes later, when Cyndi came out of the bedroom, she had changed from the blue dress into jeans and a T-shirt.

"Did you notice whether Miss Coffman's hair appeared to be wet or damp?" Haight asked.

"I couldn't tell. It was so short."

Cyndi stepped outside with Coral to move Greg's duffel bag from the Skylark into the house, then the two women left for a short trip to a convenience store to buy some cigarettes and soft drinks. Richard thought he could hear mumbling in the bedroom, something that sounded like the captive girl asking to be taken home. After the two women returned, Coral left and Cyndi joined Greg and the captive in the bedroom. Moments later, the trio emerged.

"Could you tell us whether she was handcuffed at that time?"

"Yes, she was. As they walked past me, I could see she was handcuffed." There was also a strip of duct tape over her mouth, Drinkhouse added. After the trio left Drinkhouse's apartment, he went into the bathroom to look around. The interior of the tile shower was wet.

Drinkhouse freely admitted that he had not told

the police of the incident until they came around a few days later, then he told all, because he felt a "moral obligation" to do so.

On cross-examination by Marlow's attorney Ray Craig, the witness admitted that he had seen Coffman nod or gesture in his direction when he tried to sneak a peek into the bedroom, and Marlow had charged out to order him to stay put on the couch. It was an important point to the jury, possibly suggesting Coffman's voluntary participation in the crime.

Attorney Don Jordan asked, "I think you've testified that Mr. Marlow made some comments about she's (Novis) not going to the cops, you don't have to worry, she can't tell the cops anything if she's under some rocks, things of that sort?"

Drinkhouse didn't hesitate with his one word answer, loud and clear, "Yes."

Had Drinkhouse been arrested for his part in the crime? Yes, he replied, he was charged with false imprisonment, and served 118 days in jail after agreeing to testify for the prosecution in the murder case.

Redlands Police Department officers Tom Fitzmaurice, Emanuel Smith, Russ Dalzell, and Joe Bodnar, respectively, took the stand. They produced duct tape from the Drinkhouse apartment that matched pieces found in the shower and fingerprints from the apartment that matched samples from Marlow, Coffman, and Coral Willoughby.

Also, before Corinna's Honda CRX was abandoned in the mountains, Marlow had told Cyndi to wipe it down with Armor All to get rid of prints. She had complied, but not successfully. One of her prints was left on the hood.

Detective Bodnar described how he had located the camouflaged grave, before Dick Hooper dropped to his knees and hand-scooped the sand away. Bodnar also attended the postmortem examination.

"At the autopsy, did you observe whether or not the victim was missing any earrings?" Chip Haight asked.

"Yes, I did. I observed that the right ear was absent of any earrings. However, there were holes in the ear, which are for studded (earrings). There was a yellow-stoned post earring in the left ear."

For jurors, perhaps the most difficult part of a murder trial is listening to testimony from the forensic pathologist who performed the autopsy on the victim. The gruesome details of that examination plus the hideous color photos can be extremely unsettling.

Dr. Joseph Reiber took the stand at mid-morning on Monday, November 14.

"First of all," Reiber told Haight, referring to his notes and diagrams, "there was an area of injury on the left-hand side of the neck, shaped like a *V* turned on its side. On the right wrist, there are a couple of parallel marks and some bruising.

Also, there were scattered postmortem injuries on the shins and ankles . . . appeared to be scraping after death. And the right middle fingernail had been torn off."

"Did you examine the mouth area?"

"Yes, I did. There was a fair amount of dirt in the mouth. Most of it was trapped between the inside of the lips and the front teeth. There was also a smaller amount of dirt, which was deposited over the top surface of the tongue and over the hard palate or roof of the mouth."

Gallery observers deliberately avoided looking at Bill and Donna Novis, who sat motionless in the front row. No one wanted to experience vicariously the pain the brokenhearted parents must be enduring.

"Did you perform an internal examination in the neck area?"

"Yes. There were a number of areas of bleeding in the muscles of the neck. There was one fracture . . . of cartilage."

The cause of death, Reiber proclaimed, was "ligature strangulation and suffocation. Ligature strangulation basically refers to the occlusion of . . . the blood vessels, the airways, or both. That would be some sort of a rope or similar object that can be wrapped around the neck and tightened in some manner."

Haight inquired about the suffocation. "Why did you also give that as a possible cause of death?"

"Because of the findings of soil ground into the face and the presence of soil in the mouth."

Holding up the necktie that Marlow had worn to the vineyard that night, Haight asked if it could have been the ligature used as a murder weapon. Reiber agreed that it certainly could have been.

The initial examination of Corinna's body indicated that she had been sexually molested. Haight asked Dr. Reiber about that.

"Initially, with our stain technique, I came to the conclusion that there were sperm present from all three areas: mouth, vagina, and rectum. However, with other smears, which were sent to the crime lab stained by a different technique, some question arose as to whether or not sperm were present on some of the smears. So I reexamined my slides and their slides and came to a final conclusion that there were sperm present only on the rectal smears or smears from the anal cavity."

Corinna Novis had been sodomized within twenty-four to forty-eight hours before her death, the doctor concluded.

The wrist injuries, he said, were consistent with having been made by handcuffs that Chip Haight showed him.

Chip Haight wanted the jury to clearly understand how the necktie could have been used to strangle Corinna. He handed the tie to the witness and asked him to demonstrate. "Why don't you use me rather than do it on yourself," he suggested. Reiber looped the tie twice around Chip's neck and pulled lightly.

"To be really effective in strangulation," the doctor explained, "you want to put pressure at the sides of the neck where the major blood vessels supplying blood to the brain pass." It was probable, he said, that the killer was behind the victim.

Haight was gradually building up to a critical point. With the tie still looped around his neck, he looked toward the jury, and spoke to Dr. Reiber, "Assume that at the time she was being strangled, her face was being pushed into the soil with some force. Perhaps a hand on the back of her head was pushing her face into the sand. Would that account for the soil in the back of the mouth and the ground-in dirt in her face?"

Reiber answered in the affirmative. "The dirt over the tongue and roof of her mouth indicated that the victim would have been facedown in dirt while she was still alive, making some sort of gagging or swallowing movements. . . ."

Asking the doctor to continue demonstrating, pulling on both ends of the necktie with each hand, Haight asked, "So, does it take another hand or something pressing the back of the head down into the ground to account for the dirt in her mouth and face?"

"Under this hypothetical, yes, it would."

Haight carefully articulated each word. "So, it would take three hands to account for the injuries under this hypothetical?"

The word picture he created hung in the air of the still courtroom. It wasn't difficult to imagine one of the two killers strangling the helpless girl with the necktie, while the other one mercilessly pushed her face into the soft, sandy soil until she stopped struggling, breathing, and living.

A series of criminalists, bank employees, pawn-brokers, and law officers testified all day on November 15. While they answered questions, Greg Marlow sat quietly, chewing on mints, and Cynthia Coffman looked steadily at the tabletop. Her image was one of prim vulnerability. On the following morning, an assistant manager of a Taco Bell in Laguna Beach told of behavior by Coffman quite contrary to that image.

Haight asked the nervous woman, "Do you remember an occasion in early November where soon after you closed (near midnight), a woman came up to the restaurant and demanded to get in?"

"Yes. She started to shake the doors. I said, 'Sorry, ma'am, we close.' So she tell me, 'Fuck off' or 'Fuck it,' or something like that. I say I gonna call the cops and then she run away."

"Can you tell us what she looked like?"

"She was very skinny and short hair. This was what I remember." The witness identified an arrest photo of Cynthia Coffman. She did not see Marlow that night.

The manager of the restaurant told how, on the following day, he had accepted a wallet containing identification documents for Cynthia Coffman, James Gregory Marlow, and Corinna Novis, found in the Dumpster of the adjacent Kentucky Fried Chicken store.

For the remainder of the day, Chip Haight created a chronology, through the voices of police officers, experts, and civilian witnesses, detailing the flight and arrest of Coffman and Marlow in the Big Bear area. He especially wanted the jury to pay attention to the Dial-a-Ride driver who had heard Coffman ordering Marlow to pay his own fare.

Detective Scotty Smith testified for a short time on Thursday, November 17. When he stepped down, Chip Haight announced, "That's my last witness, Your Honor. The people rest."

Judge Turner informed the jury that they would be excused for eleven days, explaining that the court had some details to work out. He wished them a happy Thanksgiving, advised them not to eat too much turkey, and asked them to return on Monday, November 28, when the defense teams would begin presenting their evidence.

Twenty-three

One of the details the attorneys needed to work out, before the defense began calling witnesses, was the issue of sodomy as related to Cynthia Coffman. Her attorney Don Jordan appealed to Judge Turner. "Now, with respect to sodomy," Jordan started, clearing his throat twice, "obviously Miss Coffman is a female. The sole evidence insofar as sodomy is concerned—must be—just in the very nature of things—I guess it may seem silly, but I do ask the court to take judicial notice of the fact that Miss Coffman cannot, personally, commit sodomy, being a female. I don't have to prove that, obviously, do I?"

Judge Turner was calm in his reply. "She cannot physically perform the act, that's true. That's not saying that she can't commit the crime of sodomy, but that is saying that she cannot perform the act of sodomy."

Jordan expressed the opinion that there wasn't enough evidence that the killing was related in any way to the sodomy, and wanted that special circumstance dropped from the list of charges against his client.

Haight also had an opinion. "Well, Mr. Jordan ignores the last part of the special circumstance allegation, which reads that the killing of the victim occurred while the defendants were engaged in the crime of sodomy by use of force. I think there's ample evidence that the killing probably occurred after the sodomy, but they were certainly in the flight stage at that time. Obviously, she's an aider and abettor in the sodomy. She's assisting, at the very least, in restraining the victim during the period when the sodomy probably occurred in the shower at the Drinkhouse residence."

The thorny issue along with the other special circumstances were just a few of the multitude of controversial problems that Judge Don Turner would try to balance between the triangle of the prosecution and the two defense teams. It was no easy task and was fraught with opportunity for judicial error that could cause the ultimate outcome of the trial to be overturned by appeals courts.

On Monday morning, November 28, before the jury was brought in, Judge Turner announced his decision to the attorneys regarding motion to dismiss the special circumstance of sodomy. "The evidence before the jury would indicate that this young woman was kidnapped for the purpose of obtaining her property and playing with her sexually.

"The evidence is clear that Mr. Marlow enjoyed lengthy showers with persons of the opposite sex, and that he took this woman into the shower shortly before she was killed . . . then the defendants killed her in order to prevent her identification of them. The motion is denied."

Haight had taken three weeks to present the state's case against Marlow and Coffman, during which he had called fifty-seven witnesses. It was now the defense's turn. Ray Craig stood to deliver the opening statement he had deferred at the beginning of the trial.

"First of all," he announced, after some preliminary comments, "I expect to show that no act of sodomy occurred. I expect the evidence to show that Mr. Marlow is not guilty of the crime of sodomy; that the special allegation is simply not true.

"Further, I expect the evidence to show that the allegation that the homicide was committed during the course of the burglary is not true. The evidence will show the burglary was much later, was an afterthought and not connected to the homicide."

Craig's strategy was apparent. He was not going to deny that Marlow was culpable for the death of Corinna Novis, but he planned to attack the special circumstances that could send his client to the gas chamber or keep him in prison without the possibility of parole.

"The evidence, I believe, is going to show what culpability there is for the offenses that may be proven, are shared equally by both defendants. One (is as) guilty as the other."

Whispers buzzed through the gallery. The finger-pointing by the two defenses was escalating.

After asking the jury to keep an open mind about penalty or punishment, Craig pointed out that Coffman's attorney planned to reveal Marlow's alleged physical domination of Cyndi. "We expect," he said, "that there will be evidence introduced to show that Miss Coffman was, indeed, quite capable of dominating Mr. Marlow. Evidence will be brought forth in the remainder of this case that far from being a prisoner, Miss Coffman had numerous opportunities to leave Mr. Marlow if she had any intention or desire to do so.

"It is anticipated that Miss Coffman's attorney will try to show you that she wouldn't be here but for Mr. Marlow. I think the evidence is going to show, by the end of the trial, that Mr. Marlow, likewise, would not be here but for Miss Coffman."

Ray Craig beseeched the jury again not to consider the issue of penalty or punishment yet and to keep an open mind until they'd heard all of the evidence. He thanked them, and sat down.

The delayed opening statement by Craig seemed to indicate that he would have a long list of witnesses to call over a long period of time. As it turned out, his defense case-in-chief would be astonishingly short. He called only one witness.

* * *

Dr. Robert Bucklin, who had started practicing forensic pathology with the Army in Europe during World War II, and who had conducted over twenty thousand autopsies, took the stand. He told the jury that he had examined the documents related to the autopsy of Corinna Novis. He had not actually seen the body or the slides containing samples of sperm found in her.

"There was evidence of sperm from the slide identified as coming from the rectum," Craig stated more than asked. "Do you have a comment on that, sir?"

"It's rather surprising to me," Dr. Bucklin snorted, "that a pathologist of the skills of Dr. Reiber would have identified sperm which were not there! What the doctor saw were epithelial cells or some kind of debris." Epithelial refers to secretions from the lining of a body cavity. Bucklin acknowledged that a second pathologist said that he had seen sperm heads on the rectal smears, in moderate numbers. Then he added, "Just because sperm are found in the rectum does not by itself mean there had been anal intercourse. If there is no sign of damage about the anus in a person who is suspected of being sodomized, it would be very unlikely that any sperm would reach the content of the rectum by penetration of a penis."

"If there had been forcible penetration," the attorney asked, "would there be injury to the surrounding tissues?"

"You would see minute tears, separation of skin

layers, at the point of the anus." There would be contusions, too, he remarked.

Following the addition of more details about his hypothesis, Dr. Bucklin also cast some possible doubt on the opinion that Corinna had died from suffocation as well as strangulation. "The only case (supporting) suffocation was some sandy material between the lips and teeth, and some sand on the face."

Ray Craig thanked Dr. Bucklin, and turned him over to Haight for cross-examination.

It took Haight only a short time to establish that Bucklin was "speculating on Dr. Reiber's speculation" about the suffocation, and that it was certainly a possibility that the dirt got in her mouth from inhalation while she was being killed.

Tackling the issue of sperm in the rectum, Haight wanted to neutralize Dr. Bucklin's opinion that there would have been injury if there had been forcible sodomy.

"Were you given any information about the circumstances under which this sodomy, or alleged sodomy, occurred?"

"No."

"No one told you that the victim was in a shower?"

"No."

"That there were lubricants available?"

"I hadn't heard that, no."

"Would that change your testimony? Let's say that somebody is consenting in the sense that their will has been overcome by a threat and in a bathroom in the shower with lubricants available, would you then expect to find signs of trauma?"

"I think less likely for trauma under those circumstances."

Haight was satisfied. After a few more questions, the witness was excused.

Ray Craig tersely announced, "We rest."

With the unexpectedly abrupt completion of Marlow's defense by Ray Craig, Coffman's attorney Don Jordan took center stage. His choice of lead-off witness delighted the gallery.

"Call Cynthia Lynn Coffman."

Looking conservative, pale, proper, and demure in a fresh skirt and a crisp blouse, Coffman eased into the witness chair and leaned toward the little microphone.

"When did you first meet Gregory Marlow?" Jordan asked.

"April 11, 1986." Her voice was soft and timid, making the attentive observers in the back row lean forward to hear. She began most answers with, "Umm . . ." and arched her eyebrows ingenuously.

"Now, Miss Coffman, about three months after that, did you participate to some degree with Mr. Marlow in the killing of a man in Kentucky?"

"Yes," came the unhesitant reply. Ray Craig's objection was overruled.

"And four months to the day after that, did you participate to some degree with Mr. Marlow in the killing of Corinna Novis?"

"Yes."

"And five days after that, did you participate in some degree with Mr. Marlow in the killing of a Lynel Murray in Orange County?"

"Yes, sir."

"Did you at any time discuss with Mr. Marlow the possibility or did he mention to you the possibility of killing still another person?"

"Yes."

"Would you tell the jury very briefly what that was about?"

"He had told me that he had a job in Phoenix, Arizona, to kill a pregnant woman." Cyndi's voice was barely above a whisper.

Once again, Ray Craig stated his continuing objection, and was acknowledged, but overruled, by Judge Turner.

For the next few hours, Cynthia's lawyer took her through a depiction of her childhood, teen years, school, pregnancy, marriage, and departure from St. Louis. Turner asked her about her stay in Page, Arizona, the move to Barstow, about meeting Marlow after her brief incarceration in jail, and how their relationship developed. She was allowed to go into considerable detail about the beatings and abuse from Marlow.

After they had stolen the pickup truck to leave Newberry Springs, Coffman said, they stopped near Lake Mead where Marlow forced her to use her lipstick brush to touch up the black paint around the white letters so that traces of red wouldn't show.

"Did Mr. Marlow help?"

"No, he just told me that I was doing it wrong. He just kept telling me how stupid I am, I couldn't do anything right."

The jury heard about the pot hunts and beatings in Kentucky and how Marlow would turn into Wolf. Coffman wound up the afternoon's testimony by describing the murder of Wildman Hill in the backwoods of Whitley County, Kentucky.

Before Cynthia Coffman resumed her testimony on Tuesday, November 29, Judge Turner advised the jury that she was allowed to answer questions about the events in which she had participated or observed, even about two other murders that were not actually part of this trial. But, he cautioned, her testimony is only to show her "frame of mind . . . to tell you the things she had seen or heard and believed to be true which influenced her thinking," and was not to be considered as evidence of the guilt of Mr. Marlow in this case.

Step by step, Don Jordan elicited from Cynthia the events in Kentucky and the trip to Atlanta. She described in detail how Marlow had cut off all her hair and thrown her out of the motel room naked, and sodomized her. More beatings occurred, she said, as they returned to the West with stops along the way to freeload on friends and to steal a safe from the parents of Sam Keam. Members of the jury squirmed along with spectators when Coffman described how Marlow had tattooed *Property of Folsom Wolf* on her left buttock.

Asked why she didn't just leave Marlow because of the beatings and abuse, Coffman's voice broke as she replied that if she deserted him, he would get revenge. "If he couldn't find me, and kill me, he would kill my son and family." He had possession of her address book, she told the jurors.

The days in California, before the murder of Corinna Novis, were described in detail by Cynthia, including how Greg stabbed her in the leg and taunted her by saying he had given her cyanide.

Dead quiet filled the courtroom when Coffman began describing the kidnapping of Corinna Novis. There were no whispers, grunts, coughs, or squeaking chairs, and all eyes were focused on the woman who answered her lawyer's short, simple questions. Each listener vicariously traveled in the little Honda with Corinna and her captors, and entered the dank apartment, saw the terrified victim being led into the bedroom, where she was forced to strip and get in the mildewed shower with Marlow. Each observer wondered if Coffman was lying when she denied being in the shower while Corinna was being molested.

When Jordan asked if she could see what was going on, Coffman replied, "Yes. He took off his clothes and was standing in the doorway and he climbed in with the shower on, and I knew what was going to happen, so I just turned around and walked away."

"What did you think was going to happen?"

"I thought he was going to rape her."

"Did you have anything to do with whatever happened in the shower?"

"No, I didn't want to watch because it brought back memories when we were in Atlanta. I didn't want to be anywhere near it."

Twelve jurors and three alternates, some taking notes, others staring intently at Coffman, listened carefully to her account of the drive to the vineyard, of leaving Marlow alone with Corinna, then returning and hearing the sounds of dirt being shoveled in the dark.

The tension in the courtroom eased as Cynthia took her audience through the burglary of Corinna's apartment and the attempts to clean out the victim's bank account. Coffman described getting a few hours of sleep at the Drinkhouse apartment, then pawning the typewriter for enough money to buy some speed, and the idyllic afternoon she and Greg spent in the wilds of Lytle Creek, using the drugs. During this narrative she cleared up one mystery on the minds of the jurors.

In the photographs of Corinna in the shallow grave, the victim wore no shoes, but so far there had been no explanation for that. Don Jordan asked Coffman, "Up to this point, had you asked Greg what had happened to Corinna Novis?"

"I didn't want to know. I didn't ask him," she replied, eyes downcast.

"Did you have an opinion as to what probably had happened?"

"At that time, I thought she was tied up at the vineyard, because he had taken her shoes. And I figured she was tied up there, and that way she couldn't get away fast."

"You say he had taken her shoes. What do you mean?"

"When he came back to the car, he had her shoes in his hand." Marlow had offered them to Coffman, but the shoes were the wrong size, so they buried them at Lytle Creek.

Once again back in Fontana that evening, Coffman said, they joined Coral to swap Corinna's answering machine for more drugs. They used the speed at the Willoughbys' house, then headed for the beach cities that night.

"Why did you go to the beach area?"

"Because Greg said it would be easier to get money down there, because all rich people live down at the beach."

Through the afternoon, no one left the courtroom as Coffman continued her chilling narrative of the search for another victim between Dana Point and Huntington Beach. She told of the several near misses, where lucky young women narrowly escaped the stalkers.

Coffman's attorney asked her about the stop at a Taco Bell. The earlier testimony from an employee of the restaurant was bothersome to him, and he wanted Cyndi to tell her version. Her account was quite different: "We went in, ordered food, went outside in the car, and ate it."

"Was the restaurant open or closed when you got there?"

"It was getting ready—after we had gotten our food, they were probably only open about five or ten more minutes."

"Did you witness anything like what was described about a person getting mad and trying to get in?"

"No, sir."

The jury would have to decide who was lying or mistaken.

That disposed of, Jordan inquired about Marlow throwing away the identification papers behind the restaurant. Coffman explained that Marlow took the cards from her, put them in a bag, and disappeared into the darkness, then came back a few minutes later. After that, she said, they drove to the hilltop, and slept in the car.

As Coffman began describing the events of the next morning, when she and Marlow parked near the Prime Cleaners where Lynel Murray worked, Judge Turner again halted the testimony to explain to the jury why Coffman would be allowed to talk about the events in Huntington Beach, even though they did not relate to the murder of Corinna Novis.

"Obviously, ladies and gentlemen, we're past the occurrences in San Bernardino County now, and we're talking about what she observed . . . in Orange County. And the purpose of this testimony is to further try to establish what she claims was the relationship she had with Mr. Marlow and his domination over her. It has no other relevance in this trial. It's not offered and is not admissible as proof against Mr. Marlow about anything and must not be accepted by you as true or as having anything to do with Mr. Marlow's guilt or innocence. . . ."

Don Jordan's questions continued, and Coffman described how they had abducted Lynel Murray from the cleaners, taken her to the Huntington Inn, and how Marlow had been outraged about her use of Murray's credit card to check in. He became Wolf, she said, then he settled down and sent her to find a bank where Murray's money could be withdrawn and to buy some food.

At that point, Judge Turner recessed until 9:30 the next morning, leaving a breathless gallery in a real-life cliffhanger.

Reporters and court watchers jammed the hall on Wednesday morning, November 30, and quickly filled the vacant chairs left after the victim's families had been seated. Don Jordan, anticipating cross-examination by the prosecutor, took Cynthia Coffman back to the shower. "Do you recall whether Mr. Marlow had said anything to you about your getting in the shower?"

"Yes, he had told me to get in."

"Did you?"

"No, sir."

"At what point did you change your clothes?"

"While they were in the shower."

"So, you had taken your clothes off while they were in the shower?"

"Yes, sir."

Jordan hoped that he had blurred any images Haight might create of Coffman disrobing while the shower incident was taking place.

Coffman's attorney then resumed the deliberate orderly questions to allow Coffman to tell her version of the killing of Lynel Murray. Coffman had returned to the motel room, she said, with food from McDonald's, gave some to Greg and Lynel, noticed that they both had wet hair, and then took a shower herself. She quoted Marlow telling her, "You are going to kill this one."

"When he said that, did it flash on you as to what must have happened to Miss Novis?" Don Jordan asked.

Cynthia didn't raise her eyes. "I don't really think I let it enter my mind. I really didn't think about it."

The jury heard her representation of ripping towels, binding and gagging Lynel Murray, and her admission that she tried to strangle the victim, but couldn't complete the act. "I couldn't do it. And so he took one side and he started pulling while I was on the other side. He just got mad because I wasn't doing it and he took the other side and told me he would do it."

Inside the crowded courtroom, it was close, stuffy, and too warm, despite the constant buzz of the air conditioner. But when the cruel account of Lynel Murray's death was unveiled, several people shivered, and quiet sobs could be heard from the rows where family members sat.

Her voice only a whisper, Coffman told of the flight from Huntington Beach, the dinner at Denny's, and the overnight stay at the Compri Hotel. After a stop in San Bernardino, she said, they fled to the mountains, bought some things at a sports store, spent a miserable night in a rocky depression, and were arrested the next day.

Don Jordan tried to exercise some damage control relating to a lie Coffman had told the police. "In the course of the interviews, did you falsely tell the officers something?"

"Yes. At the beginning I told them that Greg had dropped me off at a Seven-Eleven and he left me there when he was with Corinna Novis and was gone for about an hour and a half and he came back and picked me up."

"Can you explain to the jury why you said that?"

"Because I was afraid of the trouble I was in."

The lawyer knew that it was a gamble. The jury could either recognize her honesty for admitting the lie, or decide that the admission demonstrated her capability of lying at any time.

Before turning Coffman over to the prosecution for cross-examination, Jordan wanted to quickly address two more issues. He pulled an admission from her that she had received many erotic love letters from Marlow, and had written a large number to him. Marlow had asked her in a letter, she said, "to draw an outline of my personal areas, and he asked me to put body fluids on it because he wanted to eat the papers." She had complied with his request, she admitted.

The second matter was some personal contact she had experienced with Marlow while they were in holding cells. In February 1988, she said, Marlow had left his unlocked cell, which was back-to-back with hers, walked around to her cell, and made a request. "Should I use the exact word?" she asked Jordan.

"Yes, go ahead."

"He told me he wanted me to give him head."

"And what does that mean?"

"Means to perform oral sex. I told him no. I was sitting on the bed, cowering from him. 'No, I'm not, no.' He finally just got mad and walked away and said, 'You do remember that my friends do have your son's number?' "

There was another incident in the summer of 1988, Jordan said. "What happened on that occasion?"

"They had left my door unlocked and he was still locked in his cage, and kept screaming to me, 'Come here, come here, I got something I want to tell you. Come here.' So finally I walked over there to his cell. And when I got there, he was standing up on the bed with his jumper down and his (inaudible) sticking out the bars."

"His sex organ?"

"Yes, sir."

"And did you do anything?"

"No, I did not. I heard a deputy coming, so I went back to my cell."

Don Jordan had two final questions for his client. "Now, Miss Coffman, you have seen a report from a deputy sheriff in which it is alleged that you kissed a female inmate on the lips for some three to four seconds. You've seen that report. Miss Coffman, are you a lesbian?"

"No, sir, I'm not." Observers wondered if her answer ruled out bisexuality.

"Miss Coffman, at this point, do you feel that you have Mr. Marlow out of your system?"

"Yes, I do."

Early in his cross-examination, Haight questioned Coffman about earrings, wanting to know how Lynel Murray's missing earring got in Corinna's purse, the one Cyndi had been carrying when she was arrested, and why Corinna's earrings were in the Bavarian Lodge motel room. Coffman said she didn't know.

Lynel's maroon bra had been found in the pillowcase Marlow discarded at Santa's Village when they deserted the Honda. Chip Haight reminded Cyndi that the police had shown it to her. He asked, "Don't you remember telling them that it must be the Huntington Beach girl's bra?"

"I may have said that, yes."

"What made you say that to them?"

"Because it wasn't mine. And the belongings that were thrown in (the) Santa's Village trash can were from the Huntington Beach Hotel."

To get the drug-usage issue exposed, Haight persuaded Cyndi to admit that she had been using drugs long before she met Marlow. He asked when she started.

"I started smoking pot when I was in high school," she disclosed. "After I had my son, I did LSD a few times, hashish, things like that. And when I moved to Arizona, I did a little bit of cocaine. In Barstow is when I started using methamphetamine."

Following some questions about her experiences in Barstow, Haight inquired about Cyndi's fear that Marlow would harm her son. "Why didn't you tell the police when you were asked a direct question, 'Are you afraid for your kid?' Why didn't you say yes?"

Coffman mumbled feebly, "I don't know."

Coffman had admitted hearing Marlow shoveling dirt in the vineyard. Haight wanted to know, "When you heard him shoveling the dirt, you knew what had happened to Corinna, didn't you?"

"No, not really. I didn't want to know. I—that is why I didn't ask him when he got in the car what happened because I didn't want to know what happened."

The conversations between Coffman and fellow inmate Robin Long, while waiting for trial, were the next topic. Long had informed, and even though she had not been called to the stand yet, Haight intended to ask Coffman some questions about her meeting with Long. Over defense objections, the judge allowed Haight to proceed.

"What do you recall telling Robin Long about your case?"

"I don't know. That was a long time ago. I talked to her about different things."

"Did you tell Robin Long that when Mr. Marlow and Miss Novis were in the shower, you were in there with them?"

"No, I did not."

"When Mr. Marlow asked you to get in the shower, what did you do?"

"I turned around and walked out."

"You didn't do what he asked you to do, isn't that correct?"

"At that time, yes, sir."

Haight paused to let that sink in with the jury. Coffman's defense focused on her "state of mind" that she felt compelled to do whatever Marlow asked. Yet, if she was telling the truth about the shower, she had defied his request.

For the next hour, Haight repeatedly preceded questions with, "Did you tell Robin Long . . ." taking Coffman through every detail of the abduction, abuse, and killing of Corinna Novis. Cyndi answered in the negative to most of them. For the remainder of the day, and all of the following day, he crisscrossed back and forth over the entire relationship between Marlow and Coffman and the three killings. The jury heard several points Haight wanted to emphasize:

- Of all the beatings she described, she had only gone to a doctor once, in Pine Knot, Kentucky.
- Not only had she designed the Property of

Folsom Wolf tattoo, she had previously asked if she could have a unicorn tattoo.

- She and Marlow frequently had sex in the shower.
- A police report of her statements included a comment that Greg Hill had been shot in the head. In her testimony, she denied knowing specifics about the injury.
- Coffman had been insisting that she didn't know Corinna was dead until after the arrest. The police reported that they had asked her, when Corinna's PIN number wouldn't work, why she and Greg hadn't returned to the vineyard to get the correct number. Coffman had responded, "Because she's already gone."
- Lynel Murray wasn't killed until her PIN number had worked. Had Coffman and Marlow learned a lesson from the mistake of killing Novis too soon?
- In the Huntington Beach police report, Coffman was quoted as saying that while Marlow held the victim's hair up, Coffman had applied the duct tape to her mouth.
- After Murray's death, and the "celebration" dinner at Denny's, Coffman had sex with Marlow in the Compri Hotel.

Haight sat down, reasonably satisfied that he had exposed to the jury what he believed to be the real Cynthia Lynn Coffman.

* * *

Because of the peculiar triangle arrangement of the trial, two opposing defendants against the prosecution, Cynthia Coffman also faced being cross-examined by Mr. Marlow's attorney Ray Craig.

After a few preliminary questions, Craig asked for a conference with the judge and attorneys. He wanted to discuss the issue of using as evidence the voluminous, sexually explicit and erotic letters Marlow and Coffman had exchanged during the first six months of their incarceration. Craig said that he believed ". . . The letters from her to Mr. Marlow were for the purpose of keeping his affection with the idea that he was going to say or do something that would get her out of the case or certainly lighten the consequences she faces, by in effect, taking all the blame. When that did not work . . . she very much wanted the separate trial even at the expense of Mr. Marlow being eliminated."

Ray Craig produced a letter from Coffman to someone named "Dirty Dan." It was one of several sexually graphic love letters Coffman had exchanged with him, in which it was inferred that Dan was going to eliminate Mr. Marlow in trade for favors from Coffman.

Coffman's attorney objected to the use of that specific letter, saying, "I think that's a lot of conjecture on the part of Mr. Craig." Judge Turner agreed and sustained the objection.

The remaining few hours of Cynthia Coffman's fifth day on the stand were used by Craig rehashing the same questions Chip Haight had asked. She got a brief rest on the next day, while the jury heard from witnesses who had seen Coffman and Marlow in Kentucky and Arizona, who repeated their observations of the relationship between Cynful and Greg.

On Thursday, December 8, Cynthia Coffman began what would be four more days of grueling questions and answers from the battery of attorneys.

Haight produced a letter she had sent to Marlow, handed it to her, and asked, "What appears at the top of this letter?"

"It is a map to my son's house."

"You gave to Mr. Marlow what you thought was an accurate description of how to get to where your son was staying?" Haight's voice was incredulous.

"Yes, sir."

"You testified that one of the main things that made you commit these crimes was your fear of your son's life in Mr. Marlow's hands; is that correct?"

When she answered in the affirmative, Haight wanted to know why she sent the map.

"He sent me a letter saying that his brother lived in St. Louis . . . and would go take pictures of my son and I could have them. I wanted a picture of my son."

"Weren't you worried this was some kind of a trick Mr. Marlow was pulling to get at your son?"

"Not at that time," Cyndi replied. "I wasn't thinking that way, because that is right after someone told me that nothing would ever happen to my child. They (gangs) don't hurt children."

"That is all it took to wipe out that fear, one person in jail telling you that?" Haight didn't try to hide his skepticism.

"At that time, it went back and forth. There would be times I would be afraid and somebody would tell me, 'Cyndi, you don't have to worry, nothing will happen to him.' "

"You testified this fear for your boy was so great it caused you to participate in three murders. Correct?"

"Yes, sir." She continued to explain, but Haight was sure the jury understood the point, and went on to other questions about the contents of the hundreds of letters. He quoted a passage she had written: "I just can't wait until we get out of here so we can be together again."

"Now that's what you wrote to Mr. Marlow, is that correct?"

"Yes, sir."

"And you wrote this to a man who you claimed had beaten you for five months?"

"Yes, sir."

"A man who you say you were so terrified of, you committed murder?"

"Yes, sir."

Haight continued to grind away, using her words

in the lascivious correspondence to impeach her previous testimony. She blushed when he handed her another page she had written, and asked about the drawing in the lower left-hand corner. "What is that a drawing of?" There was no audible response.

"It's a drawing of a penis that you drew, isn't it?" Haight snapped.

"Yes, sir."

"Is it supposed to be Marlow's?" Cyndi gave the same monotonous answer.

Haight's voice was edged with disgust now. "The words that are written above it, 'Yeah, dinner. I'm starving. Hurry up.' Aren't they? What was your purpose for drawing this picture?"

Coffman's voice was thin and strained. "He had talked to me about putting a tattoo on it to cover the tattoo he already had there." She acknowledged that she had wanted the new tattoo to read *Cynful's*.

"You wanted it to show that you are the owner, that it was yours? Kind of like the tattoo on your rear end, *Property of Folsom Wolf*?"

"Yes."

The remainder of Haight's cross-examination focused on drawings, sexual references, and commitments of undying love expressed in the letters. It's always a tough call for lawyers to know exactly when to stop, and not crush the jury with too much of one subject. Haight felt that he had reached the optimum point, and turned Cynthia Coffman back over to Don Jordan.

* * *

Jordan re-covered much of the previous ground, with a focus on a key question: "Now, Miss Coffman, during the time on November 7, when you and Mr. Marlow were with Corinna Novis, did you want her to be dead?"

"No, sir."

"Did you know Mr. Marlow was going to kill her?"

"No, sir. I thought when he had gotten out of the car with her that he was going to take her in that vineyard and rape her again, and just leave her."

After several more hours of interrogation about the coded meanings in the letters and why they finally stopped corresponding, and more cross-examination by Haight and Craig, Cynthia Coffman finally ended her ninth day of testimony.

The last court day in 1988 was December 14, during which three police officers testified. Then, Judge Turner dismissed the jury until January 4. "In the meantime," he told the weary jurors, "have a wonderful holiday, and we'll see you next year."

Twenty-four

The exhaustive testimony of Cynthia Coffman was by no means the key part of Don Jordan's defense, just the foundation for it. His major assault on Haight's case started on the fifth day of January 1989, after the jury's long holiday rest, and two days after what would have been Corinna Novis's twenty-third birthday.

Dr. Lenore Walker, proclaimed one of the nation's foremost authorities on the battered woman syndrome, would be his next witness. Not a stranger to courtrooms, Dr. Walker had testified in scores of trials and she was well-known on the television talk-show circuit: Oprah Winfrey, Phil Donahue, Sally Jessy Raphäel, and others.

She marched confidently through the gates of the bar dividing the gallery from the trial officers, and raised her right hand to be sworn in. A short woman, with dark brown hair closely cropped on the back of her neck and swirled stylishly at the top, large brown eyes, flashing white teeth, and dimples that creased when she smiled, she commanded respect even without the thick stack of credentials qualifying her as an expert in her field.

"I am a clinical and forensic psychologist," Dr. Walker announced in an articulate, clear voice at about 10:30 A.M., and spent the next four hours answering questions about her professional qualifications, published works, experimental studies, procedures used, and the fundamental definitions of the battered woman syndrome. The syndrome is considered, she said, "a subcategory of post-traumatic stress disorder."

Don Jordan inquired about reliable national statistics regarding battering of women. Walker cited one research agency report that between one-third and one-half of the population of women in the United States have been battered at some point in their lives. She observed that "most battered women believe that the men who control them are omnipotent and all-knowing; they see things that other people don't see, and they can do things that other people can't do. They really see them as being extraordinary human beings."

Late in the afternoon, Dr. Walker described how she had approached the case of Cynthia Coffman. "I conducted an evaluation of Miss Coffman, administered the battered woman syndrome questionnaire, the MMPI (Minnesota Multiphasic Personality Inventory) test, a standard clinical evaluation, and the mental status examination, all during a three-day period in April 1987." She had also read police reports, analyzed Coffman's statements, read the now notorious letters, and reviewed transcripts of her recent testimony.

The objective, in doing all this, she said, was to

try to answer a relatively simple question. "If I found evidence of Coffman being a battered woman, and having the battered woman syndrome, did that have an impact on her state of mind at the time of the homicide?"

On her second day, Dr. Walker described how Coffman's childhood experiences, including possible sexual abuse, physical discipline, loss of her father, and painful hernias at birth, were factors she considered before looking at the adult experiences.

Reciting each of the major traumatic incidents Cynthia had reported experiencing with Marlow, Dr. Walker explained the impact on Coffman. The anal rape in Atlanta, she said, "caused Cyndi a great deal of physical as well as emotional pain." And Marlow's "excessive demands for sex, sometimes as much as three or four times a day," along with the fact that "he wanted sex right after a very serious beating where she was physically injured, and she did not want sex at that time," constituted sexual abuse, in spite of "a lot of very positive loving sexuality between them."

Marlow's possessiveness and jealousy caused serious problems, Walker said, resulting in a number of battering incidents. His threats to kill were present from the very first incident of battering. These, combined with several other experience factors and the results of additional tests, allowed Dr. Walker to make a diagnosis with respect to Miss Coffman.

Explaining her analysis, Walker pointed out that

if she had evaluated Coffman the year prior to her meeting Marlow, it "would have been a very different rating, with some mild symptoms, but generally functioning pretty well." After Coffman met Marlow, the doctor added, "She really changed dramatically, and that dramatic change is directly measured corresponding with the relationship with Mr. Marlow."

The barrage of scientific terms and references Dr. Walker used threatened to overwhelm jurors and spectators, but the day was nearly over. Just before the evening recess, she caught their attention sharply with one additional observation.

"Women who have battered woman syndrome often demonstrate a variety of . . . coping skills or survival skills." Cyndi, she said, intensely focused all of her feelings of love on Mr. Marlow. "She insisted that she loved him very much during that period of time and that the person who did the abuse to her, she actually had a separate name for. He was called Wolf. She understood that was Mr. Marlow, and that it was a part of his personality, but she almost encapsulated that as a separate personality. And she would talk about when Wolf would come out or she would see Wolf's eyes, or hear Wolf's voice rather than Mr. Marlow's voice. That's when she knew a battering would occur, and she would try to do things to keep Wolf away."

If the jury thought the day's end marked the completion of psychological testimony, they were terribly mistaken. Dr. Walker would occupy the witness chair for the next seven days.

They didn't have to wait long, however, for Dr. Walker to get to the point on the third morning. Within the first twenty minutes, Don Jordan asked, "Now, did the fact that you found Miss Coffman to be . . . suffering from the battered woman syndrome lead you to a conclusion as to whether those circumstances did impact, have an effect, upon her state of mind at the time?"

"Yes," came the crisp answer.

Jordan asked if Marlow exercised mental control over Coffman.

"Yes," Walker responded, "in my professional opinion the extreme amount of mind control and domination that Mr. Marlow had over Cyndi Coffman, including threats of killing her and harming her child and family, made it impossible for her to have an intent to kill Corinna Novis."

That's what Don Jordan wanted to hear and wanted the jury to hear. "I have nothing further, Your Honor."

Haight's cross-examination started with an attempt to reduce some of Dr. Walker's verbal terminology to shorter, easier to handle definitions. He asked the witness her definition of "intent to kill," but got into a gray area over legal versus psychological meanings.

Putting a little different twist on it, Haight asked, "Do you think Miss Coffman had the intent to aid Mr. Marlow in the killing of Corinna Novis?"

Still self-assured, Walker stated, "Now, in psychological terms, I believe she could not have had the intent in the way that we know it. Her intent was to protect herself, to stay alive, and to do whatever he told her to do . . . and I don't perceive that as having volitional intent."

Haight knew the waters were still muddy for the jurors. He stepped toward the stand, saying, "Okay. Maybe you are using intent differently than I think of it . . ." He suddenly dropped his pen on the floor.

Looking up at Dr. Walker, he asked, "Did I intend to drop that pen?"

"I don't know," she shot back. "I'd have to give you a psychological evaluation to find out."

Haight leaned over, picked up the pen, and threw it several feet. "What about that? Did I intend to throw that pen?"

Calmly, she answered, "Again, as a psychologist, I would have to give you a couple of tests."

Looking quizzical, while recovering the pen, Haight drilled further. "If I take this pen and throw it against the wall as hard as I can, you still are not going to tell me I had the intent to throw the pen?"

"I mean," Walker patiently replied, "if you are asking me as a psychologist, I'll have to, at this time, do an interview . . ."

"You are testifying in a court of law. Let's be a normal citizen. What do you think . . . did I intend to drop the pen?"

A little slower, Walker started her reply, "Given

the fact that you are demonstrating something and you're asking that—"

With a sigh, Haight interrupted, "You are being a psychologist. All right."

Dr. Walker could only manage a weak laugh. Haight repeated, "Did I intend to throw that pen?"

"Well, I can't separate that from what I know is happening right here. You are demonstrating something. You have purpose in your behavior."

With resignation, Haight finally said, "Okay, let's skip intent and go on to something else.

"What if it could be shown to you that Miss Coffman exaggerated the extent of abuse she suffered from Mr. Marlow? Would that change your opinion?"

"Well, I think the word 'exaggerated,' in this case, has less meaning to me because the abuse was so extensive," she said.

"What if it could be shown to you that Coffman knowingly and actively participated in these homicides? Would that change your opinion?"

"Again, it would have to depend upon what knowingly and actively in those definitions would actually be. I have no doubt that she participated in them."

After suggesting that Coffman had not been truthful during the interviews with Dr. Walker, Haight referred to a report Walker had signed. "Who wrote that Cyndi was beaten almost daily during the last six months of their relationship?"

Walker instantly perceived the error, answering,

"It should have been the last week or last six days of their relationship, not months."

Haight couldn't resist twisting the knife a little. "Kind of tough to have increase in beating lasting six months in a five-and-one-half-month relationship, isn't it?"

Quickly covering ground about the rarity of battered women who kill third parties instead of the abusers, and the short term of the Marlow-Coffman relationship before the Kentucky murder, Haight asked Dr. Walker's understanding of the shower incident involving Novis. Looking at her own summary report, which contained the story Coffman had given her, Walker read aloud, at Haight's request: ". . . Greg tried to get it up, but couldn't, so 'he told me to take my clothes off.' Cyndi complied. Greg kept trying to get it up, and every time he tried to get it, it would go soft. After several attempts by Greg, he gave up and both he and the woman exited the shower . . ." Walker read the summary, through its completion, which ended in the vineyard after the murder.

Haight wanted to know if Coffman was in the bathroom during the shower. Walker held that Cyndi was in the bedroom, so Haight asked her to read some notes prepared by her colleague who had helped develop the case. The notes included Coffman's words: ". . . Greg put handcuffs back on her, and they both got in the shower. Greg tried to get it up but couldn't, so he told me to take my clothes off. I took off my dress and still had my panties on, and Greg kept trying . . . (but) it would go soft. So then Greg gave up and got out of the shower. I put my dress on and Greg started to dry her off."

"Sounds like she is in the bathroom, doesn't it?" Haight observed. But Dr. Walker tenaciously insisted that Coffman remained in the bedroom during the shower. Haight wouldn't drop it. "Why do you think Mr. Marlow asked her to take her clothes off?"

Still maintaining her professional demeanor, the doctor replied, "She knew he was having trouble getting an erection, and that was consistent with other times that he had demanded sex from her (when he had that problem)."

"That's what I interpreted," the prosecutor agreed. "He wants (Cyndi) to take her clothes off so she can further stimulate him, correct?" Walker agreed, and Haight continued, "To do that, he has to see her, doesn't he? No point in asking Miss Coffman to take her clothes off if he is not going to see her naked. So Cyndi had to be in his line of sight, didn't she?"

Walker wasn't going to concede so easily. "Well, he could have been the one out of the shower, coming into the bedroom, forcing her to take her clothes off and watching her do that." Haight, shaking his head, asked if that was really a reasonable explanation, and went on to another topic.

Still pursuing his theory that Coffman's accounts were full of lies, Haight shifted to the Huntington

Beach murder, and pointed out that Cyndi had told Dr. Walker's colleague, and stated in her testimony, that Marlow had put the tape on Lynel Murray's mouth. "Okay, now let's look at what she told the police, just after she was arrested," Haight said, directing the doctor to a printed transcript. "One of the officers asks who put the tape on her, and (Coffman) answers, 'I did. Greg held up her hair.' Would you agree that that's a different story?"

"Yes."

"Do you see any significance in her telling a different story?"

"No."

Swallowing a sigh, Haight asked, "What kind of lies would she have to tell about the case for you to find them significant?"

"Well, she'd have to tell things that were really significant to her that would make a difference to her state of mind, things that would impact my analysis of her state of mind." Dr. Walker explained that this was an "inconsistency, but not an important one."

It was becoming apparent, in the prosecutor's belief, that the doctor, having been hired by the defense, was sympathetic to Coffman when she conducted the interviews. He also couldn't resist airing the cost of Dr. Walker's services. "How much are you being paid for your testimony?"

There were more grunts and coughs than usual in the audience, and a symphony of squeaking chairs when she answered, "My usual fee is fifteen hundred dollars a day plus expenses."

The erotic love letters Cyndi and Greg had exchanged for more than six months were discussed, but Dr. Walker saw nothing in them that would change her opinions regarding her diagnosis of Coffman. Even the map Cyndi had drawn to her son's residence, didn't bother the doctor, and she was satisfied that any assertiveness Coffman had expressed was offset by her expressions of love.

"Let's assume," Haight hypothesized, "that there is convincing evidence that Miss Coffman was actually in the vineyard physically participating in the killing of Corinna Novis. How, if at all, would that affect your opinion?"

"Just the information, those additional facts, would not affect my opinion. I would need more information in order to change my opinion," Walker answered.

One of Haight's strategic objectives gradually came into focus as he continued questioning Dr. Walker on January 11 and 12. In the spring of 1987, when Don Jordan had replaced another attorney to represent Coffman, and when Dr. Lenore Walker had tested and interviewed the defendant, Coffman had changed her behavior and had pulled away from Marlow. There had been a sudden shift in her behavior, Haight thought, in which she had started to manifest symptoms of the battered woman syndrome. Now, he wanted to convince the jury that the change was a deliberate campaign by her defense team. Another psychologist, Dr. Craig Rath had also observed this shift as well.

Dr. Walker summarized it concisely. "My knowledge of battered women would suggest that reality setting in would indeed be expected to happen at this point. It hadn't happened up until then."

Dr. Craig Rath had repeated the M.M.P.I. testing of Coffman, about three weeks after Dr. Walker had given the first test. Haight discovered that of the 566 questions on the test, Coffman had changed her answers on 113 of them. He was convinced that she had deliberately tried to answer the true and false self-assessment questions in a slant that would support battered woman syndrome. While Haight began to cite specific questions to which Cyndi had answered in direct opposition to the original test, and ask if the dramatic differences indicated mendacity, Dr. Walker vehemently opposed the tactic. "Understand," she demanded, "I would not have looked at the individual questions. It is inappropriate to look at the individual questions and make any kind of opinion based on individual questions." She added that there are scoring keys for groups of questions, and built-in criteria to assess if the subject may be lying.

Haight was incredulous. "Even if an answer to an individual question is false, totally false, that has no bearing on whether the person is telling the truth?"

"That's correct," volleyed Walker.

Despite her intractable position, during which she appealed to the judge for permission not to answer, Haight insisted on discussing many of the test questions on which Cyndi had given changed answers. Dr. Walker obeyed the court's order to answer, but steadfastly maintained that it was against her professional judgment and ethics to do so, and that examining the answers to single questions was completely invalid.

In another gambit, Chip Haight finally got an agreement from the doctor that Cyndi's alleged behavior, described in an investigative report, would be inconsistent with battered woman syndrome. In a Kentucky interview, a male witness to whom Marlow had described how he shot Greg "Wildman" Hill, claimed that Cynthia had interrupted and excitedly said, "I shot him," or "I finished him." She was quoted as saying, "You killed the last one, let me kill this one."

"Is that the kind of conduct you would have expected Miss Coffman to engage in if she was truly a battered woman suffering from the syndrome?"

"No," Dr. Walker acknowledged. "That would be inconsistent with what a battered woman would do."

In the exchanges with Dr. Walker, Chip Haight also managed to bring out that:

- To a detective's question about Corinna's death, Coffman had replied, "I guess he strangled her," indicating that Coffman was lying when she said she didn't know Corinna was dead.

- Coffman had denied ever asking Lynel Murray for her PIN number, but had answered an officer's question, "Did you have to threaten her (for the PIN number)?" by saying, "Yep, sure did."
- Haight asked Walker, "How would you expect her to act, her demeanor, a couple of hours after Lynel Murray was killed?" Walker: "To be scared, to be numb, quite frightened." Haight: "Would you expect that a couple of hours after Lynel Murray is killed that she'd be in a restaurant and observed by a waitress to be hugging and kissing Mr. Marlow?" Walker: "If she thought that would keep her alive and she wouldn't end up dead, you bet she would."

On the afternoon of Walker's sixth day of testimony, Chip Haight sat down. "I have no further questions at this time, Your Honor."

Ray Craig stepped forward to cross-examine Dr. Walker. He, too, was interested in the possibility that Coffman exhibited anti-social personality disorder characteristics. Recalling that Cyndi, in early childhood, had been caught stealing from a store, and her mother had marched her back in, whereupon the clerk had reprimanded the mother, Craig asked if that was a "critical" event.

"Well, the event itself is a critical event," Walker replied. ". . . There were all kinds of emotional overlays to that particular incident. Miss Coffman remembers it very clearly, despite the fact she has no memory of her home life."

Craig also asked about the impact of the hernias Cyndi suffered at birth. Walker explained that the pain prevented physical touching and nurturing, interfering with the bonding between mother and daughter.

One of the most interesting questions, on the minds of everyone, was asked by Craig, regarding the tendency for battered women to stay with the abusive men. "Well, if it's so bad . . . why doesn't the woman leave rather than continue in a battering situation or battering household?"

"Well, learned helplessness is an explanation for why women don't leave, and that has to do with the dangerousness of leaving. Learned helplessness (relates to) the woman's psychological perception of how dangerous it is to leave . . . and the data are very consistent that it is, indeed, very dangerous to leave." The doctor added that financial reasons also apply, and having no place to go is a factor.

"Doctor, could you tell me chronologically when did Cynthia Coffman become subject to the battered woman syndrome? At what point in the relationship of six months?"

"I'd have to analyze it more carefully," Walker responded, raising questions in observers' minds why she hadn't already done that. "But just from reviewing it in my mind right now, I would say that it was shortly after the first serious battering incident that I reported. I think it was sometime in June of 1986." After some cogitating, she decided that it was about June 18.

"Why didn't she leave then? One physical confrontation does not make a battered woman. Is that correct?"

"Not in my definition. It would take two confrontations. But there was, in this particular case, a sufficient amount of psychological conditioning going on beforehand that—and I don't know. I don't think there were any specific battering incidents. There may have been. But this was a major one." Her answer was far from definitive, but Craig didn't pursue it.

After nearly two more hours of exchanges, near the end of the day, both Craig and Walker were tired. Dr. Walker was in the middle of an answer regarding Coffman's "diminished interest in significant activities" while with Marlow. ". . . I took a look at what Miss Coffman said about her activities prior to her meeting Mr. Marlow (and) during the time that she was together with him. . . . For example, one of the things she really liked to do a lot that she had learned when she was together with Sam Keam was to ski, and that they had gone skiing different times. After meeting Mr. Marlow, there was no skiing, no possibility of going skiing. In fact, he sold her skis and Mr. Keam's skis . . ."

Restraining a smile, Craig asked, "Some other

difficulties in skiing between June and October also, aren't there?"

"Between June and October?"

"Yes."

"I don't understand."

"That's when they were together," Craig observed. "Obviously they couldn't go skiing while they were together. There wasn't any snow."

All the doctor could do was grin, and sputter, "During June—well, that's true. That is indeed true."

On Monday morning, January 23, Craig resumed his questioning. "Now speaking hypothetically, let's assume there was a contract, a killing for hire in Phoenix. Now, if Miss Coffman was insisting that the two of them undertake this mission in order to get money to go back to St. Louis and kidnap the child; and if she threatened Mr. Marlow with revealing the Kentucky homicide if he did not go through with it, would this not be inconsistent with your learned helplessness theory (and) with your battered woman syndrome?"

"No," said Dr. Walker. "I would have to know much more about the circumstances if that should have happened before I could say that."

Craig was puzzled. "Now, just that act of coercion for whatever reason on the part of the woman, would that not be inconsistent with learned helplessness?"

"No. Many battered women were quite manipulative. Some people call that coercive." She explained in detail.

"Well, on your learned helplessness and your battered woman syndrome, haven't you got a basically passive woman and a basically aggressive man?"

"No," she answered sharply.

"You don't?" Craig's voice was strained with disbelief.

"We have battered women who are lawyers, judges, psychologists, very active in their communities, as well as women who are stereotypes of the passive battered woman," Walker lectured. "This is the whole point of my research, which has been to demonstrate that the image of the battered woman, which often has been presented to us, is simply untrue." Some people in the courtroom were astonished at the exploded myth of their preconceived notions regarding battered women.

Once more, Chip Haight bored in on the MMPI tests, and once more, Dr. Walker insisted that the changed answers were of no consequence. A little later, Haight read aloud from a report the doctor had prepared, "At first (Coffman) discussed wanting to marry Greg, and she was demanding they do, so they could die together in the gas chamber, holding hands."

Dr. Walker explained: At first, that's what Cyndi thought she deserved, but later she really wanted to escape from Greg's power and control.

A little frustrated with Walker's consistent

agreement with Jordan and disagreement with him, Haight asked, "So that whole series of questions Mr. Jordan just asked you, where he'd give a hypothetical example where she was submissive, and you'd say 'Yeah, that's consistent with my opinion,' I could just turn that question around, give you an example where she's submissive and you would say that's not consistent with it?"

"You'd have to give me the context it was in," Dr. Walker told him.

"When she tells him that she's *not* going to get in the shower with him, that's also consistent with the syndrome?"

"That's correct."

With growing exasperation, Haight asked, "So if she tells him yes, that's consistent with the syndrome, and if she tells him no, that's consistent with the syndrome? I mean, what *isn't* consistent with the syndrome?"

"Again, you'd have to look at each incident and the context that it's in." The words were delivered with professional polish.

It was a little after four in the afternoon, and Judge Turner was also weary. "Would you like to knock off for the day?" he inquired.

"I'd like to knock off forever," Chip Haight growled, then grinned.

After another day and a half of testimony, Dr. Lenore Walker, a highly respected forensic psychologist, who was obviously very well educated and conversant with her specialty, and who conducted herself with absolute professionalism, finally walked out of the courtroom for good at 2:53 P.M., January 24, 1989.

Twenty-five

On Wednesday, January 25, 1989, Jordan called Elmer Lutz to the stand. Lutz recalled that Greg Marlow yanked Coffman "by the hair of the head" as they entered an Atlanta restaurant, but couldn't remember any other evidence of Marlow abusing Cynful. Even though he had occupied the room adjacent to Coffman and Marlow in the motel where Cyndi claimed a night of terror, including being shorn and sodomized, Lutz had heard nothing.

Following the innocuous testimony, Don Jordan stood, and announced, "With that, Your Honor, Miss Coffman rests."

The prosecution's next turn at bat, the rebuttal phase, followed immediately, and Haight didn't disappoint the expectant audience. One of his investigators, Hans Van DerVeen, in a yeoman performance, had located Robin Long and personally guarded her until she walked into the courtroom. She'd been missing early in the trial process.

The sullen, frightened woman settled her bulky

form into the witness chair, and turned her fleshy face toward Haight. Her expression made it clear that she'd rather be somewhere, anywhere else.

After establishing that Long had met Coffman in jail through the fortune-telling hustle, and they had conversed, Haight wanted to know what was the first thing Coffman had told her about the case.

"She mentioned to me that if she was found guilty, she would be the first woman in the State of California to be executed." (If she said that, she was wrong. Four women had been executed in California, but none since 1962.)

To Haight's questions, Long told of how Cyndi had confessed to her the events leading to the death of Corinna Novis. "The girl was in the Redlands Mall, and (Cyndi) approached her and told her that they needed a ride. They held the woman at gunpoint and took her car—had the lady pull over and she (Coffman) went around and got in and drove. They went to the fat guy's house."

"What did she say occurred after they arrived at the fat guy's house in Fontana?"

"Um, they took showers."

"Who did she say was in the shower with the victim?"

"Herself, the victim, and Wolf." There was dead quiet in the audience at the testimony placing Coffman in the shower with Marlow and Corinna Novis.

"What did she say occurred while all three of them were in the shower?"

"Um, her boyfriend fondled both of them while they took showers."

"Did Miss Coffman indicate to you in any way that the victim was bound or gagged, anything like that?"

"Yes. They had used handcuffs and duck [sic] tape."

"Did she say anything about whether they intended to kill this particular person?"

"Yes. They had—that was the plan, to kill them— kill her."

In answer to questions about the burglary of Corinna's apartment, Robin Long's recital of what Coffman had allegedly told her disagreed, in some respects, with Coffman's own testimony. Long said that Cyndi and Greg went to the apartment while they left Corinna with Richard Drinkhouse, which was also contradictory to the recollection of Drinkhouse and Coral Willoughby.

About the victim, Long said, "Cynthia Coffman told me that Miss Novis had pleaded with her not to wreck the car, that she had just gotten the car." Long said that she had also heard Cynthia say that Novis was told, while they were in the grape vineyard, that she was going to be killed.

Haight asked if Cynthia had described Corinna's response.

"She was more worried about her parents' feelings than her own."

Spectators shivered and couldn't resist taking a quick glance toward Donna and Bill Novis, who sat courageously listening to the devastating words.

"What items did she say they took personally off of Miss Novis?"

"A watch and some earrings." (Dr. Lenore Walker had rejected the idea of trophy earrings, even though Lynel Murray's leaf-shaped earring had been found in the purse Coffman carried.)

Robin Long remembered that the answering machine had been "sold for two quarters of speed."

"What did she say occurred when they arrived at the grape vineyard?"

"She said that once they was at the grape vineyard, that Wolf took Miss Novis out of the car and strangled her . . . with a piece of clothing." She added, "After that, he walked back to the car, got out, went to the trunk, took out a folding shovel, went back into the grape vineyard, and proceeded to bury Miss Novis."

"Did she say whether they both went into the vineyard or just one?"

"They both." Long placed Coffman at the grave site as it was dug, and recalled that it was a shallow grave.

"Why didn't they dig it deeper?"

"She said they didn't want to go through all of that trouble."

"Did Miss Coffman tell you how she felt when she thought about Corinna Novis being killed?"

"Yes. She told me that it made her feel really good." To demonstrate that, Long said, Coffman had asked Robin to look into her eyes. "Cyndi said, 'You see how my eyes get?' She goes, 'They get just like Greg's. I'm becoming part wolf, too.' "

Proceeding to the Huntington Beach murder of Lynel Murray, Haight asked if Coffman had told of binding or gagging the victim. "Yes. They had taken her and used goose tape." This time, Haight clarified that it was duct tape. Handcuffs were also used, Long said. Haight had her run through the facts again.

"Did Coffman ever tell you that she participated in these crimes because she was afraid of Mr. Marlow?" Haight finally asked.

"No."

"Did she ever tell you she'd participated because she was afraid he would hurt her son?"

"No."

"Why did you contact the police after talking to Miss Coffman?"

"I felt like it was something I wanted to do, because I had two friends that were killed, and it's just something I wanted to do."

"Did they promise any deals in return for your testimony?"

"No, sir."

"Have I promised you any deals?"

"No, sir."

With a sense of accomplishment, Chip Haight declared, "No further questions, Your Honor," and returned to the prosecutor's table.

* * *

It fell to Ray Craig to reveal, through questioning of the witness, that Robin Long was a convicted burglar and drug addict whose violation of parole had landed her back in jail where she met Coffman. The two women had talked over a period of two weeks. Long had contacted Det. Scotty Smith on February 6, 1987, shortly after her release. She had also "snitched" on another woman.

Flirting with the possibility that Long might have read details in published accounts to get the information that she attributed to Cynthia Coffman's confession, Craig asked if Long had seen anything in the newspapers. Long squelched that with a surprising admission. "No. I don't know how to read, sir."

Long also reiterated to Craig that she could remember no stories from Coffman about being beaten by Wolf.

Alan Spears, who had sat silently for most of the trial while Don Jordan carried the ball for Coffman's defense, stood to cross-examine Robin Long. A veteran defender, the forty-year-old former pro-motorcycle rider, whose dark curly hair tumbled over his ears down to his shoulders, and whose beard and mustache were neatly trimmed, had handled twelve capital murder cases.

Taking her through a number of questions about her history, her attempts to lighten her jail sentence, and false claims of having contacts in the Aryan Brotherhood, Spears found himself raising his voice at the reticent woman whose answers were slow and faltering. Haight asked the judge to invoke a rule preventing yelling at the witness. Turner dutifully cautioned the lawyer.

Using a transcript of her interview with Scotty Smith, Spears asked a series of questions and read parts of it to Long. The witness had said to Smith, "She tried telling me she was afraid of him and he stabbed her and beat her up and hit her in the face with a clutch plate and different things, but I didn't buy that." Long admitted those were her words.

The impeachment of her earlier statements, claiming that she couldn't remember Coffman telling her of any beating incidents, led Spears to seek other inconsistencies, then to reveal that Long had been corresponding, by mail, with Greg Marlow.

Marlow had written to her first, she said, and admitted to Spears that it was a love letter, received just before her release from jail in February 1987.

The attorney asked if Long had conspired with Coral to "cook up any type of scheme to take any heat off of Mr. Marlow." She denied it.

Fighting back tears, Robin Long listened as Spears asked, "You told this jury how badly you felt for the family, for the parents?"

"Yes, I did."

"And you cried, didn't you? As you are doing

now. And you felt so badly and so horrified by
Corinna's death, it just compelled you to come forward, correct?"

"Yes, sir," Long sniffled.

"Did you become so sensitive about this case and
about the parents of Corinna Novis that you decided to adopt Greg Marlow as a pen pal and exchange love letters with him?"

"No. He wrote me and I wrote him back. . . ."

With little effort to hide his contempt, Alan
Spears released the witness back to Chip Haight.
A female juror had watched Alan Spears's cross-
examination with more than admiration.

By means of the prosecutor's questions, the jury
heard that Robin Long had sent one of Marlow's
letters to Cynthia Coffman to expose Greg "because she was telling me that he was real true-blue
and she was going to go to the gas chamber for
him."

Recognizing the jurors' confusion about how
Long could correspond by mail if she couldn't
read, Chip Haight asked, "You mentioned yesterday that you don't have much ability to read or
write; could you tell us exactly what ability you
have along those lines?"

"I have a third-grade reading average," she
sighed. "I have dyslexia, and at birth I was prema-
ture and the lack of oxygen to the brain gave me
a learning disorder."

Long revealed that she had also told Coffman,

via telephone several times, that she did not want Marlow to write to her anymore. She told how Coffman had demonstrated the strangling of Lynel Murray, information which Long used to pose in the photos. And she said that Coffman had shown no remorse for the killings. Haight asked how she knew that.

"Because at one point I asked Cynthia Coffman, 'How do I know you have heart? How can I tell that you have heart?' She told me, 'Robin, if you get me out of here and you want someone killed, I'll kill them for you.' "

That dramatic, startling statement gave Haight the perfect place to sit down, let the jury digest it for a moment, and tell the judge that he had no more questions.

Ray Craig took the helm again, and wanted to reestablish that Coffman, from what she had told Robin Long, was not really afraid of Marlow. Long explained that in the beginning she believed that Cynthia was truly afraid of Greg, but later it appeared to her that Coffman was just feigning fright.

Keeping Long for only a few more minutes to recapitulate some of her earlier testimony, Craig gave way once more to Alan Spears. After an exchange about the shower and rehashing Long's quote that "he (Marlow) took her out there to kill her," Spears asked, "When you were locked up with her, did you perceive her to be streetwise?"

"I perceived her to be manipulative," Long retorted.

After a few more minutes, Alan Spears completed his probe, and Robin Long was excused.

On the last day of January, Det. Richard "Hoop" Hooper and Det. Scotty Smith both testified about their interview of Cynthia Lynn Coffman on November 14, 1986. "Did you and Sergeant Smith continue talking to Miss Coffman even though she invoked her Miranda rights?" Haight asked.

"Yes, sir," Hooper openly acknowledged. "We were hoping we would find Corinna Novis alive. I wanted to do anything I could, legally possible, to get her to tell me where Corinna Novis was, because we did think she was still alive, or there was that chance." Smith's testimony agreed with Hooper's.

The words of the two officers carried the jury through Coffman's reluctance to talk, to her admission of the crimes, the wild-goose chase to Lytle Springs with Coffman in the intensive search for Novis, and finally, the tragic discovery of the body, facedown in a shallow grave in the midst of a deserted vineyard.

Twenty-six

Reporters, observers, and jurors wondered if they would hear from the last major defense player during Ray Craig's surrebuttal. So far, James Gregory Marlow had sat silently, staring at the table in front of him, occasionally scribbling something on a yellow legal pad, or whispering to Craig. Curious onlookers would have to patiently wait through a parade of fourteen more witnesses over the next week before Craig would announce Marlow's decision whether or not to speak.

Paul Donner and his wife, Marlow and Coffman's hosts at Newberry Springs, led off Craig's procession on the final day of January.

Paul said he couldn't recall ever seeing Greg lay a hand on Cyndi, nor had he heard her complain of being beaten, during the month-long tenancy in June or the two-week stay in October. The only exception was a single incident: He saw Greg push her down at the bathroom door. She didn't appear to be harmed, and since Cyndi's apparel during the hot month of June was usually "shorts or a bikini," Paul probably would have noticed any bruises or injuries on her body. When the couple returned from Kentucky in October, Paul noticed little difference in Cyndi other than her short haircut.

Observers were surprised when Paul Donner revealed that he had not only been a friend of Marlow's for some time, but was also the ex-husband of Greg's wife, Beverly.

Donner did recall that he had accompanied Cyndi and Greg on an expedition to help Coffman collect money owed to her for drugs, but the debtors they visited were all broke.

Mrs. Donner stated that she hadn't cared much for Cyndi, who was "hard to get along with." In her account of the pushing incident, she stated that "he pushed her and she slipped and fell on the concrete floor." There were no ostensible signs of injury or beatings to Coffman during the two periods the couple stayed there, Mrs. Donner said.

Cyndi had accompanied Mrs. Donner to work one day in June, at Calico High School, the woman said, where she was "flirtatious" with a male student, and gave the youngster the Donners' phone number so he could call Cyndi. It didn't surprise Mrs. Donner, though. In her opinion, Coffman flirted with "anyone" outside of Marlow's presence.

Both of the Donners were angry when they discovered, after Marlow and Coffman left in October, that two rings were missing.

* * *

An ex-con friend of Marlow's, who had helped him paint the pickup truck in Newberry Springs, swore to tell "the whole truth," and then denied having told a private investigator that Coffman "came across like a tramp, used a lot of profanity, and dressed like a hooker." Neither could he remember telling the P.I. that Cyndi sometimes got mad and screamed at Marlow.

The private investigator, Patti Smith, contradicted his denials and affirmed all of the alleged statements. She noted that he had changed his mind about saying those things on the stand possibly because he had recently been in jail, and some folks he met there had suggested that he shouldn't "snitch" on Miss Coffman.

The lengthy testimony by Dr. Lenore Walker, Ray Craig felt, may have been injurious to his client Marlow, so he called his own expert, Dr. Michael Kania. After citing impressive credentials, Kania said that he considered himself a clinical psychologist and that he knew his purpose in this trial was to comment on his own evaluation of the data Dr. Lenore Walker had used to form her conclusions and to discuss any differences of opinion.

Tall and trim, with a neat beard matching his dark hair, Kania's first conflict with Walker's strong opinions regarded use of individual questions on the MMPI tests. "I partially agree" with Dr. Walker, he said, but argued that it is certainly

402 *Don Lasseter*

useful to examine the answers to singular questions in some cases. He cited several possible answers that might stimulate the need for additional probing. For example, if there was an item on the MMPI stating, "I like to lie a lot," and the person answered, "True," Kania said he might want to learn more about why the person gave that answer.

Specifically, on Coffman's tests, Kania thought that some of the profiles developed were in a range, "where you would want to at least consider the possibility that a person might be exaggerating their symptoms."

Craig asked, "Is it your testimony that on the basis of the MMPI, you would be most suspicious of (a) presence (in Coffman) of anti-social personality disorder with also a drug-abuse factor?"

"From what I've reviewed, yes. Those would be the two diagnoses that would be foremost in my mind and would be the ones I would want to question so I could either rule it in or rule it out."

While Dr. Michael Kania did not absolutely contradict the opinions of Dr. Lenore Walker, he did dispute some of them, and clearly suggested that portions of the material developed on Cynthia Coffman indicated the need for additional inquiry and analysis.

When Chip Haight cross-examined Kania, the doctor positively agreed on the necessity of a psychologist being skeptical when dealing with a criminal defendant.

* * *

Two witnesses who had observed the behavior of Marlow and Coffman in Big Bear stores gave their accounts to the jury on Monday morning, February 6. Then Ray Craig recalled Coral Willoughby. Going over the period again of the three weeks prior to Corinna's death, Willoughby said that Coffman was "wired" nearly every day, meaning under the influence of methamphetamine, and she was always "bitching" at Greg. She quoted Coffman's words to Marlow: "We have got to get money . . . 'cause we have to go score some speed."

Once, they were arguing in her car about money, Coral said, and Greg slapped Cyndi. Coral ordered them "to get out of the car if they wanted to fight." They exited and continued to quarrel outside, until Greg got back in and told Cyndi if she wanted to leave, she could leave. Coffman begged, "Please don't leave me, I love you, please don't leave me," and was crying. Five minutes later, Greg readmitted her in the car, but told her to get off his back. The argument took place near the corner of Sierra and Jurupa, Coral said, near a connection's house. She did not mention that it was next to the grape vineyard where a brutal murder happened a few days after the incident.

Perhaps the most damaging comment Coral made about Coffman came in the next exchange. Coffman had gone into the Drinkhouse bedroom, Coral said, and then returned to the living room. Craig inquired, "At that time, did you notice anything unusual about Miss Coffman's hair?"

"Nothing, except she was wet!"

"You say she was wet?"

"Her hair was wet, and she had changed clothes."

On cross-examination, Don Jordan tried to blur the image Coral had verbally painted. Referring to the wet hair, he asked, "What did it look like?"

"Wet," was the terse answer.

"Just plain wet? Can you describe it in any more detail than that?"

"Wet hair is wet hair," Coral snorted.

A private forensic criminalist was next, appearing on the stand for just a few minutes. He made some vague comments about the crime scene in the vineyard being inadequately protected by the investigators, but left the audience confused about his purpose. Within minutes after he stepped down, there was a rumble of excitement. Chairs filled rapidly following the afternoon break, and observers watched James Gregory Marlow shuffle to the witness stand, where his leg shackles were removed before the jury returned.

The first thing Ray Craig wanted to dispel was the notion that Marlow was a member of, or associated with, any prison gang. Marlow said that he was not nor had he ever told Coffman that he was. Methodically, Craig gave Marlow the opportunity to say that he had never threatened Cyndi's life nor the life of her son. "At any time did you ever threaten her with harm of any sort if she left you?"

"I tried to get her to leave me sometimes," Marlow replied, with a slight snicker. His voice varied from soft to nearly inaudible, and his intense gaze rarely left the face of his attorney.

To a query about his arguments with Coffman becoming physical, Marlow responded, "A couple of times it was . . . on both sides."

Marlow's narrative took listeners through his first day with Coffman: meeting her at the apartment she shared with Sam Keam, Marlow's efforts to help fix Sam's station wagon, a trip to find some marijuana, and parking with her in Greg's El Camino near a microwave tower. "And we just kind of got together right there. . . . We made love right there."

Marlow's story was presented matter-of-factly, with seeming candor and touches of whimsical humor. Court watchers could begin to see the charm of the muscular man, whose jailhouse pallor accentuated his heavier face and his receding, short hair.

"At Newberry Springs, how did you feel about Miss Coffman?" Craig inquired.

"I loved her." He had started feeling that way "a few days after I was with her at Paul's."

He had neither killed anyone in prison, Marlow asserted, nor told Cyndi that he had.

Bringing up the incident where Marlow had pushed Coffman down in the Donners' home, Craig asked him for the reason. "I can't remember if it was because of guys calling on the phone or exactly what it was," Marlow replied, giving a hint of his jealousy. His voice grew softer, causing the judge to repeatedly ask him to please speak up. Greg had pushed Cyndi with one hand, to her shoulder, he said, and she fell after taking two steps backward.

The other incident of physical confrontation acknowledged by Marlow was also in Newberry Springs. He had been painting the trailer while she was inside repairing her long, red fingernails with superglue. "I ended up biting her fingernail off," Marlow admitted, "and got some clippers and trimmed the rest of them."

There were no other incidents of violence toward Cyndi while in Newberry Springs, the defendant insisted.

Marlow told of leaving California, the zigzag trip to St. Louis where Cyndi was unable to see her parents or son, and the run to Kentucky to discover there was nothing left of his deceased grandmother's property. He admitted making a deal to kill Greg "Wildman" Hill, but asserted that while he and Cyndi waited on the ridge above Hill's house, he wanted to back out. Cyndi, Marlow said, demanded that he "deal with it."

According to Marlow, he told her he couldn't do it, "so she said, 'Well give me the gun. I'll deal with it.' I gave it to her and told her, 'I'm going back up by the truck. I'm not telling you to do anything. I'm not doing anything. If you do anything, do it on your own. You're not going to blame me later for it.'"

Continuing his chronicle, Marlow said that Coffman tied a bandanna around her chest, put the gun in the back of her pants, and went down to the house. In about a half hour, he heard someone coming, and hid. He saw Coffman and Hill go to the open truck hood. He watched as she acted like she was trying to start the engine, and as she twice tried to aim the gun at Hill, but didn't succeed. Marlow came out of the bushes yelling, "What are you doing here with my sister?" and grappled with Hill after the man drew a gun. "I grabbed his hand, we jerked around, and he got shot."

Asked what happened then, the defendant whispered: "She came up and kicked him a couple of times and said, 'Are you sure he's dead? Shoot him again.'" He refused and they left the scene in the pickup.

The following weeks, Greg recalled, were taken up with spending the $5,000 payment for a motorcycle, clothes, and drugs. They had a biker wedding, then ran out of money. Cyndi thought they could get some more by doing another job for Killer. And she wanted to get even with her ex-in-laws for taking her son.

"Did she say what she meant by that?"

"She wanted me to kill them. I told her I can't do that. And she said she would tell on me for what happened to Wildman." Her threat, Marlow said, caused most of their fights after that.

Yes, he told the lawyer, they had gone to a doctor after a bike wreck, but it was not because he had beaten Cyndi. And he had never hit her in the face with a clutch plate or kicked her with steel-toed shoes. (Marlow would later comment to a journalist, "Can you imagine me kicking that skinny little thing with steel-toed shoes? I would have broken all of her bones.")

In Atlanta, Marlow said, he didn't want to go out with his coworkers that night. Asked why, he explained, "I was concerned about some of the things, the Wildman thing, that we had done shortly before we came there to work, and about arguing in front of my boss and stuff over Cyndi flirting around, and then getting into something worse. I was afraid to."

"You said something about Miss Coffman flirting. What did you mean?"

"Just . . . she would flirt with a lot of my friends and would make you get in bad situations. Happened in Newberry, happened in Kentucky."

That night, he said, "I told her, 'Cyndi, if this time you make me look bad in front of my boss, and all this other stuff . . . ,' I would cut her hair." Marlow knew that Coffman was proud of her hair and spent a lot of time grooming it. Maybe the threat of losing it would keep her in line. "She just laughed."

At the Atlanta bar, he and Cyndi drank several shots of straight tequila. "There was an argument between me and these two big guys with cowboy hats and Cyndi (was) on the dance floor while Elmer and the two guys from Texas were playing pool."

"What was the argument about?"

"About Cyndi. The two guys were arguing over

her. I was drunk and I told her to come on, let's go. And she didn't want to. She was just laughing and drinking. We all finally left the bar and went to a place to eat." He was not beating on Cyndi, he insisted. "I was just scared. Ever since that time in Kentucky, I was scared."

Inside the restaurant, Marlow muttered, something happened that caused the explosion. "Cyndi said she was going to be with Elmer."

"What did that mean?"

"That she was going to sleep with him that night, or something. That is the way I took it."

"How did that make you feel?"

"I grabbed her hair. I pulled her back and let them guys go in. And we walked back to the car."

Just as Marlow started to talk about the incident back at the hotel, Judge Turner called the evening recess, ordering resumption at 9:30 the next morning. It was like the old Saturday matinee serials, leaving the viewer in suspense.

On Valentine's Day, Tuesday, Marlow resumed his story, taking listeners to the Atlanta motel room. "I told her I was going to cut her hair because she was flirting around with my friends and starting trouble. She laughed at me and said I wasn't going to do it. She got me the scissors and sat down in a chair. We were both drunk." He vehemently denied threatening to cut her eye out or sodomizing her that night. After the haircut, he could only remember lying down, then hearing someone knock at the door in the morning.

"What happened when you woke up?"

"She got up and went to the bathroom and started crying and said, 'You really did cut my hair.' I told her I was sorry, and she could cut mine, too, if she wanted to."

Back in Kentucky, according to Marlow, Shannon Compton (Killer) made another offer. "He said there was a lady in Arizona who some people back there wanted killed for twenty thousand dollars. I told him, 'No way.' Cyndi said she would do it."

In a hectic return to California, they stopped at Page, Arizona, penniless again, Marlow complained. "Cyndi said that Sam's parents had a safe they kept thousands of dollars in, and that they didn't use banks. We went to their house and she told me about a window they kept open in the back. We took the safe and a couple pieces of jewelry." They were sorely disappointed to find only a few silver dollars in it.

Once more in California, according to Marlow, they stayed with his friends and he tattooed Cyndi. "She wanted one in Knoxville, and she wanted one in Kentucky. And she kept wanting one and I put some on her ring finger. Then she drew up a pattern that she wanted on her—"

"Buttocks?" Ray Craig interrupted, protecting the dignity of the court.

"Yeah."

When they had moved in the Willoughbys house, Marlow testified, they began to argue again over money and about getting her son. "And then I—a few times before in Kentucky I would tell her that (I) would go ahead and send her to Missouri or whatever, and she could wait for me. And she said she didn't want to do that."

He explained the stabbing incident: "We were arguing in the bedroom and she laid down and pulled covers all around her and asked me to come to bed. I didn't want to. I was on edge . . . near panic. She told me if I didn't get her to Arizona . . . and we were getting loud . . . and I tried to tell her that I didn't mean to do that in Kentucky . . . we were getting loud and you could hear in the other room. I didn't know what to do . . . I don't know how to describe it . . . I was losing touch."

"So what happened next?"

The witness's voice faltered again, "I . . . I grabbed my knife and stabbed the bed and the covers and she jumped and said, 'You stabbed me!' I thought she was faking it, and I pulled the covers off. I didn't intentionally stab her. With a knife like that, it would have been a lot worse if I meant to." She asked for some pills for the pain, and one of the Willoughbys produced some. No, Marlow asserted, he never said anything about cyanide.

Because he had agreed to try to get Cyndi to Arizona, Marlow worried about it all night while they stayed at the Drinkhouse apartment, he said, trying to figure out how to acquire enough money.

"I went to a friend's house, borrowed a suit, and she put on a dress, to do some robberies."

At the Redlands Mall, "That little white car pulled up right in front of the car we were sitting in. And Cyndi said that she wanted that car . . . it would be a good little car to go to Arizona. The lady came out of the mall, and Cyndi went up to her and asked her for a ride, to the college, I think. And then we took off down the road, and Cyndi nudged me a few times to pull the gun out. We pulled over, and Cyndi got out and went around to the driver's side and told her to scoot over. She (Novis) got in my lap and Cyndi drove."

Spectators were anxiously waiting to hear what Marlow would say about the shower. He didn't disappoint them. "Cyndi got in the shower with that lady. She asked me to get in, and I got in there, too."

"Who disrobed first?"

"Cyndi did. She helped me take the girl's clothes off."

"Who first said anything about getting in the shower?"

"Cyndi did. She wanted to see me be with a girl. She pushed us together. And, I couldn't . . . a lot of times I couldn't . . . get it up. Cyndi gave me oral sex."

"Did you climax?"

"With her I did."

Craig wanted to know if Marlow meant he climaxed with Coffman, but Greg was looking at

Cyndi, sitting down at the defense table. Indignantly, Marlow said, "I don't see how she can laugh."

"What did you do after you climaxed?"

"Got out of the shower."

"Were the two women still in there?"

"Yes. She was kissing around on Miss Novis."

"Where was she kissing her?"

Marlow flushed, and gestured toward his lower body. "Down here. Around her private parts and stuff. Then they got out and we all got dressed."

Each excruciating step leading to the vineyard was reviewed, like the dramatic climax of a suspense movie being shown in gripping freeze-frame shots. The only sounds in the courtroom were the voices of Greg Marlow and his attorney Ray Craig.

"All right," Craig enunciated, "you stopped in the vineyard, is that correct?"

"Yeah. Um . . . we sit there for a little while and Cyndi said she wanted to go to the speed lady's house and get some speed, for us to wait there. So I got a sleeping bag out and put it on the ground a little ways from the car. And that lady and I sat there and she (Coffman) took off."

Cynthia Coffman had previously testified that Greg had sent her to the connection's house, but she didn't go because she didn't have enough money. Craig asked Marlow, "How much money did she have at the time?"

"I thought she only had five or ten dollars that she got out of the lady's purse, but I didn't know if they (Coral and Cyndi, earlier) went and got some out of the machine, or what."

What did Marlow and Corinna Novis do in Coffman's absence? Marlow, nearly inaudible again, said, ". . . (We were) just sitting there and talking about Miss Novis's car, and Cyndi, and her coming back, and where did she go. I didn't want the lady to be hurt and I was trying to think of some kind way to come out of all this."

Bill and Donna Novis sat still behind the rail, their rage and hurt concealed.

In about fifteen minutes, Marlow professed, Coffman returned to the dark vineyard. "She said, 'You still haven't done anything.' And I said, 'What do you want me to do?' She wanted me to kill the lady."

"What did you say?"

"I told her to kill the lady if she wanted the lady killed. And we argued right there about Arizona and Kentucky and she said, 'You already killed somebody there and we are going to Arizona to kill somebody else. You're either going to have to do this . . . You might have to kill Richard and Coral too.' " He stood there, in confusion, Marlow said, arguing and noticing that "there was a lot of stars."

"Then what next occurred?"

"I put my arm around the lady and it was like choking her. I was sitting behind her, and I put my arm around her. Cyndi was standing in front of us a few feet away. I tried to tell her just to lay still, but I didn't know what to do. I tried to tell her . . . 'Just lay down, don't do nothing until we get out of here and get up and run away.' And then I let go of her and she was lying on her side and still breathing. I know she was still alive. I didn't want to kill her or anybody else."

"What did you do with the dirt?"

"I pulled it right up there while (Cyndi) was watching, and there was some bushes right there, and I laid those by her head so she would . . . I just put dirt up around the rest of her. It was like on top of the ground."

Marlow took listeners out of the vineyard and through a night of burglary and attempts to profit from the death of Corinna Novis. He reiterated his confusion and desperation. At Corinna's apartment, he didn't want to go in because he didn't think the victim was dead, and she might be there with the police. He quoted Coffman as saying, "Don't worry, she's dead."

After they were arrested, and during the long wait in jail, Marlow divulged, Coffman spoke to him when they had the opportunity. "She told me that if I went against her in this, that deputies and inmates would make sure that I was killed before I made it through trial."

Before releasing the witness for cross-examination, Craig asked about the holding-cell incident where a deputy had seen them "having some oral activity."

Marlow spoke candidly. "She came over to my cell, like a lot of other times, and I was all for it, myself. It was fifty-fifty. She gave me oral sex through the bars."

Alan Spears cross-examined for Coffman's defense team, but got off to a rocky start. Nine of his first fourteen questions drew objections, all sustained, with a caution from Judge Turner, at sidebar, to stop badgering the witness and start asking legitimate questions. Within minutes, he drew the judge's ire again. Spears crossly snarled at Marlow, ". . . You are deliberately speaking slowly and softly because you want the jury to believe that Miss Coffman was dominating you or—"

Judge Turner interrupted. With no voiced objection from the other attorneys, the judge uncharacteristically scoffed, "Objection sustained! Counsel, shame on you. Purely argumentative. Now if you have any questions you wish to ask, ask them. But don't argue your case."

Spears shot back, "If you want to criticize me before the jury, we can go to side-bar." The judge calmly deflected the remark, and Spears asked Marlow, "Your purpose in speaking this way, Mr. Marlow, is to make the jury think that Cyndi Coffman controlled you, is that correct?"

Now Marlow joined in the fray, replying, "I want the jury to believe what is true. That my voice has anything to do with it—if you like me to shout, sir, then I'll try to do that."

Spears wanted to know if Marlow had spoken that softly with Shannon Compton when making a deal to kill Wildman Hill for "five grand." Marlow thought that he probably had.

Had he spoken that softly when interviewed by police officers, and had he been trying to convince them that he was "just a big, dumb oaf?"

After a few more questions about the first sex encounter with Coffman, Alan Spears suggested adjournment for the day.

Before open court proceedings started on February 15, Judge Turner met with the attorneys to rule on an objection to allowing the letters Marlow and Coffman had exchanged into evidence. He profoundly summarized the tone of the trial:

"The two defendants have chosen to, starting with Miss Coffman, to make this primarily a trial of their mental relationship to each other, and their ability to control or be controlled by each other. And much of the time we have devoted in this trial has been expended on those issues. There's sort of some evidence having to do with the actual killings—killing, but primarily the evidence seems to relate to who is controlling whom. I do think you are entitled, since that has become a very significant issue, to explore that issue to the fullest. And I think those letters . . . give an insight into part of the thinking process of each one of the defendants. Many of the letters were admitted . . . to show the real Miss Coffman behind the facade which some people were claiming she was putting up here in court. And this is an effort on behalf of her attorneys to try to show the real Marlow behind the facade they claim he is putting up here in court. I think that's legitimate evidence. The objection is overruled."

Spears questioned Marlow about his sexual experiences with Coffman. "Did Miss Coffman have sex or try to have sex with all your friends, Mr. Marlow?"

"She flirted with all of them."

Spears finished the morning with queries about Marlow's letters, tattoos, understanding of gangs and bikers, and thoughts about marrying Coffman with intent to keep her from testifying.

Marlow's appearance on the stand would continue for three more days.

Twenty-seven

When Alan Spears continued his acerbic cross-examination of James Gregory Marlow on February 16, the defendant still had a few more surprises for the fascinated audience.

Spears asked, ". . . Miss Coffman told you that if you went against her in this, that deputies and inmates would make sure that you were killed. Do you remember that?"

"Sure do."

With obvious disbelief, Spears inquired, "Has anyone made any attempt on your life?"

"Several times!" Marlow was suddenly animated and mentioned examples of near-miss attacks by other inmates. "I've got away so far. That's why I live in isolation." It would be a continuing problem for him, and Marlow would later produce documents that seemed to support his claims of assassination attempts.

After the torrent of sizzling letters the two defendants had exchanged, their relationship finally began to crumble, Marlow informed the jury, and the correspondence tapered off with a Nestlé's candy bar wrapper, which was produced as evidence. Written on the crumpled paper was a note from Coffman to Marlow. She had handed it to him during a bus ride between jail and court. Her words told him, "The reason I have not been writing you is because my lawyer says I can't or shouldn't. Because they will really stick it to me." She informed him that she would still write, but through a third party. It marked the final stages of the love affair, and Marlow received his last letter from Coffman in September 1987, ten months after they were arrested.

A six-day hiatus in the trial passed before Chip Haight cross-examined Marlow again. He was curious about the couple's fading passion for each other. Mentioning Marlow's initial interviews with the police, in which he had tried to take "all of the heat," Haight noted that something had since changed.

Marlow explained. "Well, some of the things she said . . . the part about killing her son, things like that. I'm not going to sit over there and just be quiet while everybody thinks stuff like that." Also, Marlow remarked, ". . . She's been working with other people and trying to get me killed behind my back, while she's telling me she loves me. I've heard her tell people on the bus, 'If he doesn't make it to court, I'll beat this.' "

Chip Haight dragged out of Marlow his view of Richard Drinkhouse's complicity in the crime. The prosecutor asked if Drinkhouse demanded money for the use of his place to hold Novis captive.

"I thought he wanted a thousand dollars," Marlow complained. "And he is the first one who (protested) letting her go. He said, 'You can't do that. You can't let her go because she will bring the cops right back here to me.'" Marlow did not deny responding to Drinkhouse, "How is she going to talk when she is under a pile of rocks?"

Bouncing back to Marlow's early attempts to take most of the blame, Haight asked, "Now you're blaming Miss Coffman for these crimes, aren't you?"

Marlow thought about it for a few seconds. "I'm not blaming her one hundred percent. I'm saying that . . . it's fifty-fifty. I'm saying that anyone involved in any part of this is just as much to blame as anybody else."

Alan Spears took up the same theme, sensing the opportunity to show that Marlow was now wrongfully shifting the blame to his client. "Are you mad at Cyndi as of today?"

"I don't think I'm mad at her," Marlow said, looking at Coffman. "I'm more hurt than anything else." Then, tearing his gaze away, "I don't want anything else to do with her."

On his last day of his testimony, Monday, February 27, Marlow continued to deny that he had taken a shovel into the vineyard and buried Corinna Novis. He had only "pulled a little dirt over her," he maintained, so that "she could still breathe."

Twenty minutes later, James Gregory Marlow left the stand.

Redlands Police Department detective Tom Fitzmaurice was called by Chip Haight in a final rebuttal on February 28. Now that Marlow had testified, there was no legal problem in allowing the officer to quote from Marlow's post-Miranda violation confessions.

Fitzmaurice and Det. Odie Lockhart had intensively interviewed Marlow on the night of his arrest. They listened to Marlow's hints, denials, and cryptic comments, such as, "I guess I could blame all this on my mom." After Corinna's body was discovered in the early morning, they had rested for a while, then began questioning the suspect again.

Chip Haight walked to the witness stand, handed Fitzmaurice a transcript of those interviews, and asked him to read aloud from it. The detective quoted his own words. "Whose idea was it to kill that girl?"

"She . . . man, she just . . . I have to say it was both. It was fifty-fifty," Marlow had blurted out.

"Was it to keep her from being a witness?"

"Yeah."

"How did the girl die?"

"Strangulation."

"Who strangled her?"

"I did."

The jury riveted their eyes on Fitzmaurice, in rapt attention, and spectators dared not breathe. All of Marlow's denials during his testimony were being methodically shredded.

"What did you use?" Fitzmaurice had demanded of the suspect.

"A tie."

"Is the tie there with her (in the grave), or what did you do with it?"

"I threw it away somewhere." Some of the spectators glanced at the evidence table, where the brown tie had been for several days.

The reading continued. "Why did you take her in the shower?"

"I don't know exactly why. We took her in there and I couldn't do anything. I half tried, and thought maybe I could, but I couldn't."

"What was Cyndi doing?"

"She was playing with me, trying to get me hard. And I couldn't . . . I just couldn't do nothing, and I don't know why."

Haight asked the detective to skip over to more questions about the vineyard. Fitzmaurice complied, and read:

"Who dug the hole?"

"I did," Marlow had admitted.

"What did you use?"

"A little shovel."

"Can you remember how you laid her in the hole? Was she on her back, stomach, or side?"

"On her stomach, I believe." The jurors winced. They had seen the enlarged full-color photos of the pitiful young woman, lying facedown in the sandy grave.

In the recorded confession, Marlow admitted taking Corinna's shoes and giving them to Coffman, but they weren't her size, so they had buried them at Lytle Creek. His memory about the disposition of the necktie also improved. He had given it back to the friend from whom he had borrowed it, where detectives had seized it with a search warrant.

Near the end of the interview, Fitzmaurice and Lockhart had let James Marlow ramble and express his thoughts about Cyndi Coffman: ". . . And I never beat on her or nothing like that. It was always her. Driving me nuts. It was—man, flirting around, messing around, or . . . Goddamn. Go through all kinds of shit, man. I'd do it all again . . ."

The detective's voice stopped, and there was heavy silence in the courtroom. No one wanted to break it. It was a moment of profound human drama, a culminating peak of the trial.

Chip Haight had saved the best for last.

Final summation opened on Monday, March 6. Chip Haight paced back and forth in front of the jury and proclaimed, ". . . Both defendants were

the actual perpetrators of the murder of Corinna
Novis. They were both actually out there in the
vineyard with their hands on her when she was
killed. But there's one crime where Miss Coffman
can only be found guilty as an aider and abettor.
And that's sodomy. That's anatomical. We all understand."

Regarding the believability of the defendants,
Haight commented, "Let's face it, to some extent
their stories are mutually exclusive. You have to
disbelieve one or disbelieve the other. I'm suggesting to you to disbelieve both of them and look at
the objective evidence."

Shrugging off most of Dr. Lenore Walker's
psychological testimony, Haight branded the couple as "classic sociopaths, whose synergistic effect
on each other produced a violent crime spree."
There was no real mental illness, he said, and
the killers were not incapacitated by drugs. Coffman was part of a killing team, not a battered
woman.

"Let's look at examples," Haight said. "First,
that little nod at the Drinkhouse residence. That's
very revealing, isn't it?" He summarized how Coffman had signaled Marlow of Drinkhouse's attempt
to peer into the room, and characterized it as a
team effort. And in the Kentucky killing, "they had
divided but complementary roles," with Coffman
as the "lurer." In the murder of Lynel Murray,
Haight argued, "The net result is you again have
a team effort, and you don't have anybody dominating the other.

"Corinna Novis wasn't here to speak to you," said Haight, invoking mental images of the beautiful young woman when she was alive and able to speak. "But in a way, she told you what happened in that vineyard." Reminding the jury of the injuries on Corinna's neck, and the sand in her mouth, Haight invited the jurors to "work on it in the jury room." He asked, "How are you going to use that ligature . . . with two arms pulled away and another hand pressing (her head down) unless there are three hands actually killing her? The evidence Corinna is telling you is that two people killed her. This is tangible evidence."

Corinna's earrings, Haight asserted, were found in the possession of Coffman and "were taken for either trophies or mementos."

Pounding away at the veracity of Coffman and Marlow, Haight proclaimed, "I think both are liars. They have no idea what the truth means, let alone the oath to tell it."

Haight was well known in the legal community for quoting from Charlie Chan, and he finally found the opportunity in this trial. "Necessity mother of invention, but sometimes stepmother of deception," he enunciated. "I think that is really what went on in a nutshell, with the Coffman defense."

Knowing that he would have one more crack at the jury following final summation by the two defenders, Haight scanned the jurors' faces, looked toward the defendants, and said, "You've probably all heard the old saw about attorney arguments. If you have the facts, you argue the facts. When you have the law, you argue the law. When you don't have either the facts or the law, you just argue.

"In summation, I'm going to ask you to . . . convict the defendants for what they did to Corinna Novis, not for what they may or may not have done to each other. Thank you."

Ray Craig stepped to the lectern next. After some preliminary comments about instructions the jury would hear from the judge, Craig said, "One of the most upsetting, chilling accusations against Mr. Marlow was that part of his hold on poor Miss Coffman was this constant threat to kill her and her child. Interesting, though, the first time anything like this came to light was approximately April 27, 1987, when Dr. Walker came on the scene. Lots of things were said at the Redlands Police Department the night of November 14, 1986, by Miss Coffman, (but) not a thing came up about Mr. Marlow threatening or taking any action against that child."

Bringing up the letters, Craig reminded the jurors that Coffman had drawn a map for Marlow to where her child lived. "Such fear," he hissed.

"And how about Robin Long? Lots of things were said to her. Anything about fear regarding the child?"

Having dealt with the fear issue, Craig moved on

to the alleged physical abuse. "Now, how about the beatings, which were described to you with such intensity, such chilling detail?" Summarizing some of the incidents, Craig pointed out that Coffman had opportunities to leave Marlow very early in the relationship, but didn't. "The amazing thing is, all this beating, kicking in the shins and legs with steel-toed boots—certainly Mr. Marlow is a good-sized individual—where are the broken arms? Where are the scars? It just wasn't that serious.

"That knife," Craig continued. "You've seen that knife. A stab with that knife would certainly do a lot more harm than that cut. And the cyanide capsules, I suggest to you, is the height of melodrama."

The murder, Craig conceded, had obviously happened, and certainly, so had the robbery. "That's not what this case is all about. If it was, we wouldn't have devoted the last more-than-half-a-year of our lives to this case. There is much more to be decided."

It became clear that Ray Craig was not hoping for complete exoneration for Marlow, but perhaps a finding of a lesser degree of murder or manslaughter. He was also making a concerted effort to save his client's life by invalidating the special circumstances allegations that could send Marlow to the gas chamber. To do this, he pointed to the possibility that Marlow was crazed by methamphetamines when he made the admissions to Detective Fitzmaurice. And he wanted the jury to believe that Marlow's confession was an attempt to protect his lover, Coffman.

One of the special circumstances, sodomy, was never proved, Craig argued, questioning the quality of the pathologist's findings. Two others, burglary and robbery, happened after the murder as separate events, Craig said. "As the special circumstances are worded, I submit to you . . . they are not true."

The evidence that Marlow intended to kill Novis was highly circumstantial, according to Craig, and the jury would be instructed how to weigh that.

"This has not been an emotional summation by any means," Craig concluded, "nor has it been intended to. Logic is oft times the opposite of emotionalism. I ask you, beseech you, to not base your decisions on passion, prejudice, or caprice."

Reminding the jurors that "what happened in Orange County will be determined and dealt with by the proper tribunal," Craig ended his plea with, ". . . The last time Mr. Marlow saw Corinna Novis, no matter what else he may have been guilty of, he didn't have the intent to kill her nor did he kill her. Thank you."

Don Jordan acknowledged that "this has been a very long trial. All of you have been very patient." He, too, commented on the jury instructions they would receive. In doing so, he stated, ". . . and then there is the last series of findings, and that is whether or not Mr. Marlow suffered a prior conviction or actually two . . ."

"Whoa," shouted Chip Haight. "Objection!"

"Move for mistrial," joined Ray Craig.

Judge Turner frowned toward Jordan, saying, "There is not an issue before the jury as to whether he has a prior conviction." After a discussion at the bench, Turner sustained the objection and denied the motion for a mistrial. Jordan resumed his summation.

"I believe that the facts show that Miss Coffman was so dominated by her relationship with Mr. Marlow, by the sheer force of his personality, and her limited experience beforehand, that she did not know what she was doing insofar as allowing herself to get involved and specifically that she did not and was not able to form any intent to kill." Despite this, he told the jury, "I do not think it would be unreasonable for a jury to return a verdict of guilty as to first degree murder on Miss Coffman."

He did think, he stated emphatically, that, "it would be unreasonable for a jury to come back with true findings on the special circumstances, all four special circumstances." He listed them again: kidnapping, robbery, burglary, and sodomy. Jordan systematically outlined the reason for his beliefs, then tackled Chip Haight's key accusation. "Now Mr. Haight has developed a theory that it must have taken two people to kill Miss Novis. I'm going to offer a suggestion . . . That's nonsense." Again, he gave his supporting reasons. Jordan also rejected the theory of trophy hunting for earrings.

Taking the jury through chronological events of the relationship again, Jordan compared Coffman's experience with Marlow as a "boot camp" of indoctrination. "By comparison to Marlow, she was naive. The man had been to prison, and even built his nickname around prison. Folsom Wolf, what a nickname. What does that say about a person?"

Marlow's regaling of Coffman with his prison experiences impacted her, Jordan said. "Miss Coffman was like a bowling pin knocked over by a bowling ball, like a palm tree in a hurricane. This man came down and surrounded her with love."

Don Jordan began his speech to the jury in midafternoon of Monday, March 6, and spoke all day Tuesday. He recapitulated the trial and the chaotic relationship of Coffman and Marlow, focusing on the beatings and mind control. With an eloquent plea to find the special circumstances not true, Don Jordan completed his summation.

Because the burden of proof is on the prosecution, Chip Haight had one more shot at the jury.

"If you look at both defendants," he said, "it seems pretty clear that he is the muscle, and she is the brains of that team. These two dropped out of normal society. And they adopted alter egos. He became Folsom Wolf, and she became Cynful Cyndi, and that fit her image of herself."

Hitting lightly on all of the evidence, and the highlights of the synergistic relationship, Haight talked of the excitement they sought, resulting in murder. He regretted, he said, that he had to call a jailhouse snitch to testify. "Let's face it, I want all of my witnesses to be Boy Scouts and nuns, or the President of the United States. But when you cast a play in hell, you can't expect the actors to be angels."

To deal with the issue of intent to kill, Haight said, "It isn't like the intent to build a bridge or write a book. It's not a very complicated thought process, is it? I mean think about it. Isn't it one of the most primitive thought processes we, as human beings, have? Sharks form the intent to kill. My cat, when he goes after a bird, intends to kill the bird. It's not very complicated."

Another facet of the defendants' alleged behavior defied logic, according to Haight. "Isn't it weird that they both separated at the key moment in these crimes? I mean, according to their stories, they are together all the time. Everybody described them as being inseparable. But the key moment, when you are going to kill your victim and cover her up and bury her, they both say they separated. Is that consistent with their prior pattern of conduct?

"These two were hunters of human beings," Haight reiterated. "They intended to kill their victims just as surely as hunters do." With emotion now clear in his voice, Haight said, "Mr. Craig refers to the killing of Corinna Novis as a tragedy.

Now, when I think of a tragedy, I think of floods. I think of earthquakes. This was not a tragedy in that sense. This was cold-blooded murder to get rid of a witness. That's what this was. Thank you very much."

That afternoon, after over four months of grueling testimony and exhibits, the seven men and five women listened first to the long jury instructions read by Judge Don Turner, then filed into the jury room to begin deliberations. They elected one of the women to act as foreman.

On Tuesday, March 14, they signaled the bailiff that they had reached a decision. The sixty courtroom seats were quickly filled, and more than forty people stood along the walls to hear the verdicts. Marlow, in shackles, shuffled to his chair. Coffman, wearing a blue striped dress, appeared nervous. The couple still would not speak to each other. When the jurors were seated, the tension grew. Court clerk Nancy Dugas read the findings.

"We, the jury in the above entitled action, find the defendant James Gregory Marlow, guilty of the crime of murder in the first degree in that he did murder Corinna D. Novis, a human being."

The clerk paused for a moment, then peeled the second sheet from the stack.

"We, the jury in the above entitled action, find the defendant Cynthia Lynn Coffman, guilty of the crime of murder in the first degree in that she did murder Corinna D. Novis, a human being."

In a monotone befitting court dignity, Dugas continued to read, while tears began to roll down Coffman's cheeks and Marlow grimaced.

"Guilty" was repeated for the charges of kidnapping, robbery, burglary, sodomy, and twelve counts of using a firearm. The announcement that Coffman was guilty of sodomy drew gasps from the gallery.

While the clerk read for fifteen minutes, everyone in the courtroom sat in suspense, waiting to hear the jury's decision on the special circumstances that could send the trial into a penalty phase to decide whether the convicted killers would serve life without the possibility of parole, or be sentenced to death.

At last, Nancy Dugas came to the twenty-fifth form in the stack.

"We the jury . . . find the special circumstances that the murder of Corinna D. Novis was committed by the defendant James Gregory Marlow with the intent to kill while said defendant was engaged in the crime of kidnapping." And . . .

"We the jury . . . find the special circumstances that the murder of Corinna D. Novis was committed by the defendant Cynthia Lynn Coffman with the intent to kill while said defendant was engaged in the crime of kidnapping."

Donna Novis clenched her fist, smiled broadly, and hugged Bill, who whispered, "Thank God."

Continuing to read, the clerk revealed that the

jury had convicted Marlow and Coffman on all counts, including the remaining three special circumstances, robbery, burglary, and sodomy.

The same seven men and five women would have to reconvene on April 17 for the beginning of the trial's penalty phase to decide if the two convicts would spend the rest of their natural lives in prison, or would face execution for killing Corinna Novis.

Twenty-eight

"Welcome back," Judge Don Turner greeted the refreshed jurors on Monday, April 17, 1989. "We're going to begin the second phase of this trial . . . the penalty phase." He explained that the purpose was to weigh aggravating and mitigating circumstances "to help you more intelligently decide which of the two potential penalties that are available is the proper one for each defendant in this case."

A broader scope of evidence could be presented in this segment to illuminate the behavioral history of the defendants, including previous convictions. Additionally, facts about the killing of Lynel Murray, for which Marlow and Coffman still faced a possible trial in Orange County, could be aired. "Also, in this trial, it's perfectly appropriate for you to allow your sympathy and emotions to help you with your decision," Turner told the jury.

He did not tell them that the decision they would make, after hearing ninety witnesses over the next two months, would be, for the most part, just a recommendation. The final decision would actually be in Turner's hands. Even if the jury recommended the death penalty for either defendant, it was within the power of the judge to reduce it to life without parole if he believed that to be more appropriate.

Following opening statements by Chip Haight and Ray Craig (Alan Spears deferred until later), a series of witnesses began the long parade.

Chip Haight summoned the victims of three 1979 robberies Greg Marlow had committed with his partner, George Tinnly, in 1979. The two young women frightened by the intruders, and the bachelor whose apartment they had raided, told of Marlow's callous treatment. The proprietor of the Leathermart, her customer and witnesses, described the young bandit's plunder of the store. Employees of the methadone clinic testified about the shotgun-wielding young bandit, and the clinic manager, Wilson Lee, spoke "from the grave." He had died several years earlier, but his testimony from the preliminary hearing was read to the jury. Finally, they heard that Marlow had copped a plea, and ultimately wound up in Folsom Prison for the crimes.

Witnesses who had seen Coffman and Marlow around the Prime Cleaners just prior to the kidnapping of Lynel Murray, along with investigators, were heard. People with whom the fugitive pair came in contact after Lynel died came forward to describe the couple's conduct.

Ray Craig summoned relatives and acquaintances of Marlow, including his sister, Coral, some foster parents, and an ex-wife. Alan Spears brought in Coffman's friends and relatives, including her mother and stepfather. And, of course, the jury was subjected to more testimony from psychologists.

Detective Richard Hooper, who had made the horrifying discovery of Corinna Novis's body in a dark vineyard, nearly three years earlier, stepped down from the witness stand shortly after the morning recess, on Wednesday, June 14, happy to be the last person to testify.

Three exhausted attorneys, in turn, stood before the drained jurors on June 20 to present closing arguments. Donna, Bill, and Brenda Novis grimly watched from the jammed gallery.

"Why should we vote the death penalty in this case?" Chip Haight asked. "Because the defendants have shown that they didn't just kill their victims to get rid of a witness . . . they enjoyed killing them! They took pleasure in causing pain to their victims, and they even went one step further. They took pleasure in demeaning and debasing their victims."

With new intensity, Haight attacked the method used to kill Corinna and Lynel—strangling. "A very personal means. You really have to want to kill your victim. You want to be able to feel the life ebb out of your victim." He criticized the "celebration" at a restaurant "a couple of hours after Lynel Murray is kidnapped, beaten, strangled to death, and urinated on." Haight was indignant

that the defendants had bought champagne to take
to the hotel room paid for with Lynel's credit card.

"I have always been struck by the similarity in
the manner of the killings of the two victims. Both
strangled from behind. I don't think one person
could have killed Corinna, ground that dirt into
her face and forced it down in her mouth. Both
of them did it."

Once more, Haight expressed his belief in a synergistic effect when Marlow and Coffman came together, resulting in serial murder.

"This battered woman syndrome," he scoffed,
"is subtle and designed to exploit . . . you. I think
Miss Coffman's defense team is hoping there are
one or more of you simply unable to sentence a
woman to death." Coffman was a sociopath before
she met Mr. Marlow, said Haight, and sociopaths
lack any conscience or sense of true remorse.
"Doesn't that describe Miss Coffman and Mister
Marlow to a tee?"

Pointing to the planning and teamwork used by
the killing couple, Chip Haight cited examples:
bringing a shovel to the vineyard, having handcuffs
and a gun available before abducting the two girls,
and Coffman's practice in forging the signatures.
"That planning and teamwork destroys any domination and control theory."

Marlow's pathetic background was no excuse,
Haight said, because he still could make choices.
"Do you see any indication that he made a choice
to try to better himself, to become law-abiding? If
anything, he sunk lower, lower than his mother and

all those other people." Referring to the benevolent Sydnes family, who gave Marlow a chance in his early teens, Haight pointed out that Marlow clearly had a choice. "You saw what happened. Stabs them in the back and chose to become a violent criminal, a renegade."

Coffman had better opportunities, with "fine relatives, some of them really upstanding, decent people. But she, even more than Mr. Marlow, made the decision to sink into hell."

"I think in the final analysis, society must, from time to time in the criminal justice system, protect itself. And I'm talking just about punishment. Pure punishment.

"The defendants have made their decisions. Twelve of you are going to make the final few decisions in this case. In making that decision, I ask you, as the prosecutor, to bring back a verdict of death as to both defendants.

"I think you, as the conscience of the community, have to say these kinds of crimes, this kind of conduct, this kind of violence and humiliation, they deserve the death penalty. . . ."

After a ten-minute recess, Ray Craig gripped both sides of the lectern and faced the jury. He strongly disagreed with Chip Haight's closing comment. "He seemed to say that you are the conscience of the community, of society. I submit to you that is not your duty. Your duty is to apply the law, consider all the evidence, make a just decision. And if you have done so, you're answerable only to your own conscience. You're answerable only to yourselves, Jim Marlow, and Cynthia Coffman."

Imploring the jury to consider Marlow as a person, to consider his motives, his manner, his background, and then to apply the evidence and the law to their decision, Craig spoke softly. "And then, once you've made that decision, sink to your knees and thank God that you are not that person . . ."

As Chip Haight had done, Craig attacked the battered woman syndrome defense by Coffman's team. On the contrary, he noted, "The woman, albeit of slighter stature, is certainly able to manipulate men. Go back to Adam and Eve, Samson and Delilah, David and Bathsheba. Culpability in this case was joint, mutual, and equal." Cyndi Coffman, he said, "was perfectly capable of acting independently."

Citing the tight confinement of a small cell, bland food, few privileges, and endless years in prison as apt punishment, Craig pointed out, "There are many who committed worse crimes who are now serving life sentences. Such as Manson, Richard Speck who killed seven nurses in one night back in Chicago, (Angelo) Buono, Jr., and (Kenneth) Bianchi, (L.A.'s notorious) Hillside Stranglers.

"He was a man that never had a break in his life. And today, I'm asking you to give him one—

one break, even though it means he'll be in prison forever.

"I'd like to leave you with just one thought, parable as it were. There was a wise old Indian man in years gone by. Seemed to always know the answer to every question. Two young men decided to fool the wise old man. One of them got a bird and held it in his hands and came to the wise man and said, 'Is the bird alive or is it dead?' Knowing if the wise man said it was alive, he would crush it. If he said it was dead, he'd free it. When asked that question, the wise man looked at the young one and said, 'It's in your hands.'

"And as the fate of James Marlow goes, his fate is indeed and in fact in your hands. Thank you."

The final turn belonged to Alan Spears. After thanking the jury for their patience, he said, "It's been my observation that a focus of this penalty phase has been on Cyndi Coffman, not Greg Marlow. I surmise that is because the prosecution feels that Greg Marlow's fate (was) sealed at the other phase of this trial and that Cyndi's fate was less certain." Much of the strategy of Haight and Craig, Spears hinted, was simply to find something negative or bad about Cyndi.

Spears looked in the eyes of each juror, trying to transmit to them, through more than words, his determination to save his client. The woman who had been foreman earlier gazed back, entranced with the attorney. Something electric seemed to come alive when their eyes locked momentarily. She hoped the other panel members didn't notice.

Chipping away at Haight's "two-person" theory, Spears referred to the testimony of Detective Fitzmaurice to support his view that Marlow, alone, killed Corinna Novis. Coffman, he said, had cooperated, led the police to the victim's body, and freely told the whole story. Spears reminded the jurors that due to Coffman's admitted complicity, Don Jordan had even accepted the reasonableness of a first degree murder finding. He stated that her admitted status as an accomplice entitled her to mitigation consideration.

Alan Spears produced a towel he had subpoenaed from the Huntington Inn. Acknowledging that the jurors couldn't take it into deliberations with them, because it wasn't in evidence, Spears observed, "Suffice it to say that even as worn as this one is, it's probably extremely unlikely that the ladies on this jury could tear it into strips. When you pull those other strips out of the bag, (it's) going to be . . . pretty graphic for you. That's human hair embedded in those knots. You are going to have a tough time dealing with it emotionally, trying to sort all this out." He implored them to find Coffman's part in Lynel's murder as "that of a nonparticipant aider and abettor."

Summarizing portions of the testimony in favor of his client, Spears noted that the taking of human life was inconsistent with Coffman's beliefs, as shown by her opposition to the thought of abortion when she was a pregnant teenager.

"Because of the sanctity of human life, the courts in this country have ruled, in deciding whether or not to impose the death penalty, that you may consider mercy, sympathy, or even sentiment in arriving at a proper and just penalty. I told you in the opening statement there's nothing I can say about Cyndi Coffman that minimizes the tragic deaths of Corinna Novis and Lynel Murray. Their deaths are a tragedy of the highest order. I can't present mitigation evidence that's going to bring them back. It just can't be so.

"That isn't the object of this penalty phase. The object is to determine an appropriate punishment in light of aggravating and mitigating circumstances."

Spears forged ahead. "I can't help but tell you how I feel, and that is that we have two dead girls on our hands already and I . . . we really don't need a third at this juncture. The punishment of life without the possibility of parole is an awesome punishment. And that was the best Cyndi Coffman could hope for from the moment you rendered your verdict finding the special circumstance true. So, I ask you and I beg of you, ladies and gentlemen, to spare her life. Thank you."

Once more, on June 21, the jury listened to ponderous instructions, and retired for the most serious discussions they would hold in their entire lives. Lawyers, families, reporters, and observers whispered in the corridors, lingered over cold coffee in the cafeteria, and generally found ways to kill time over the next few days, waiting for the decision.

Word spread quickly on Thursday, June 29, at 1:45 P.M., that the jury had reached a decision, and within an hour, the courtroom was packed with people who had been screened carefully with a metal detector. Several of the investigators, including Scotty Smith, were among the crowd. Bill and Donna Novis, holding hands with Brenda, sat in the front row with friends of Corinna. Near them were Don and Jacque Murray, and Lynel's mother, Nancy. Cynthia Coffman's parents sat across the aisle.

At 2:45, Marlow, wearing a brown sport coat, brown slacks, and a newly shaved head, was led in by several deputies, arms and legs shackled. The parallel creases in his forehead seemed deeper and his full mustache droopier. Cynthia Coffman, in a blue dress, followed minutes later, also with shackles on her legs which remained in place during the hearing. She began to cry as her handcuffs were unlocked and slipped off.

Court clerk Nancy Dugas held the verdict form up and began to read, and some of the jurors, holding hands, began to cry.

Dugas read the legal language, but one word resounded through the silent room. "Death!" Cynthia Lynn Coffman, as well as James Gregory Marlow, should suffer the death penalty, the jury had decided.

Cynthia Coffman's head fell forward to her folded arms, on the table, and she sobbed loudly while Alan Spears patted her back in an effort to console her. James Marlow put his right hand to his cheek and stared dejectedly at the tabletop.

After Judge Don Turner had complimented the jurors and thanked them, the condemned pair were led out. The jurors filed slowly from the box they had occupied for so many months, and several of them stopped to hug Donna and Brenda, and shake hands with Bill. "God bless you guys, all of you," Donna smiled.

The Murray family had little to say, for they still faced an agonizing wait for Orange County officials to decide whether or not to try Marlow and Coffman for the murder of Lynel Murray.

Eight months of living in a camper parked outside of San Bernardino, in a KOA campground, had been more than enough for the Novis family. Now, they could finally pack up and head home at last, back to Gooding, Idaho, where they would always have precious memories of their beloved daughter, Corinna.

They planned to return to California in July, though, to hear Judge Turner pronounce the sentence. "I think they should be hung at sunrise tomorrow, just like they did in the old days," Bill declared before their departure. He and Donna hoped and prayed that Judge Turner would accept the recommendation of the jury, and not exercise his prerogative to reduce the sentence to life without parole. They would just have to wait and see.

Twenty-nine

After a one-month postponement, Judge Don Turner heard appeals to save the lives of both defendants on August 30, 1989. When the attorneys were finished, he heard Cynthia Coffman speak. "I'm sorry for what happened and I'm ashamed for letting it happen . . ." she sobbed. "I don't think I should have to die."

Turner told the assembly, "It's difficult for juries to vote for death for an attractive young woman, but this jury got to know her too well." Looking toward Marlow, Turner continued speaking of Coffman. "For (her), here was a man who was thrilling, who was exciting, who was dangerous . . . the court is satisfied that these two people make a team . . . I am convinced that any jury, anywhere, would have convicted Mr. Marlow and the same for Ms. Coffman. I can find no basis for reducing it."

The sentence for each of them was death.

"I'm glad it's over, and I am pleased with the outcome," Bill Novis told reporters. "I would like to have asked Coffman if Corinna pled for her life . . . not that she would have given me a truthful answer." Donna and Bill could now go home, to Gooding, to stay.

If James Gregory Marlow had been transported immediately to Death Row in San Quentin prison, overlooking San Francisco Bay, he would have been the 258th condemned man in the California system. There had been no executions since voters restored the death penalty in 1976, and the Death Row cells were crowded with men in various stages of the convoluted appeals process.

But Marlow was not taken to the site of California's gas chamber. Instead, he was bussed to the Orange County jail in Santa Ana to await a decision by the district attorney.

Cynthia Lynn Coffman had the unenviable distinction of being the first woman to be condemned to death in the state since the 1976 law became effective. Susan Atkins, Patricia Krenwinkle, and Leslie Van Houten, all members of the Charles Manson family, had faced the death penalty in 1970, for the grisly murders of actress Sharon Tate and six other people, but like Manson, their sentences had been reduced to life, with parole eligibility, when the U.S. Supreme Court had overturned the old law. A new prison was being built in central California with a special facility for condemned women, but Coffman, too, was sent to Orange County to wait.

The issue of a second expensive trial was controversial. A sizable contingent of taxpayers figured that another trial would be a waste of money. After all, how many times can you execute convicted killers?

District Attorney Michael Capizzi knew very well, though, that the court of appeals with jurisdiction in California, had a reputation for liberal interpretations of Constitutional law. The complexity and length of the San Bernardino trial, with two defendants pointing fingers at each other, might give the appellate justices some reason to overturn the jury's decisions. The D.A. did not want to see Coffman and Marlow on the streets again.

Another important consideration was on his mind. Didn't the family of Lynel Murray deserve justice, too? Was her killing any less important than other murders?

In a press conference, D.A. Capizzi announced that Orange County would try Coffman and Marlow for murder, and would seek a second death penalty for each of them.

Deputy District Attorney Robert A. Gannon, Jr., despite an already overloaded work schedule, inherited the assignment to prosecute from an assistant D.A. who had decided to enter private practice. Tall, slim, articulate, and intellectual, Gannon was one of the top prosecutors in the county at age forty-six. His high cheekbones and narrow face, emphasized by round rimless glasses, full dark neatly trimmed hair, pin-striped suits, and the deliberate, measured movements of Henry Fonda, enhanced his conservative image perfectly. A combat pilot in the Vietnam war, Gannon was known among peers as having a skill for "filling the courtroom with righteous indignation."

Diagonally across the street from the Superior Court building in Santa Ana, which housed the D.A. and his staff, the Public Defender's Office occupied the second floor of a modern office building. Leonard A. Gumlia, Deputy P.D., assigned to defend Cynthia Coffman, had collected an office full of files on the case. Gumlia, thirty-six, had joined the P.D. staff in 1982, following graduation from U.C.L.A. and Stanford. Six-feet, one-inch and slim at 175 pounds, with a mop of curly chestnut hair, Gumlia moved, spoke, and worked with quick energy. He understood the appeals process, having spent more than a year working in the appellate office assisting in the research and writing of appeals.

With help from his bright, efficient, and attractive paralegal, Kristen Widmann, twenty-five, Gumlia immersed himself in the case with unprecedented vigor and passion. Hector Chapparo, thirty-seven, also a Stanford graduate, who had taken his law degree at University of California, Berkeley, would assist in the courtroom. Before the trial started in February 1992, Leonard Gumlia traveled to Kentucky, Missouri, and Ohio, to locate and interview friends, relatives, or anyone else who could support the theory he was forming for the defense of Cyndi Coffman.

The defense team from San Bernardino provided documents from their case, too. Alan Spears had recently surprised some of his colleagues, Gumlia learned. The glances between Spears and the woman who served as jury foreman had developed into a romance, and the couple had recently been married.

Gumlia was absolutely convinced that Coffman's love for Marlow was the single most important factor in her behavior during their six-month relationship. Her fear of Marlow and concern for the safety of her son were important elements as well, but her searing, passionate, consuming love had compelled her to obey his every wish, Gumlia believed. Marlow had manipulated the vulnerable woman into a bizarre acting out of sexual and homicidal fantasies.

The battered woman syndrome had not worked for several reasons, Gumlia decided, so he would not mirror that defense. Certainly many elements of it were worth repeating, but his plan to save Coffman would not include prolonged testimony from psychologists. Certainly, he would use them, but in abbreviated presentations. Instead, he would rely on observations by witnesses who had seen the result of Marlow's dominance, some from the previous trial, and some never before contacted.

Partially agreeing with the allegation that the motive for killing Lynel Murray was to eliminate a witness, Gumlia planned to convince the jury that Marlow had a dual motive. "Intellectually, he was eliminating a witness. Psychologically, he wanted to destroy women . . . and vent his hatred for women," which, Gumlia felt, came from the love-hate relationship with Marlow's mother. To blunt any suggestion of Coffman's intent to kill, Gumlia proposed to argue that her primary motive was a desire to please Marlow, both out of love and fear.

Kristen Widmann prepared for the trial by performing most of the clerical and administrative work for Gumlia (her mother made all of the posters and charts he would show to the jury). The energetic Widmann also became a confidante of Cynthia Coffman and brought the prisoner's daily clothing changes, some of which came from Kristen's own closet.

Private attorneys George Peters and Charles Margines were court-appointed to defend James Marlow. Affable, resourceful, and proficient George Peters, was determined to save his client from a second death penalty. A highly successful twenty-year veteran in criminal law, Peters had served with the Orange County prosecutor early in his career, and remembered losing his first case to a brilliant defense attorney named Donald A. McCartin.

Now a famed, veteran superior court judge, Don McCartin's calendar included the oft postponed Coffman-Marlow trial for the murder of Lynel Murray, scheduled for February 1992. With a reputation for irascibility mixed with compassion, and a caustic wit frequently aimed at lawyers, McCartin had presided over some of the most publicized and controversial trials in the county's history. He had sent seven men to Death Row, including Randy Steven Kraft who was convicted of murdering sixteen young men, several of whom were sexually mutilated.

When jury selection began on February 19, Judge McCartin was in true form during jury voir dire (questioning of potential jurors). After asking the panel if any of them had friends who were lawyers, he smilingly apologized, "I know, attorneys have no friends." A few minutes later, with twinkling eyes telegraphing the arrival of more tongue-in-cheek acrimony, he asked, "Any one of you ever study law, then go into an honest profession when you regained your sanity?"

So there would be no misunderstanding, the judge explained that he deliberately used humor to relax the courtroom tension, and it was not to be interpreted as compromising the serious intent of the trial.

James Marlow, wearing a blue pin-striped dress

shirt and dark slacks, sat with an impassive expression, slowly chewing mints and occasionally yawning. His fourth wife, Brenda, age twenty-nine, whom he had married while waiting for this trial, fidgeted in the first row of the gallery. She and Marlow had met, briefly, prior to the murders, when he admired her ability to play baseball. She had visited him in jail following the first trial, had become a court runner for the defense attorney, and they had married in a jailhouse ceremony on December 2, 1989. A tattoo of his name adorned the third finger of her left hand.

Cynthia Coffman, with dark brown hair falling in waves halfway down her back, kept her eyes straight ahead or focused on the table in front of her. She wore a gray pleated skirt, white blouse, spike-heeled black shoes, and an adhesive bandage over her ring finger, concealing her lightning bolt and *Wolf* tattoos.

A major surprise rippled through the courtroom on March 2, when Judge McCartin announced that he had accepted motions to sever the trial, to allow each defendant a separate trial. Marlow would go first, then Coffman.

Following the completion of Bob Gannon's opening statement on March 4, George Peters rocked jurors and spectators again when he said, "We are virtually conceding the guilt phase. I will cross-examine very little, and we may plead guilty." His primary goal, he explained, was to convince the jurors that Marlow's life should be spared because of a horrific childhood and background.

One week later, Bob Gannon rested the prosecution's case after the thirty-third witness stepped down. Among those who had testified were police officers, the near-miss victims who saw Marlow and Coffman near the Prime Cleaners, Lynel's boyfriend, and pathologists who contributed chilling details about Lynel's death. Soft sobs came from the row where the victim's parents sat while full-color pictures of the savaged girl, wrapped in bloody towel strips, rested mutely on an easel near the witness stand.

George Peters stood and calmly announced that James Marlow was changing his plea to guilty. The jury would now face only the responsibility of hearing the penalty phase and deciding if Marlow should be locked up forever or face execution.

To legally clarify the plea, Gannon was given the opportunity to question Marlow outside the jury's presence. "With respect to the killing of Lynel Murray," Gannon said, "you were the person who strangled her, with the assistance of someone else. Is that right?"

"Well, I can comment on my participation at the time . . . when I did it," Marlow hedged. "I obviously must have meant to do it."

"Did you have the help of anyone else?"

"I can plead to my own participation at this point in time. I am guilty of murder." Gannon repeated the question, but Marlow was unwilling to reveal what part Cynthia Coffman had played. "I strangled Lynel Murray and I plead guilty to that."

George Peters quickly stepped in to explain, "My client's reluctance is that he's concerned about his security in jail." Nothing was lower, among inmates, than an informer, and Marlow, already fearing attempts on his life, wanted to avoid that tag. Peters requested a court order to place Marlow in protective custody during the trial, which "will give him the confidence to answer the question." Judge McCartin agreed. But Marlow would acknowledge only that he had the assistance of another party, a female.

In George Peters's opening statement in the penalty phase, he summarized Marlow's "horrific" life, emphasizing the bizarre relationship with his mother, Doris that made him an emotional cripple. "I think you will see," the attorney said, "that (in) his involvement in the deaths of Lynel Murray and Corinna Novis (he) was trying to kill himself or kill his mother. . . ." Give him life without parole, Peters begged, "because we as a society do not kill cripples."

Among the seventeen witnesses in this phase, Dr. Michael Kania was summoned again. He told the jurors that Marlow had been sexually abused during a "chaotic" childhood by an adult male in the family, in addition to being seduced by his own mother. Marlow was "head over heels in love with Coffman" and saw many "likenesses" in her to his mother. Therefore, he would do anything to please Cyndi, including killing. He "didn't want to, but felt compelled to." Marlow had told Kania, the doctor reported, that Lynel Murray "came on to him," and was agreeable to sex with him because she was in fear of Cynthia Coffman or possibly to placate him in an effort to save herself.

Observers rumbled with indignant rejection of the idea that Lynel Murray "came on" to Marlow.

According to Kania, Marlow had also revealed to him that Coffman was the one who had planted her knee in Lynel Murray's back during the strangulation.

The parade of witnesses ended on March 27, and Bob Gannon addressed the jury. Starting in a dry recital of the facts, Gannon built to a powerful, emotional crescendo, creating word pictures of Lynel Murray trembling in the grip of two predators. "Did she struggle? Did she cry out for help?" Gannon asked, his voice quaking. When the prosecutor displayed enlarged color photos of Lynel and Corinna, both smiling with innocent radiance, there were audible sniffles in the gallery, and tears ran down jurors' cheeks.

George Peters was faced with a painful decision. Would he make his final appeal for mercy while those beautiful photos of the victims were still in the jury's view, or risk alienating everyone by taking them down? He really had no choice. With words of respect, he removed the devastating pictures.

"By pleading guilty," Peters told the jury, "Mr. Marlow has shown remorse and placed himself in the doorway of the gas chamber. Please do not push him in."

It took the jurors less than six hours of deliberation to make a decision.

On March 30, court clerk Gail Carpenter read from the signed form. James Gregory Marlow, the jury had recommended, should suffer the penalty of death. Judge Don McCartin scheduled the formal sentencing for July 1, to give himself enough time to consider whether or not to reverse the jury and reduce the punishment to life without parole, and to complete the trial of Coffman. As it turned out, he would not be Coffman's judge.

Leonard Gumlia had sensed, prior to the severance, that Judge McCartin was not going to allow extensive evidence or testimony about the relationship between Coffman and Marlow, and was going to set time limits on the trial. Charging that McCartin was not impartial, Gumlia filed a motion to have him replaced. A supervising judge found no evidence of McCartin being partial to one side or the other, but "in an abundance of caution," reassigned the case to Judge Jean Rheinheimer.

Now unburdened with the Coffman trial, Judge McCartin moved up Marlow's sentencing to May 8.

In the meantime, just before dawn, on April 21, a convicted killer named Robert Alton Harris inhaled deadly cyanide fumes in San Quentin's gas chamber, becoming the first inmate to be executed in California in twenty-five years. There was a firestorm of news media coverage and widespread controversy over last-second delays. The majority of Californians had voted, twice, for a death penalty law, but a clamorous, protesting minority still made headlines. Would the reality of execution affect Judge McCartin's decision, or inhibit the next jury in Coffman's trial?

Cynthia Coffman heard of the execution while sitting in a court holding cell and began to cry uncontrollably.

On Friday, May 8, James Marlow stood before the assembled court, dressed in the orange jumpsuit of inmates, trying to hold back tears, and stammered, "I have been involved in some evil things. I am sorry is very inadequate . . . If you gave me a thousand lifetimes, I couldn't . . . compensate for any part of this." He told of his fear of assassination, noting that he'd be lucky if he ever made it to the gas chamber. "The fear of death has got to be worse than death itself. I am sorry to God and I am sorry to society and I am very sorry to the Murray family. If I could give myself to them to torture me, I would do that."

Judge McCartin had obviously struggled with his decision, and seemed stressed as he spoke. "This has been an extremely difficult case for me. It doesn't seem like the fellow sitting in front of me could have committed these crimes." The judge was convinced, he said, that Marlow was truly a changed person. "I have no doubt that he is sincere and remorseful."

Onlookers felt it coming. There was going to be no second death penalty, they were sure.

The volatile relationship between Marlow and Coffman created a chemistry that made them a deadly team, the judge commented. "When these two people got together . . . a third person arose and did these horrendous crimes.

"It's a given that he's a victim of abuse," McCartin continued, convincing observers that he would defy the jury. But Don McCartin was a judge unafraid of doing his duty. "The jury's verdict was proper," he concluded. He approved the sentence of death, ". . . as much as I would like to do otherwise."

Within three days, James Gregory Marlow was whisked away to San Quentin prison to take his place on Death Row.

Thirty

The *Los Angeles Times* ran a comprehensive story on Cynthia Lynn Coffman, covering seventy-one column inches with full-color photos, on Sunday, April 26, 1992, before her second trial. Local and network television reporters clamored for information, and shared the output from the single video camera allowed by Judge Jean Rheinheimer.

A petite, articulate, precise woman whose graying brown hair and easy smile, which squinted her eyes, giving her a kindly look, Rheinheimer ran a no-nonsense courtroom.

Raphael Abramowitz, producer from the NBC show, *Hard Copy*, spoke to the judge requesting permission to place a second camera in the courtroom. Rheinheimer denied the request, but Abramowitz was not only a producer, he was a lawyer. Before completing his coverage of the story by using file footage and interviews filmed at other sites, he appealed Rheinheimer's decision and eventually won his legal point when the judgement was reversed.

The *Hard Copy* show aired on May 20, 1992, utilizing filmed interviews of Chip Haight, Leonard Gumlia, and Robert Whitecotton, along with a dramatized re-creation of the biker wedding in Kentucky, and the murders.

On Wednesday, May 13, Cynthia Coffman's trial started with the reading of charges by Judge Rheinheimer. In addition to the murder of Lynel Murray, Coffman would be tried for the special circumstances of kidnapping, burglary, robbery, and rape during the murder.

James Marlow wouldn't help. In a special pre-trial hearing, he had informed court officers that if forced to testify, he would invoke the Fifth Amendment on any questions related to the death of Lynel Murray. He would not be a part of Coffman's trial.

Don and Jacque Murray were in attendance nearly every day, and Nancy, with Lynel's sister, Stacey, attended as often.

Five of the jurors from the last Marlow trial had developed a fascination with the case, and most of them began attending Coffman's trial to see the whole story through to completion. Susan Dolstra, an attractive gregarious woman with a wicked sense of humor, who was the center of the group, never missed a day. She took detailed notes, and became acquainted with many of the principals in the case.

Prosecutor Bob Gannon's whole week had been rotten. On the previous Thursday, he had heard another judge overturn a hard-fought case Gannon had won, dramatically illustrating just how fragile a conviction can be, and how easily it can be reversed.

If that wasn't enough, on the day of the reversal,

his teenage daughter had been taken to the hospital with a collapsed lung that required surgical insertion of a breathing tube. She survived with no damage, but Gannon had felt the strain and panic of any loving father.

In his opening statement for the Coffman trial, Bob Gannon spoke only thirty-five minutes, succinctly outlining the facts, summarizing them crisply, and presenting a list of witnesses he would call. He was finished by eleven o'clock that morning.

Leonard Gumlia stepped to the lectern with a thick sheaf of papers. It soon became evident that he had performed extraordinary research, and was passionately convinced that Coffman had no intent to kill, but had acted under Marlow's manipulating domination and the spell of her love for him. Gumlia began reading his opening statement from a 150-page history he had written. He used giant charts to illustrate his points. His words were clear, but extremely fast, causing the court reporter to glance often in his direction with silent pleas to slow down. In exhaustive detail, he covered the life and background of Marlow, a full chronology of Coffman's life, and commentary about the forces that shaped both of them. After three hours of reading, Gumlia's rapid-fire voice faltered, and Hector Chapparo took over for an hour. When Gumlia replaced Chapparo, the judge appealed to him to slow down, but within minutes he was racing along again. His presentation used up the rest of the court's day.

The defense strategy unfolded. Leonard Gumlia

intended to show that James Marlow had manipulated the judicial system by utilizing his bizarre childhood and twisted relationship with his mother in a continual plea for sympathy. Some would call it the "Mommy" defense. Now, Gumlia asserted, Marlow was repeating the pattern by "restructuring" his relationship with Cynthia Coffman, as a stand-in for his mother, blaming her for his behavior.

The proposition that Coffman had dominated Marlow was preposterous, Gumlia argued. On the contrary, Greg had manipulated and controlled Cyndi with physical beatings, threats, promises, and lies, and had exploited her love for him. Gumlia would use a series of witnesses to substantiate his theories, including three of Marlow's ex-wives, a woman Marlow had raped, the cowboy recipient of Cyndi's sexual favors at Marlow's bidding, and her relatives and friends who had seen changes in her in Kentucky and afterwards.

Characterizing Chip Haight's synergistic theory as a compelling argument, but untrue, Gumlia planned to use Marlow's criminal history as evidence that the man was "a runaway train, headed for death," long before Cyndi climbed aboard.

Methodically and efficiently, with never a folder or document out of place, Bob Gannon presented the case against Coffman. While she sat quietly, with a pale, demure look, the jury heard thirty-nine witnesses, including police officers, pathologists, and players from the previous trials who told their stories again.

Marlow's ex-wife Beverly answered "No" when Gannon asked her if Greg had forced her to rob, rape, or murder anyone. She had chosen to leave him. The prosecutor made his point crystal clear that abuse doesn't necessarily lead to complicity in crime, that the woman had a choice.

One short, stocky young man, with a fuzzy beard and a high pompadour, told the jury he had observed Marlow and Coffman at a restaurant where he worked, and had seen them hugging and kissing on the same evening Lynel Murray was killed. Observers familiar with the case were puzzled, not being able to remember a waiter at the restaurant, until they learned that the witness had been a waitress in 1986, and had undergone a sex change.

Jurors watched a silent videotape, lasting forty-five minutes, of Marlow and Coffman sitting in a San Bernardino jury box, accompanied only by two deputies across the room, during a break in the proceedings. Unaware they were being filmed, the couple seemed relaxed and affectionate, fondly touching and kissing. There were no signs of Coffman being afraid of Marlow.

The red-hot, racy letters were aired again, with Gannon attempting to show the jury that Coffman's words were evidence of her independence and initiative in the relationship.

Bob Gannon had planned to put Robin Long on the stand, but the nervous, elusive woman had disappeared yet again. Having foreseen this possibility, the prosecutor had previously taken advantage of a short period during which Long was available to get her story on record. Now, as his last witness in the trial, Gannon had the transcripts of Long's words read to the jury. Leonard Gumlia listened carefully, noting several discrepancies in her story as compared to the previous accounts of what Coffman had told her. Part of Gumlia's focus would be to demonstrate those discrepancies, placing weight on the errors.

From May 26 to June 12, Gumlia questioned thirty witnesses, including Cynthia Coffman who spent a little more than four days on the stand. Once more, in a whispery voice, Coffman enthralled the audience with details of the brutality of James Marlow. Her attorneys felt confident that the physical evidence, such as a photo of three soft drink cups found in the trash, Lynel's bruised back as described by a pathologist, and her broken fingernail found in Marlow's pocket, all corroborated her account of the events in the Huntington Inn motel room.

Cross-examination by Bob Gannon was fierce. He asked Coffman if her relationship with Marlow was more important to her than the lives of Corinna Novis and Lynel Murray. Her answer to both questions, with eyes downcast, was "Yes."

A great deal of Gumlia's presentation had seemed to be a retrial of Marlow, and the judge had been lenient in her decisions related to witnesses and evidence presented by the defense. Bob Gannon, ordinarily quite patient, was nearly fed up. In the fifth week, Gumlia sought testimony from a psychologist whose expertise was "conjugal terrorism." Gannon objected.

"Your Honor," he appealed, "I don't believe it's relevant. Mr. Marlow is not on trial here." There were grunts of assent in the audience, people who were weary of hearing repetitions of charges against Marlow. Gannon hoped to avoid another long history of Marlow's childhood. "There is no question he is a violent man, but I don't think it's relevant how he got there. The issue is, was he violent to Coffman? Did that affect her behavior?"

After hearing from Gumlia, Judge Rheinheimer ruled. "Well, I believe it's borderline, but in a case where someone is on trial for their life, I have to make a borderline call in favor of the person who is on trial. . . ."

Dr. Daniel Sonkin testified for the next five hours, during which the gallery yawned and shifted in squeaky chairs, jurors looked confused and perplexed, and the judge angrily banged her gavel for the first time to intercede in bickering between counsel. Gannon had been right. The five hours was another mini-trial of James Marlow.

On June 22, while Leonard Gumlia scribbled little concentric circles on a yellow legal pad, and Judge Rheinheimer sat with hands neatly folded in front of her face, Bob Gannon made his final argument to the jury. Attacking Coffman's credibility, Gannon scoffed, "The only direct evidence that she did not intend to kill Lynel Murray is her word. That's it. That's all."

Gannon brought up Coffman's words in one of her letters to Marlow: "Anybody who touches my Roscoe is dead meat." When he had asked Coffman if she meant that anyone who touches Marlow's penis is dead, she had answered, "Yes."

"There was no attempt to explain the answer," Gannon told the jury, "and none of the nonresponsive answers that we had extensively. It was a simple yes."

Reminding the jurors that Coffman had admitted pulling on the towel around Lynel's neck, Gannon related it to Robin Long's story, showing no discrepancy.

Cynthia Coffman faced making some choices, and chose to kill, the prosecutor said.

Gannon spoke a little more than an hour, then relinquished the floor to Leonard Gumlia. Gannon would have another turn.

"I hope the distinction about intent to kill matters to you," Gumlia began. He explained that everything he had offered about Marlow was to help jurors understand why Cyndi was still in the relationship at the time of the murders. "As far as blaming Mr. Marlow, Cyndi Coffman has confessed to you, and to the police, a first degree felony murder. She's not blaming anyone for that." What she denied, Gumlia emphasized, were the special circumstances because there was no intent to kill.

Marlow had controlled and manipulated Cyndi, Gumlia insisted, and made her a possession that he would even share with other men, if he so chose, or to coerce her into participation in the crimes. Marlow's ex-wives had clearly shown his pattern of abuse and domination. And Marlow, at last, was tired of Cyndi and was no longer sexually attracted to her.

"When he sent Cyndi Coffman away in Huntington Beach, what he's telling you is, 'I know Cyndi Coffman doesn't want to have sex with these girls and I know she doesn't want me to have sex with these girls, and I want to enjoy this one a lot more than I had to go through with the first one.' And that's why Lynel Murray was beaten. Probably didn't resist at all . . . When Marlow wraps the bindings . . . ," Gumlia hesitated, and for the sake of the Murray family, inserted, "This is a very difficult subject to talk about and look at . . ." After a respectful pause, he continued.

"When Marlow wraps the bindings around Lynel Murray, it is not just to gag her so she can't make noise. And it is not so that she can't see who her assailant is, because Marlow knows she is going to be dead. He binds her because he knows it's going to be a horrifying act for Cyndi Coffman."

Someone sarcastically whispered, "Poor Cyndi."

After lunch, Gumlia resumed his argument, designed to show the jury that everything Cyndi did, including her subject matter in the letters, was in response to demands or requests by Marlow. Then, Gumlia tackled the issue of Robin Long. He itemized a list of inaccuracies in what Long told police, and years later, included in her testimony. Observers would later wonder how important those errors were, noting that few people can recall every detail of a story that someone else has told, and recite it with perfect accuracy.

Leonard Gumlia, though, was convinced that he had exposed Long as an unreliable informant. "That church burglar was probably more helpful than harmful to Cyndi in Orange County, and what negative facts she added were easily neutralized."

Regarding Marlow's history, Gumlia observed that ". . . with the death of his mother, he was determined that no woman would ever leave him again, no woman would ever be disloyal to him again." To illustrate the point, Gumlia took the jury through the experiences of Marlow's first three wives once more.

As the afternoon rolled on, Gumlia hoarsely presented a litany of the abuse, threats, and lies to which Marlow subjected Cyndi, and commented that, "common sense should tell you that is only the tip of the iceberg. . . ."

To counter Gannon's observation that Coffman had admitted refusing Marlow on several occasions, including his request for her to get in the shower with him and Corinna Novis, Gumlia said that Cyndi didn't refuse, she just pointed to the bandage covering the stab wound on her leg. No one had ever challenged Marlow directly, Gumlia asserted.

"Greg Marlow directed Cyndi Coffman to kill. That's why he kept Lynel Murray alive. He was going to involve this woman for his own reasons: One, to make her less of a threat to him if she was ever apprehended, and two, for the psychological pleasure of having one woman do this act against another woman for him."

Winding down, Gumlia brought up the bruise in the middle of Lynel's back that Coffman had said was made by Marlow when he put his knee there while strangling her with the towel. "When Cyndi told you that she did not pull (on the towel) until death, she was telling the truth . . . because that injury in (Lynel's) back cannot be explained unless you're going to believe Cyndi Coffman climbed up there and did that. But there's no evidence of that. That was Greg Marlow." At least two observers wondered if Gumlia had created a damaging word picture of what his client might have done.

Perhaps sensing that, Gumlia pursued the subject. "Cyndi Coffman is on record as saying these two things: One, I pulled on the towel for a matter of seconds, and two, I pulled for about a minute. . . . I think it's fairly clear that she probably pulled for at least thirty seconds, off and on. And she may have pulled longer." Gumlia reiterated that Lynel was still alive "when Greg Marlow climbed up on her back, put his knee in her back . . . just like the physical evidence shows. . . . If she had been already dead, the bruise wouldn't have formed."

To be certain that the jurors understood the technical distinction of the charges, Gumlia explained once more. "In order to find that the special circumstance is true, it must be proved the murder was committed in order to carry out or advance the commission of the crime of robbery, or kidnapping, or rape by force, or burglary, or to facilitate the escape therefrom to avoid detection." It is *not* established if the robbery, kidnapping, rape, or burglary was merely incidental to the commission of the murder. The distinction was important. It could mean the difference between life or death for Coffman.

Weary and hoarse, but still pounding home his sincere belief in Cynthia Coffman, Gumlia concluded, "This is the case of two different stories, and one is a story of a man who's created out of an abused childhood and then spent the remainder of his life seeking revenge against the chief architect of the abuse, his mother. And he sought his greatest compensation from Cyndi Coffman, abusing her, lying to her, testing her, terrorizing her, until she gave herself to him completely and became just a shell of the girl he had met. In the process, he killed three people, twice trying to make Cyndi Coffman do the killing.

"In the end, the sexual assaults of Corinna Novis and Lynel Murray were the most visible evidence of his contempt to Cyndi Coffman, and their deaths were his final statement against all women, everywhere. . . . Inside room 307, that same man focused all of his energy and power directly on Cyndi Coffman and told her to kill Lynel Murray. . . . And despite her pathetic love, her pathetic desire to please, Cyndi Coffman ultimately decided in the only way she could, by compromising and finally believing that she did not want to kill and would not kill. And that's a choice she made, Mr. Gannon, a choice when you talk about free will."

The jury had all night to digest the words of both attorneys. On the following morning, Bob Gannon had their attention for his final argument.

To undermine the theory that Marlow had forced Coffman to kill for him, Gannon pointed out, "There is not one piece of evidence that Marlow recruited or solicited any of his wives . . . to commit a violent crime on a third person. They . . . stood up and got away from him." The implication was clear that Coffman had a choice to do the same thing.

Using the analogy of fire and gasoline mixing, Gannon insisted that the partnership was, as Marlow had stated, a fifty-fifty arrangement. Quoting from a Coffman letter, Gannon read, "I'm a lean, mean, moving machine. I know I'm bad. We're two of a kind." After reading more, Gannon commented, "She liked his sexual performance, and she liked his power, and he met those needs in her."

It was absurd, Gannon argued, that Coffman had been concerned about Lynel Murray, as Gumlia had indicated, by bringing food back to the motel for her. "If she's so solicitous . . . what in God's name is she thinking about when she helps Mr. Marlow kidnap her and take her to the hotel?"

Raising more questions about the defense's scenario of the events in room 307, Gannon, with righteous indignation, declared, "All we have as to what happened in that room . . . is the word of the lean, mean, moving machine sitting over there. That's it."

Tracing Coffman's relationship with Marlow, Gannon pointed to evidence and testimony that he thought supported her culpability in the crimes, right up to the moments before Lynel Murray died. Coffman put the towel strips around the victim's neck, not Marlow, Gannon said, bringing up the issue of intent, and pointing out that, according to testimony, the towel-ligature was pulled for up to a full minute. "When she puts that around her neck, she pulls once. That's the act. What's she intending? Is she intending to pull when he pulls? You bet. She's not intending to walk out of the room. She's not intending that Lynel Murray live happily ever after. She's intending to pull on that towel."

Summarizing the high points of his contentions once more, Bob Gannon reached into a paper sack marked "Exhibit 67" and pulled out the terrible strips of towel. "This is what the defendant had in her hands with Mr. Marlow on the other end," Gannon growled. "You can look at this and you can still see Lynel Murray's hair tied up in the binding."

Pausing to let the image sink in, Gannon softly said, "Now, I'm going to sit down and I'm going to look at the clock for a minute, and I'm going to put this down, and I'm going to wait sixty seconds. Let's just stop for a minute and think, starting right now."

The silence seemed to last forever. The minute hand was in slow motion. Dead silence.

"That's a minute," Gannon thundered. "If there is a question in your mind about whether or not she intended to kill, I ask you to recall the evidence and the testimony that you have heard in this trial, and to look at Exhibit sixty-seven, and to think about sixty seconds.

"Thank you very much, ladies and gentlemen, for your time and patience."

After three days of pondering and arguing, the jury announced that they had reached a verdict on June 29. Bailiff Sam Black ushered them into the jury box, and the foreperson (a woman) handed the verdict form to Black to give to the court clerk Chris White. In a steady voice, she read their unanimous decision. Cynthia Coffman was guilty of first degree murder with the special circumstances of kidnapping and robbery.

The penalty phase lasted only two days. A recent Supreme Court decision overturned an old rule preventing victim-impact testimony in trials. Previously excluded as prejudicial, the new ruling stated that barring such testimony deprived the state of "the full moral force of its evidence." Bob Gannon decided that he would call only three witnesses, Lynel's two parents and her sister.

Stacey Murray, who was seventeen when she lost her sister, took the stand on Wednesday, July 1. In six minutes of testimony, during which her family cried, Stacey told of how she is painfully reminded each day of her beloved sister's death, because she still lives in the same condominium just a five-minute walk from the Prime Cleaners. She and Lynel would often wave to each other through the windows of the cleaners where they worked across the street from each other. Lynel had always been "motherly" to Stacey, cooking her dinner and leaving her notes reminding her to do her homework.

With soft sobbing coming from the gallery, Stacey told of identifying Lynel's gold ring when detectives came to the house, and of the intense pain when she passes the Huntington Inn, just a couple of miles from her home.

Nancy Murray was sworn in next. Controlling the urge to cry by courageously smiling instead, Nancy recalled the last time she had seen Lynel. "We had a ritual, and she would wake me up every morning before she went to school and tell me the coffee was ready and to get up and go to work.

And that's when I saw her, every morning at seven o'clock when she was on her way to school."

Theirs was a special relationship. "We all learned to ski together, and she would share things with me. If she went to a movie, I never had to go see it, because she would tell me the entire plot." They would sit for hours, talking and sharing everything. ". . . The texture, the color of your life changes. The joy goes out of it. It's very difficult to hold onto things. You are constantly searching for that hole, that void. It's still there. And it's not filled." Nancy had been undergoing sporadic counseling ever since Lynel was killed, nearly six years earlier. The heartbroken mother stepped down after fourteen minutes.

Don Murray saw his daughter frequently after he and Nancy were divorced, he told the court. He had last talked to her on the day she was killed, at about 4:30 in the afternoon, on the telephone. Then, later, he was summoned to the Huntington Beach condominium when Lynel was missing.

"There was a knock on the door, and these two men came in suits, and I knew this wasn't going to work. They were very quiet, and all they wanted to know was, 'Are you the parents of Lynel Murray?' So I knew that this wasn't—this wasn't a good thing."

Gannon asked about Lynel's personality. Don, eyes moist but voice strong and proud, said, "She was real bubbly, bouncy, outgoing, very verbal, very talkative. I was still Daddy to her. Just a nonstop, go, go, go kid. Very warm." Don, too, had been in counseling, and lived in constant fear of losing another of his daughters. "Part of the problem, you know, I can't tell these kids how safe they need to be. They are young kids still. But I know what's going on out there, and I have to hold that in and feel it."

Gannon asked Don to describe how he had been affected. He, too, felt a vacuum that wouldn't go away. "The hardest thing for me is the word 'Daddy.' That's the thing I miss the most." Of course, his other children used the word, he said, but sometimes "Daddy" would trigger deep sadness. "And, of course, I would probably be a grandfather by now . . . and I don't have that." Don Murray had talked for nine minutes before he stepped down.

On Monday morning, July 6, 1992, Leonard Gumlia called his witnesses for the penalty phase. He, too, would need only three. His paralegal assistant, Kristen Widmann, led off by describing her daily close contact with Cynthia Coffman. Cyndi, Kristen said, maintained frequent telephone and mail contact with her family and son. The defendant also was completing a correspondence course in American history and hoped to eventually earn a degree so she could teach other inmates.

After some brief cross-examination, and twenty minutes of testimony, Kristen was excused.

* * *

Leonard Gumlia called Brenda Marlow, James Marlow's fourth wife. Gumlia only wanted to know when she was married, asked her to display the tattoos on her ring finger, and turned her over to Gannon.

The prosecutor asked if Marlow had forced her to marry him. No, he hadn't.

"Since you've been married to Mr. Marlow, he hasn't asked you to go rob anybody, has he?"

"No."

"And he hasn't directed you to commit any crimes? . . ."

"No."

Whose decision was it to tattoo her finger? Hers, Brenda said. Yes, she told Gannon, she had children and took them frequently to visit Greg. Did she have any concern about him having contact with the children? No.

"Since you've known him, has he forced you to do anything at all?"

"No."

On redirect, Gumlia heard Brenda say that she intended to move to the (San Francisco) Bay area to be near Marlow.

Both sides rested, but after the lunch break, Gumlia asked permission to reopen with a witness that surprised several people—including the author of this book. He called me, Don Lasseter, to testify.

When the *Los Angeles Times* ran the Sunday edition article on Coffman, I read it carefully and noted a comment that she wanted to learn more about the victims. Coffman had been told that I was writing a book. On the next court day, she sent word to me asking if I knew anything about the two victims. I replied that I had written a draft chapter about Corinna Novis. Coffman wanted to know if I would allow her to read it.

My immediate reaction was absolutely not. Then I reconsidered. Maybe it would be just retribution for her to know about the sweet innocent life she had helped snuff out. I agreed to send her a photocopy of the chapter.

Within a few days, Cynthia Coffman sent a note to me, which read: "Thank you for letting me read about Corinna. It was a very painful reminder of some very painful events, but it's something I need to do. I hope some day you will let me read your chapter on Lynel. Cyndi Coffman."

As his last witness, Leonard Gumlia called me to the stand, and asked me to read the card aloud. His intent was simply to show the jury that Coffman was remorseful. Bob Gannon, on cross-examination, asked if I knew the defendant.

"No."

"Are you familiar with her handwriting?"

"No."

"Have you had any other correspondence with

the defendant other than this?" (I hadn't yet interviewed her.)

"No."

"Of your own personal knowledge, do you know that, in fact, the note was written by Cynthia Coffman?"

"No."

Leonard Gumlia asked if I had read the letters Coffman and Marlow had exchanged. I answered that I had seen photocopies of them.

"Does the handwriting look similar?"

I replied that I had no way of knowing if it was the same. My testimony lasted four minutes.

And, following short closing statements by the prosecution and defense attorneys, the last trial was over.

While the jury deliberated, pondering the fate of Cyndi Coffman, an odd event took place. One of the jurors, a woman, sent a note to Judge Rheinheimer, saying:

"Judge, last night when I got home from jury duty there was a threatening phone call left on my message phone directed specifically at me. I do not know if it has anything to do with this case. It has been reported to the Fullerton Police Department and they have the tape. I didn't know if I should poll the others to see if they were also called or if you prefer to do that."

Judge Rheinheimer was seriously concerned. She called the juror into a special hearing, and asked for more details. The woman had not told the other jurors. Asked what the message said, the shaken juror answered, "Basically said this call is for (juror's name). 'You know who I am. You don't—' something about you aren't doing things in a very womanly manner, and if you don't take care of things the way you are supposed to, then you know what's going to happen."

She had no idea who it could have been. The mysterious person had called again, later in the evening, and talked to her husband. She and her husband speculated that it might be related to a bad debt for someone with a similar name. "But it's nothing we know of."

After a few more minutes of discussion, Judge Rheinheimer asked if the incident could affect the juror's ability to continue serving. The woman said she was upset, but wasn't sure that it would influence her ability to serve.

Judge Rheinheimer heard input from Gumlia and Gannon about possibly replacing the juror with one of the alternates. Rheinheimer asked Cynthia Coffman her preference on the matter, and Coffman wanted the juror replaced.

In "an abundance of caution," Judge Rheinheimer excused the juror and replaced her with one of the three alternates. Additionally, in a highly unusual move, she sequestered the jury, commencing Thursday evening, July 9, in a local hotel, until they reached a verdict.

They needed to deliberate only a few more hours. On Friday morning, bailiff Sam Black telephoned court officers, family members, and reporters. The court was assembled by four P.M. Cynthia Coffman sat at the defense table wearing black jeans, a pink blouse, and white tennis shoes. Her cheeks were already tearstained.

Judge Rheinheimer asked the foreperson if the jury had reached a unanimous decision. They had, she replied. The forms were collected again by Sam Black, and handed to Chris White to read aloud.

"We, the jury in the above entitled case find the appropriate . . ."

Sitting next to Cynthia Coffman, staring at the blank tabletop, Leonard Gumlia abruptly shot his right fist into the air, triumphantly, in a gesture of victory, and Coffman began sobbing. Gumlia recognized the prefacing words to the penalty for which he had fought.

". . . find the appropriate penalty is life in prison without the possibility of parole."

A reliable source later revealed to the author that the juror who had received the strange phone call, and who had been replaced on the deliberating panel, was the only one who was willing to hold out for the death penalty.

On Friday, September 25, Coffman stood before Judge Rheinheimer one last time, flanked by Leonard Gumlia and Hector Chapparo. Rheinheimer spoke firmly, making the sentence official. She added, "I have never tried a case in my courtroom where the killing was so debased, so wanton, so senseless, so brutal, and so avoidable. It is my hope that the conviction of the jury in this case withstands any and all appellate challenges, because it is my belief . . . that you should never return to society."

Cynthia Coffman, in her soft whisper, murmured, "I just hope one day the Murrays can forgive me."

In California, the procedures for sentencing allow the responsible judge to rely partly on reports and recommendations from the probation department. Interested parties may contact the county department, in writing, to express anything that may influence the sentence.

On May 1, 1992, just prior to Judge Donald McCartin's sentencing date for James Gregory Marlow, Donald E. Murray, Lynel's father, wrote a three-page letter to Ms. Kathy Diddier, Orange County Probation Department. In it, he said:

"This is a letter to introduce my daughter Lynel Murray. It is intended to inform those who find it necessary to acquaint themselves with her . . . I hope these few lines will help to personalize Lynel, both as a daughter and as a young woman just beginning to blossom as a wonderful, joyous human being. And, additionally, I will share just how her death at the hands of another has impacted us, the living victims, who alone know fully what has been taken from them."

In the next seven paragraphs, Don Murray wrote a touching, humorous, personalized biography of his beloved daughter, expressing his glowing pride and love for the bright, happy young woman. His last paragraph was:

It has been five and one-half years. How have I changed? There is the constant refocusing of my life to accent the positive things the Lord gives me—accept the wonderful gift of children, be thankful for what time we have, realize there are no guarantees to life or happiness except as we find them from Faith. To finally look at photo-albums from the past without pausing to go around pages where Lynel is displayed. And, finally, the learned ability to accept and even laugh at myself when some special song on the radio sends tears streaming down my cheeks as I sit at home or drive in a car. Because, to isolate one's self from the pain of losing a child is to lose a piece of our lives. To let the child live in our memories allows the laughter and pain to keep the memory vivid, for that is the most horrible fear I have—that of forgetting that laugh, Lynel's way of saying ". . . Daddy," her rapid-fire speaking and mimics. No matter what, I never want to forget that kind of pain, Lynel, and no one or thing will take away my love of life and the important people in it. She was my first daughter, and lives on without getting any older. I pray for the day I will see all my daughters again, in one place and time, with the pain and hurt gone forever.

Epilogue

The appeals process for convicted murderers, especially those sentenced to death, is perhaps the most convoluted, complex, and prolonged labyrinth in the entire judicial system. By the end of 1994, nearly 400 condemned killers were lodged at various stages in California's pipeline of appeals. Five of them, including Cynthia Lynn Coffman, were women.

Between 1967 and 1994, only two executions were carried out. After a twenty-five year hiatus, Robert Alton Harris died in the gas chamber in April 1992 and David Edwin Mason, rejecting all appeals, inhaled the lethal hydrogen cyanide in August 1993. Ten of the condemned committed suicide, one was murdered in the exercise yard, seven died from other causes, and forty-seven were resentenced to prison terms after courts decided to overturn the death sentences.

It is unlikely that any of them will ever step into the gas chamber, since the state passed a law in 1992 giving Death Row convicts a choice between cyanide gas and lethal injection.

In California's history, only four women have

been executed. Juanita Spinelli, a gang leader in San Francisco, drowned a "squealer" in the Sacramento River, and was executed for it in 1941. Six years later, Louise Peete, a housekeeper who put a bullet in the brain of her female employer, died in the gas chamber. Perhaps the most famous and controversial of the four was an ex-prostitute named Barbara Graham, who was convicted of joining two men in the murder of a wealthy Burbank woman. Susan Hayward won an Oscar for her portrayal of Graham in the 1958 motion picture, *I Want To Live,* and Lindsay Wagner repeated the role in a 1983 made-for-television movie. In both productions, it was suggested that Graham was framed. When she was finally strapped into a chair in the apple-green execution chamber, on June 3, 1955, a guard advised her, "Take a deep breath and it won't be so bad."

Barbara Graham snapped back, "How the hell would you know?"

In the 1959 capital murder trial of Elizabeth Duncan, her own son acted as co-counsel on her defense team, even though the victim was his wife. Duncan had paid two men $6,000 to kill her. The three conspirators were executed on August 8, 1962, seven months after Cynthia Lynn Coffman was born.

Legal experts agree that it will be a long time, if ever, before either Coffman or James Marlow will face execution. The complex trial in San Bernardino will be examined microscopically to determine if there were any violations of Constitutional guarantees, and then the same scrutiny will apply to the Orange County trials.

Meanwhile, Cynthia Coffman is an inmate of a new prison in Central California, near Chowchilla, where she waits with four other condemned women. She has a private room with a small black-and-white television set, a bunk, and minimal furniture. Library and exercise facilities are available.

James Marlow is still concerned about being murdered in San Quentin prison, where he is confined with the scores of men on Death Row. He has collected reams of documentation to prove that paid hit men have tried to kill him. He has avoided assassination, he says, only by his own careful wiles and by the grace of God. Marlow underwent psychological examination in the prison hospital, in 1993, and was returned to Death Row.

Leonard Gumlia still firmly believes that Cynthia Coffman had no intent to kill, and simply acted under the emotional and physical influence of Marlow. He has handed over his extensive files to her appeals attorneys who will pursue motions for reversal, up to the U.S. Supreme Court, if necessary. Gumlia's paralegal assistant, Kristen Widmann, has visited Coffman and maintains correspondence with her. In July 1993, Leonard and Kristen were married.

Alan Spears, who married the San Bernardino jury foreperson, accepted a position as court commissioner in Los Angeles County. He and his wife live on a comfortable boat in Newport Harbor, not far from the bank where Cynthia Coffman withdrew Lynel Murray's savings.

Raymond "Chip" Haight III continues prosecuting major cases in San Bernardino County, and supervises a special D.A. unit to combat gangs. In 1991, he convinced a jury to bring in a verdict of first degree murder against the brutal killer of a homosexual victim. The defendant was represented by Alan Spears.

Bob Gannon accepted a promotion to supervise a unit dedicated to consumer and environmental protection. He returned to a courtroom in 1993 to again prosecute the child killer whose case had been overturned by a judge. Gannon's efficiency and skills resulted in another conviction of first degree murder with special circumstances, and a new death sentence.

Susan Dolstra, the juror in Marlow's trial who became so fascinated with the process that she kept a journal during her daily attendance of Coffman's trial, turned over all of her notes to the author. In mid 1993, she accepted a position on the county payroll, in an office directly across the street from the courthouse.

Judges Don Turner and Don McCartin retired from the bench in 1993. Both men periodically preside over trials on a contract basis.

George Peters is one of the busiest and most successful attorneys in Orange County. His cocounsel for Marlow, Charles Margines was promoted to the municipal court bench in May 1993.

Dick Hooper continues to chase felons for the Huntington Beach Police Department. Scotty Smith left Redlands and joined the Police Department of Pismo Beach, a peaceful oceanfront town on California's central coast. Asked if he still works homicide cases, he answered, "We don't have any."

Trooper-Detective Colan Harrell has spent more than twenty-three years ferreting out criminals in Southern Kentucky, and wishes that he could continue for another twenty-three years.

The State of Kentucky considers the murder of Gregory "Wildman" Hill solved, but is holding possible prosecution of Marlow and Coffman in abeyance. It is unlikely that the case will ever reach a court, since key players Killer Compton and Lardo Lyons are both dead.

Jerome and Joanne Hill, the parents of Greg Hill, reside in rural Wayne County, Kentucky, still convinced that some of the local boys had more to do with their son's death than was ever revealed.

* * *

Donna and Bill Novis live in the modest little home in Gooding, Idaho, where Corinna was raised. In the wholesome small-town atmosphere, they frequently spend Sundays with William, Jr., Brenda, and five beautiful grandchildren.

Don Murray and Jacque, with their two daughters, Holly and Erin, live in La Habra, and remain active in his trucking business and the church.

Nancy Murray and her daughter, Stacey, reside in Huntington Beach, in the same condominium where Lynel lived. Nancy supervises food operations for a major chain.

The Huntington Inn, where Lynel Murray died, sits empty in a weed-choked, fenced parking lot, ready to be razed and replaced by a modern glass-and-steel structure.

The squalid apartments where Corinna Novis was held captive have been demolished.

Author's Note

When I had completed interviewing Det. Richard Hooper for a different project several years ago, we began chatting about another murder case he had investigated. He would never forget it, he said, and described to me how he had dropped to his knees in a cold, dark vineyard, and touched the hand of Corinna Novis.

I realized that I would never forget it either, and knew before I left his office that I would write the story.

In the process, scores of people sat patiently for interviews, or contributed information in conversation. The list of people to whom I am indebted is much too long to include here. All of you, please accept my heartfelt thanks.

Among the interviews, I spent more than ten hours talking to Cynthia Lynn Coffman and James Gregory Marlow. Marlow was astonishing in his articulate verbal skills, quoting presidents and philosophers. He acknowledged that in years of isolated protective custody, "I don't have anything else to do but read." He wished that he had educated himself earlier, because, "A lot of my problem was ignorance. I've learned to hate it. When you broaden your knowledge, your thinking changes." Perhaps education might have prevented his descent into the hell of drugs and murder.

READ EXCITING ACCOUNTS OF
TRUE CRIME FROM PINNACLE

HORROR FROM HAUTALA

SHADES OF NIGHT   (0-8217-5097-6, $4.99)
Stalked by a madman, Lara DeSalvo is unaware that she is
most in danger in the one place she thinks she is safe—
home.

TWILIGHT TIME   (0-8217-4713-4, $4.99)
Jeff Wagner comes home for his sister's funeral and uncov-
ers long-buried memories of childhood sexual abuse and
murder.

DARK SILENCE   (0-8217-3923-9, $5.99)
Dianne Fraser fights for her family—and her sanity—
against the evil forces that haunt an abandoned mill.

COLD WHISPER   (0-8217-3464-4, $5.95)
Tully can make Sarah's wishes come true, but Sarah lives
in terror because Tully doesn't understand that some wishes
aren't meant to come true.

LITTLE BROTHERS   (0-8217-4020-2, $4.50)
Kip saw the "little brothers" kill his mother five years ago.
Now they have returned, and this time there will be no es-
cape.

MOONBOG   (0-8217-3356-7, $4.95)
Someone—or some*thing*—is killing the children in the little
town of Holland, Maine.